DEVELOPING AND SUPPORTING MULTICULTURALISM AND LEADERSHIP DEVELOPMENT

INNOVATIONS IN HIGHER EDUCATION TEACHING AND LEARNING

Series Editor: Patrick Blessinger

Previous Volumes:

INNOVATIONS IN HIGHER EDUCATION TEACHING
AND LEARNING   VOLUME 30

DEVELOPING AND SUPPORTING MULTICULTURALISM AND LEADERSHIP DEVELOPMENT: INTERNATIONAL PERSPECTIVES ON HUMANIZING HIGHER EDUCATION

EDITED BY

ENAKSHI SENGUPTA

Centre for Advanced Research in Higher Education,
New York, USA
International HETL Association, New York, USA

PATRICK BLESSINGER

St. John's University, New York, USA
International HETL Association, New York, USA

MANDLA S. MAKHANYA

University of South Africa, Pretoria, South Africa

Created in partnership with the International Higher Education Teaching
and Learning Association

https://www.hetl.org/

United Kingdom – North America – Japan
India – Malaysia – China

Emerald Publishing Limited
Howard House, Wagon Lane, Bingley BD16 1WA, UK

First edition 2020

Reprints and permissions service
Contact: permissions@emeraldinsight.com

British Library Cataloguing in Publication Data
A catalogue record for this book is available from the British Library

ISBN: 978-1-83909-461-3 (Print)
ISBN: 978-1-83909-460-6 (Online)
ISBN: 978-1-83909-462-0 (Epub)

ISSN: 2055-3641 (Series)

ISOQAR certified
Management System,
awarded to Emerald
for adherence to
Environmental
standard
ISO 14001:2004.

Certificate Number 1985
ISO 14001

INVESTOR IN PEOPLE

CONTENTS

PART II
HUMANISTIC PEDAGOGY

LIST OF CONTRIBUTORS

Patrick Blessinger	International Higher Education Teaching and Learning Association, New York, NY, USA
Luisa Bunescu	European University Association (EUA), Brussels, Belgium
Alison Robinson Canham	Independent Higher Education and Professional Learning Consultant, York, UK
Timothy J. Fogarty	Case Western Reserve University, Cleveland, OH, USA
Hope J. Hartman	The City College of New York and The Graduate Center of the City University of New York, New York, NY, USA
Leanne R. Havis	Neumann University, Pennsylvania, PA, USA
Moeketsi Letseka	University of South Africa, Pretoria, South Africa
Vimbi Petrus Mahlangu	University of South Africa, Pretoria, South Africa
Mandla S. Makhanya	University of South Africa, Pretoria, South Africa
Veronica Margaret Makwinja	Botswana Accountancy College, Botswana, Africa
Victor Pitsoe	University of South Africa, Pretoria, South Africa
Carolyn L. Sandoval	University of California San Diego, San Diego, CA, USA
Jennifer Schneider	Southern New Hampshire University, Manchester, NH, USA
Enakshi Sengupta	International Higher Education Teaching and Learning Association, New York, NY, USA
Cameo Lyn West	San Diego Community College District, San Diego, CA, USA

SERIES EDITORS' INTRODUCTION

INNOVATIONS IN HIGHER EDUCATION TEACHING AND LEARNING

The purpose of this series is to publish current research and scholarship on innovative teaching and learning practices in higher education. The series is developed around the premise that teaching and learning is more effective when instructors and students are actively and meaningfully engaged in the teaching–learning process.

The main objectives of this series are to:

(1) present how innovative teaching and learning practices are being used in higher education institutions around the world across a wide variety of disciplines and countries;
(2) present the latest models, theories, concepts, paradigms, and frameworks that educators should consider when adopting, implementing, assessing, and evaluating innovative teaching and learning practices; and
(3) consider the implications of theory and practice on policy, strategy, and leadership.

This series will appeal to anyone in higher education who is involved in the teaching and learning process from any discipline, institutional type, or nationality. The volumes in this series will focus on a variety of authentic case studies and other empirical research that illustrates how educators from around the world are using innovative approaches to create more effective and meaningful learning environments.

Innovation teaching and learning is any approach, strategy, method, practice, or means that has been shown to improve, enhance, or transform the teaching–learning environment. Innovation involves doing things differently or in a novel way in order to improve outcomes. In short, innovation is positive change. With respect to teaching and learning, innovation is the implementation of new or improved educational practices that result in improved educational and learning outcomes. This innovation can be any positive change related to teaching, curriculum, assessment, technology, or other tools, programs, policies, or processes that lead to improved educational and learning outcomes. Innovation can occur in institutional development, program development, professional development, or learning development.

The volumes in this series will not only highlight the benefits and theoretical frameworks of such innovations through authentic case studies and other empirical research but also look at the challenges and contexts associated with implementing and assessing innovative teaching and learning practices. The volumes represent all disciplines from a wide range of national, cultural, and organizational contexts. The volumes in this series will explore a wide variety of teaching and learning topics such as active learning, integrative learning, transformative learning, inquiry-based learning, problem-based learning, meaningful learning, blended learning, creative learning, experiential learning, lifelong and lifewide learning, global learning, learning assessment and analytics, student research, faculty and student learning communities, as well as other topics.

This series brings together distinguished scholars and educational practitioners from around the world to disseminate the latest knowledge on innovative teaching and learning scholarship and practices. The authors offer a range of disciplinary perspectives from different cultural contexts. This series provides a unique and valuable resource for instructors, administrators, and anyone interested in improving and transforming teaching and learning.

Patrick Blessinger
Founder, Executive Director, and Chief Research Scientist,
International HETL Association

Enakshi Sengupta
Associate Editor, International HETL Association

PART I

DIVERSITY AND INCLUSIVITY

CHAPTER 1

INTRODUCTION TO DEVELOPING AND SUPPORTING MULTICULTURALISM AND LEADERSHIP DEVELOPMENT: INTERNATIONAL PERSPECTIVES ON HUMANIZING HIGHER EDUCATION

Enakshi Sengupta, Patrick Blessinger and Mandla S. Makhanya

ABSTRACT

Education needs to be viewed in a holistic manner; it does not end when one simply acquires a degree or a job. Education creates human beings, shapes them into what they are and influences their behavior and attitude toward life. It contributes to creating a long-lasting effect on people's mind and attitude. Developing a curriculum is not an easy task as it involves various dimensions of life, and one of them is to inculcate the idea of inclusivity and multiculturalism in the minds of young learners and help them to become effective leaders in the future. The process of teaching, delivery of lessons, assessment, evaluation and various pedagogical approaches needs to be aligned to deliver multicultural education. Society's values, beliefs and goals should be translated into a curriculum that is relevant and connects students to society. Humanizing education to instill values that supports inclusivity and equality

Developing and Supporting Multiculturalism and Leadership Development:
International Perspectives on Humanizing Higher Education
Innovations in Higher Education Teaching and Learning, Volume 30, 3–13
Copyright © 2020 by Emerald Publishing Limited
All rights of reproduction in any form reserved
ISSN: 2055-3641/doi:10.1108/S2055-364120200000030002

should be built around the cultural context synthesizing opinions and facts derived from the work of researchers and academics. This book aims to review research work conducted by academics across the world. Authors argue how social justice education and inclusion should be an inherent part of the curriculum. Strategies and tools are suggested that can strengthen the learning abilities of students and create an attitude of appreciation toward inclusivity. Case studies and interventions that have been effective are cited from Africa to the USA and UK, which can help create an intentional design of a classroom environment supporting multiculturalism. The book illustrates the importance of appropriate curriculum development involving all stakeholders and the integration of multicultural education in the curriculum. Concepts such as Ubuntu and academic freedom toward leadership development have also been stressed in this book.

Keywords: Curriculum; multicultural; inclusivity; pedagogy; classroom environment; cultural context; leadership development; equality; interventions; intentional designs

INTRODUCTION

Creativity is considered one of the most important resources that can become the driving force for our future society. Education is changing to give way to creative thinking and enhancement of soft skills which emphasizes higher-order thinking and problem-solving skills. Curriculum, which can be viewed as a knowledge base that directs the educational setting of society, is undergoing a paradigm shift from blackboard lectures to student-centered learning that emphasizes inclusivity and multiculturalism. Education, as an extended learning community, is moving to the center of the community to align education to the needs of society. Community-based learning activities, for example, have become a key element to help humanize the curriculum to include elements that accommodate critical thinking and meaningful problem-solving abilities.

The term education has been defined by many, each giving a new meaning to it. Education needs to be holistic in nature and provides accessibility to all. Gautam and Singh (2015) defined education as a key component that enhances social, economic and political transformation in all societies. Education is considered as an integrative force in society that can be used to impart values to foster individual excellence, generate social cohesion and enhance nation-building. A curriculum has to be developed in a manner that is targeted at improving educational settings, improving teaching practices and enhancing learning activities. The curriculum is not aimed only at the students but toward faculty and staff members to develop inclusive leadership skills and an ethical and humane mindset toward developing the human potential of students.

Humanistic education needs to be holistic involving both individual and society as academics and those involved in imparting higher education need to have a sense of responsibility toward self, the learners and community at large

(Blessinger, Sengupta, & Makhanya, 2019). Developing the person's knowledge, skills, competencies and ethical habits should remain as the foremost priority of every academics no matter which stream of education they are involved in. A humanistic-oriented education that is learner centered should be the aim of a multicultural curriculum where students are capable of directly experiencing and interacting with various cultures.

Multicultural education should be capable of recognizing, understanding and sympathizing with cultural diversity that would impart a unique learning experience to students from all fields (Yun & Zhang, 2017). True experience can be achieved only when new changes are induced in the learning methods by exposing the students to concrete experiences outside the four walls of a classroom (Kim & Lee, 2001). Experiential learning is not about blindly accepting what the teacher has advocated, but rather a complete process that helps enhance the overall development of the learner (Lee, 2013).

LITERATURE REVIEW

Muacin (2017) defined the concept of multicultural education as the place that is capable of harboring the voice of a multitude in a society that is multicultural in nature and is also a place that nurtures the dreams of others. The concept of multicultural education permeates at all levels from primary school to secondary and in the field of higher education. It is not confined to developing only an inclusive curriculum but encompasses teaching methods, staff selection, policies, programs, activities and teaching methods. It ought to raise and address queries pertaining to gender, race, equality, religious tolerance, xenophobia, elitism and classism.

Multicultural education places students at the center of education and recognizes that students' experience is paramount in building up the concept of inclusivity, which can happen when the student is exposed to real-life issues outside the classroom premises and understands and perceives a world devoid of human biasness and prejudices. Students should be encouraged to express their opinion and thoughts and should be free to analyze the prevailing oppression in society and understand the power relationship. Classroom technique should be suited to develop a multicultural context by integrating students from all quarters and having culturally competent staff who are unbiased in their freedom of thought and expression.

The concept of multiculturalism has the term equity or equality inherent in it. As Edtrustorg (2017) commented, equality can be considered synonymous with leveling the playing field, while equity is for those who need it, the ones who are vulnerable or had been maltreated in past. Multicultural education hence should include a level-playing field for those who are in need of it. The category reservation process in higher education is one such approach that gives an opportunity to those who had been oppressed in the past. Right from the admission process involving everyone in the same manner and administering a curriculum that is free of biasness can be adopted to become a step toward inducing multiculturalism and the humanistic approach toward higher education.

Sleeter and Grant (1991) advocates five approaches that can be adapted to create a multicultural education:

(1) *Teaching the culturally different*: This approach when adopted helps to raise the academic achievements of students from diverse backgrounds. No segregationist policy is followed by the higher educational authorities and being inclusive in nature it treats students from all cultural and ethnic backgrounds in the same manner who are taught under the same premises inequitable manner.

(2) *Human relations approach*: Social and cultural differences are identified and celebrated instead of treating "others" as somewhat superior or inferior to the outgroup. Institutional and economic power are not given any preference and students are not treated differently on the basis of such power.

(3) *The single group studies approach*: Histories and contemporary issues which talks about oppression and suppression marginalization of groups in the past are explained to all in the same manner, eliminating all kinds of differences.

(4) *The multicultural education approach*: Educational processes both classroom and those that are experiential in nature including instructional methods are taught to value cultural knowledge and differences.

(5) *Social reconstructionist*: Students are exposed to social issues such as oppression and discrimination. With the help of creative and critical thinking students are made to realize their role in their own society as agents of social change.

Content cannot be multicultural if it is controlled by few with vested interest who purposefully ignores and demeans the culture of a particular group of people from different ethnicity. A distorted image of those who are represented in our books can even distort the multicultural perspective. Certain groups are presented in our books, mainly history books as stereotypes and their contribution trivialized, these in turn chisels the views carried by students and equitable representation of diversity is grossly ignored. Students fail to respect and understand the inclusive spirit and themselves grow up harboring biases as it is not inculcated in them.

Students require a broader understanding of world education embedded in multiculturalism without the filter imposed on them by the faculty members. Content developers are responsible for representing facts as they are way negating the filter and including material which tells the story of everyone, mainly the oppressed and the underprivileged as opposed to serving the cause of the powerful. "The manifestation of ethnicization is not limited to the domain of the political party and party system but extended to the area of economy as well" (Holst, 2012, p. 84). "An integrative approach to internationalization of curriculum is understood as the integration of inter cultural dimension into an already existing curriculum" (Joseph, 2012, p. 241).

A transformative approach to such curricula should include inclusive education, feminist pedagogies, anti-racist and post-colonial pedagogies (Joseph, 2012), which are rarely included in the curriculum of the universities. The concept of cultural diversity and inclusive pedagogy should be an important component of humanizing curricula which is often neglected by educators:

> Curriculum can be enhanced by adding in or integrating different cultural perspectives and experiences. The work of an educationist is to understand power and culture as played out through identity strategies and pedagogical practices within educational spaces. (Joseph, 2012, p. 246)

Education activities falling under the purview of multiculturalism and inclusivity should enhance student's engagement with different cultures and environments, which is often ignored in higher educational institutions. As Spivak (1990, p. 62) argues, while working critically one must work through one's beliefs, prejudices and assumptions:

> we need to do our homework, to work hard at gaining some knowledge of the others who occupy those spaces most closed to us and also attempt to speak to others in such a way that they might take us seriously and be able to answer back.

In a university it is often noticed that the faculty members in the way they incorporate multiculturalism in their curriculum are "filling the bag with some international bits," which ultimately affects "the way in which knowledge is organized and ultimately the ways in which the curriculum is implemented" (De Vita & Case, 2003, p. 388). Studies in the past have revealed that "inter cultural learning is not just a topic to be talked about, it is also about caring, acting and connecting" (De Vita & Case, 2003, p. 388).

The approach to multiculturalism in higher education is dominated by entities rather than academics who sit in privileged positions, who can direct faculty in adding and implementing diverse cultural practices to curricula and draw on the experience of the students as native informants (Joseph, 2012):

> We need to interrogate the complexities of our position as educators and academics and help to transform the world that we share to be more equitable, more inclusive, more just and more human. (Joseph, 2012, p. 253)

Universities are moving away from the principles of cultural exchange, altruistic internationalism and reciprocity (Shinn et al., 1998).

As argued by Hodson and Thomas (2001, p. 110):

> this lack of cultural sensitivity in existing collaborative audit approaches ... constrains diversity and is likely to drive the system down the compliance end of the quality continuum and away from quality enhancement.

Worries over the risk of offering a mono cultural model of education ... or even worse, of engaging in a form of ideological manipulation through the promotion of, "western packaged global problems and seemingly global solutions" (Anyanwu, 1998, p. 18) are present everywhere and no institution has been able to escape the "uncritical and decontextualized presentation of western managerial fads and fashions" (Howe & Martin, 1998, p. 449).

As Volet and Ang (1998) point out, interacting with the content and with each other would help create a learning environment, where students are exposed to multiple perspectives and foster cultural understandings. Hence, well-crafted policies are not enough unless a:

> challenging hybrid culture is developed whose multifarious cultural perspectives and experiences of those who make up the faculty are themselves seen as the material which inspires the creation of new learning practices. (De Vita & Case, 2003, p. 394)

CONCLUSION

The concept of multiculturalism and inclusiveness is being recognized by world leaders, academicians and visionaries. Equity pedagogy in higher education is adopted in the classrooms which can accommodate diverse students who can be empowered and sensitized against the existing prejudices in society. Academics are trying to inculcate tolerance, understanding and respect among future leaders (Koshy, 2017). Social psychologists believe that stereotyping and segregation is a normal cognitive functioning of humans. It is only through correct understanding of culture, the ways of life and social relations that values and attitudes toward multiculturalism can be achieved.

Students should be exposed to the real-life context through experiential learning giving them a chance to understand and experience the diverse nature of world and thus create future leaders whose thinking is not compartmentalized with racial biasness. Education is one of the most vital social institutions of the society and a process by which society transmits its cultural heritage through the learning institutions. Multicultural education is a critical aspect of the curriculum, and students can gain competence with the help of teachers' understanding and ability to think, communicate and interact in a multicultural way inculcating different perspectives and world views.

CHAPTER OVERVIEWS

"Humanizing Learning Outcomes for Diversity Requirement Courses: Advocating for and Supporting Social Justice Education," by Cameo Lyn West and Carolyn L. Sandoval, speaks about research I universities who are increasingly requiring a "diversity" course as part of the general education curriculum. In this chapter, the authors explore how diversity requirement course (DRC) proposals are framed at their institution and share how instructors at their university are framing their own student learning outcomes for these courses: from the perspective of multiculturalism, or from the perspective of social justice? The authors describe how a lens of multicultural education frames discussions of diversity as appreciation, awareness and tolerance, and contend that this approach alone is not sufficient to meet either the intent of DRC initiatives or the goals of equity and inclusion in academia. The authors argue that social justice education is a more appropriate instructional framework for DRCs, as it is a humanizing approach that necessitates the crafting of student learning outcomes which specifically address actionable strategies toward opposing marginalization. The authors include selected results from a campus-wide DRC outcomes survey and separate focus group feedback, emphasizing the critical assessment and campus climate aspects of these data. Finally, the authors examine how their faculty development programs and resources are currently assisting DRC instructors with identifying and meeting their needs, and how other faculty developers can expand their support structures in the future to align with the philosophy of social justice education.

"Improving Classroom Engagement and Learning: Adaptable Tools, Strategies, and Resources for Nurturing Diversity Appreciation and a Mindfully Multicultural

Environment in the Online Classroom," authored by Jennifer Schneider, seeks to help and support online educators in their efforts to improve tomorrow. Specifically, the chapter shares practical strategies and tools that online educators can easily apply, adapt and/or personalize in order to help promote a mindfully multicultural classroom in their online classrooms and programs. The chapter includes a wide range of actionable tools and exercises to help online instructors optimize the learning experience for all students by building upon the unique strengths and diverse cultural backgrounds of all students in their online classrooms. The strategies help instructors leverage diversity as a means to promote equity and social justice in online programs and, ultimately, the world as a whole. The chapter relies upon Gollnick and Chinn's (2017) six beliefs that are fundamental to multicultural education and presents strategies from two perspectives or lens (student focused and faculty focused). Approaching the issue from a dual-sided lens is intended to best support the ultimate goal of improving the student learning experience. Emphasis is placed on both public and private interactions between faculty and students. Public interactions include all discussion board and announcement communications. Public interactions also include resources that are shared in the online classroom for all students' benefit.

"Advancing Inclusivity and Citizenship: Adapting Theory, Changing Practice," by Alison Robinson Canham and Luisa Bunescu, is about the European Forum for Enhanced Collaboration in Teaching (EFFECT, 2015–2019) (EFFECT, 2019), a project co-financed by the European Commission, through its Erasmus+ program, has been exploring effective methods for university teachers' development at the European level, including pedagogical staff development "modules" to support inclusivity and citizenship in teaching and learning practice. Throughout the project and this chapter, the authors have taken "inclusivity" to convey an attitude and appreciation for principles which inform "inclusion" as a practice – in the context of reflective and reflexive practice the words become largely interchangeable. The way academic staff teach is of critical importance in any reform designed to enhance inclusion and citizenship in higher education. Conveying these values-related topics in an academic context hardly lends itself to a traditional pedagogical training model. Promoting inclusion means stimulating discussion, challenging stereotypes and unconscious biases, as well as improving educational and social frameworks. The Change Laboratory methodology (Engeström, 2001) was chosen for the pedagogical staff development workshops under EFFECT, with a view to engaging teaching staff in a deeper reflection about the topics and about their teaching practice.

Change Laboratory is an intervention-research methodology that aims at reconceptualizing activity: it intends to provoke authentic reactions, responses and disagreements among the participants and provides opportunity for them to work together to reimagine their activities and to identify "concrete" solutions that address persisting issues in their practice. The theory takes a broad conceptualization of "activity" and "practice," which is not specific to the education sector or the "classroom." The Change Laboratory is a methodology designed to support the "expansive learning cycle" described by Engeström, and as such can be understood as a theory of change which the EFFECT project team applied to a pan-European higher education learning and teaching context.

In 2017, the project team designed and implemented four physical/face-to-face pedagogical staff development workshops on inclusivity and citizenship skills based on this methodology, attended by over 100 participants from across Europe. In 2018, the workshop model was adapted to a virtual learning environment and three online sessions on inclusivity and citizenship skills for higher education teaching staff were offered. The pedagogical staff development workshops enabled participants to use open reflective questions to provoke discussion about the challenges faced in their own learning and teaching contexts, think about their pedagogical practices and identify their unconscious biases. Most of the participants rated the workshops as very good and innovative, and considered the methodology an effective vehicle for promoting meaningful open discussion. In this chapter, the authors reflect on the design, implementation and lessons learnt from the pedagogical staff development workshops on inclusivity and citizenship skills. The authors propose a set of recommendations for individual teaching staff and institutional leadership to consider when addressing continuous professional development for inclusivity and citizenship.

"Inclusive and Multicultural Education: The Dynamics of Higher Education Institutions in Botswana – Inequality and Exclusion of Students," by Veronica Margaret Makwinja, is about higher education in Botswana which is believed to transform life through the provision of job opportunities for those with the privilege to access it. Parents believe that when their children graduate with degrees, this will alleviate them from poverty, and hence encourage their children to work hard and perform to their best ability. Higher education is viewed as the pinnacle a good life – an assurance of a better future for the extended family kinship. Unfortunately, access to higher education institutions is a prerogative of those who can attain high marks in their last national or international examinations. When students do well, they receive full scholarship from the Botswana government to attend any institution of higher learning of their choice. However, most students from the marginalized or minority groups tend to fail to access higher education due to various challenges socio-economic challenges they face.

"Holistic Faculty Development: A Learner-Centered Approach," by Hope J. Hartman, is about a holistic approach that has been applied to teaching the whole student, yet rarely emphasized in faculty development in higher education. Similarly, learner-centered instruction has become more prevalent in higher education as a way of teaching students, but less so as a concept for faculty pedagogy. This chapter examines the psychological underpinnings of holistic, learner-centered instruction and describes strategies and materials for applying these principles to faculty development so that higher education environments are humanized for culturally diverse faculty and students. Conceptual frameworks underlying the approaches emphasize humanistic theories and the needs of adult learners. Topics addressed include motivation, cooperative learning, culturally responsive teaching, active learning, metacognition, teaching for transfer, nonverbal communication and instructional technology. Faculty development efforts described include both interdisciplinary activities and a special project with the School of Engineering. While modeling holistic, learner-centered teaching in faculty development, university instructors are engaged in their own learning of effective pedagogy, and their experiences and knowledge can be used subsequently to enhance student success in their courses. A holistic, learner-centered approach enables higher education faculty to create stimulating, nurturing, safe and respect-ful classroom environments which promote student engagement, content mastery, cognitive skill development, intrinsic motivation and attitudes which foster think-ing and learning. Consequently, this chapter provides faculty, administrators and policymakers with tools that can be used to help students, especially at graduate and post-graduate levels, learn academic material and become enlightened global citizens with enhanced thinking abilities and affect to meet current and future personal, professional and societal needs.

"Active Learning Strategies for Promoting Intercultural Competence Development in Students," by Leanne R. Havis, talks about students entering higher education who often lack a sense of cultural awareness and a basic under-standing of what diversity, multiculturalism and intercultural competence have to do with their future goals. Ironically, student populations tend to be diverse in and of themselves. Yet the critical element that is often missing is their ability to inter-act across these differences and to confront (and engage with) their discomfort in the face of something new and unfamiliar. Getting students to overcome this discomfort so that meaningful learning and critical skill-building can take place is challenging a number of reasons. Students are typically more motivated to expend effort in a course if they can recognize and appreciate the value and relevance that the material may have on other areas of their lives, most notably their professional pursuits. This appreciation can best be cemented though the use of active, rather than passive, learning strategies. This chapter introduces strategies for the inten-tional design of a classroom environment that will engage students and promote the development of intercultural competence. Activities and assignments desig-nated as promoting the accumulation of specific knowledge (K), the development of particular skills (S) or the exploration of certain attitudes (A) are shared.

"Applying Freire and Ubuntu to Humanizing Higher Education Leadership," by Victor Pitsoe and Moeketsi Letseka, explores the relationship between higher education leadership and humanizing pedagogy. It is premised on the assumption that higher education leadership, as a social construct, is both a philosophical problem and policy imperative. Yet, the fourth industrial revolution and artificial intelligence imperatives have far-reaching implications for the "dominant" higher education leadership theory and practice. With this in mind, this chapter advocates for a broader and culturally inclusive understanding of higher education leader-ship perspectives. Among others, the thesis is that in a developing country context such as South Africa, for example, the dominant approach of higher education leadership should be guided by the Ubuntu principles and humanizing pedagogy. The authors shall argue that the humanizing pedagogy and Ubuntu principles, in a culturally diverse setting of the fourth industrial revolution era and artificial intelligence, have the prospects of changing the current unacceptable levels of per-formance and bring change in a larger scale in higher education institutions.

"Academic Freedom at the Business School: Teapot's Tempest or Modernity's Knife Edge?," by Timothy J. Fogarty, is about the development and progres-sive refinement of the concept of academic freedom that has generally occurred without material participation by the American Business School. Whereas the business school looms large as a component of higher education in the twenty-first century, most believe that it is indifferent or perhaps hostile to the concept of academic freedom. For the most part, business school faculty fail to share the liberal political leanings of their colleagues from across the university, and therefore are less likely to find themselves to need academic freedom protection from those who would like to squelch opinions that run contrary to government and establishment elites. This chapter recognizes the fundamental alignment of what is taught in the business school and what business faculty research. However, that does not gainsay prospects for academic freedom protection when such is not the case. The chapter explores public interest dimensions of being a faculty member in a business school and how these might be manifested. Examples of controversial work are offered for each of the major business disciplines.

"Humanizing Higher Education through Ethical Leadership to Support the Public Service," by Vimbi Petrus Mahlangu, focuses on humanizing higher education by infusing ethical leadership in the curriculum to improve the public service. Its design is qualitative in nature and literature reviews and document analysis were employed in compiling the chapter. It followed an interpretive paradigm and used Kolb's Experiential Learning Theory as a lens in understanding humanizing education in higher education. Nowadays ethical leadership is of paramount importance in higher education and in the public service. Ethical leadership should be based on the moral person and the moral manager. The moral person component focuses on desirable personal qualities of leaders such as being perceived as honest, fair and trustworthy. The moral manager focuses on the leader and uses transactional efforts such as rewards and punishments to reinforce desired behaviors. Soft skills are very important in higher education and should be transferred through coursework. Students need to be supported in all aspects of education including the academic, emotional and social demands in higher education.

REFERENCES

Anyanwu, C. (1998). Transformative research for the promotion of nomadic education in Nigeria. *Journal of nomadic studies*, *1*(1), 44–51.

Blessinger, P., Sengupta, E., & Makhanya, M. (2019). Creative inclusive curricula in higher education. Retrieved from http://www.patrickblessinger.com/creating-inclusive-curricula-in-higher-education/

De Vita, G., & Case, P. (2003). Rethinking the internationalization agenda in UK higher education. *Journal of Further Higher Education*, *27*(4), 383–398.

Edtrustorg. (2017). The education trust. Retrieved from https://edtrust.org/the-equity-line/equity-and-equality-are-not-equal/

EFFECT. (2019). Project page and resource repository. Retrieved from https://eua.eu/101-projects/560-effect.html

Engeström, Y. (2001). Expansive learning at work: Toward an activity theoretical reconceptualization. *Journal of Education and Work*, *14*(1), 133–156. doi:10.1080/13639080020028747

Gautam, M., & Singh, S. (2015). Entrepreneurship education: Concept, characteristics and implications for teacher education. *International Journal of Education*, *5*(1), 21–35.

Gollnick, D. M., & Chinn, P. C. (2017). *Multicultural education in a pluralistic society* (10th ed.). Boston, MA: Pearson Education.

Hodson, P. J., & Thomas, H. G. (2001). Higher education as an international commodity: Ensuring quality in partnerships. *Assessment and Evaluation in Higher Education, 26*(2), 101–112.

Holst, F. (2012). *Ethnicization and identity construction in Malaysia.* Routledge Malaysian Studies Series. London: Routledge.

Howe, W. S., & Martin, G. (1998). Internationalization strategies for management education. *Journal of Management Development, 17*(5/6), 447.

Joseph, C. (2012). Internationalizing the curriculum: Pedagogy for social justice. *International Sociological Association, 60*, 239.

Kim, J. H., & Lee, C. (2001). Implications of near and far transfer of training on structured on-the-job training. *Advances in Developing Human Resources, 3*(4), 442–51.

Koshy, R. S. (2017, April–June). Multicultural education: Significance, content integration and curriculum design. *International Journal of Advanced Research in Education & Technology (IJARET), 4*(2). ISSN: 2394-6814 (Print).

Lee, J. Y. (2013). The use of the field experience learning in a college liberal art course: A case study of the field experience learning of reconsidering the awareness of unification. *The Review of Korean Studies, 7*(5), 495–521.

Muacin. (2017). Purpose Need and Principles of Teaching And Learning In Multicultural Society. Retrieved from http://results.mu.ac.in/myweb_test/MA%20Education Philosophy/ pdf. Accessed on February 16, 2017.

Shinn, M., Weitzman, B. C., Stojanovic, D., Knickman, J. R., Jimenez, I., & Duchon, L., et al. (1998). Predictors of homelessness among families in New York City: From shelter request to housing stability. *American Journal of Public Health, 88*, 1651–1657.

Sleeter, C. E., & Grant, C. A. (1991). Race, class, gender, and disability in current textbooks. In M. W. Apple & L. K. Christian-Smith (Eds.), *The politics of the textbook* (pp. 78–101). New York, NY: Routledge.

Spivak, G. C. (1990). *The post-colonial critic.* New York, NY: Routledge.

Volet, S. E. & Ang, G. (1998). Culturally mixed groups on international campuses: An opportunity for inter-cultural learning. *Higher Education Research and Development, 17*(1), 5–23.

Yun, H., & Zhang, J. (2017, May–August). The significance of the multicultural education based on the experiential learning of a local community. *European Journal of Social Sciences Education and Research, 4*(4). ISSN 2411-9563 (Print)

CHAPTER 2

HUMANIZING LEARNING OUTCOMES FOR DIVERSITY REQUIREMENT COURSES: ADVOCATING FOR AND SUPPORTING SOCIAL JUSTICE EDUCATION

Cameo Lyn West and Carolyn L. Sandoval

ABSTRACT

Research I universities are increasingly requiring a "diversity" course as part of the general education curriculum. In this chapter, the authors explore how diversity requirement course (DRC) proposals are framed at their institution and share how instructors at their university are framing their own student learning outcomes for these courses: from the perspective of multiculturalism or from the perspective of social justice? The authors describe how a lens of multicultural education frames discussions of diversity as appreciation, awareness, and tolerance, and contend that this approach alone is not sufficient to meet either the intent of DRC initiatives or the goals of equity and inclusion in academia. The authors argue that social justice education (SJE) is a more appropriate instructional framework for DRCs, as it is a humanizing approach that necessitates the crafting of student learning outcomes which specifically address actionable strategies toward opposing marginalization. The authors include selected results from a campus-wide DRC outcomes survey and separate focus group feedback, emphasizing the critical assessment and campus climate aspects of these

Developing and Supporting Multiculturalism and Leadership Development:
International Perspectives on Humanizing Higher Education
Innovations in Higher Education Teaching and Learning, Volume 30, 15–31
Copyright © 2020 by Emerald Publishing Limited
ISSN: 2055-3641/doi:10.1108/S2055-364120200000030004

data. Finally, the authors examine how their faculty development programs and resources are currently assisting DRC instructors with identifying and meeting their needs, and how other faculty developers can expand their support structures in the future to align with the philosophy of SJE.

Keywords: Learning outcomes; diversity, equity, and inclusion (DEI); social justice education (SJE); emotional labor; general education (GE); neo-liberalism;

INTRODUCTION

The purpose of general education (GE) diversity requirement courses (DRCs) at Research I (R1) universities[1] can be broadly understood as a humanistic enterprise (Koopman, 1987). Undergraduates attending these institutions are expected to demonstrate some degree of fluency with the foundational principles in the sciences, the social sciences, and the arts and humanities. This comprehensive education plan is typically designed by requiring a certain number of courses outside the student's major, with subjects such as composition being required for all students. DRC course subjects vary across institutions, because they grow out of a variety of campus contexts, with many of them becoming required only after a racist inciting incident (Williams, 2013), as was the case on our campus. The formal purpose of these courses should ideally align with the university's mission and values, but at the core of these requirements is the hope that students will be challenged to think critically about their own identities, and that they will learn communicative skills to help them collaborate with their peers and colleagues in an increasingly diverse society (Espinosa, Turk, Taylor, & Chessman, 2019). Additionally, DRCs are typically guided by a humanistic philosophy which encompasses the goal of helping students develop an understanding of and compassion toward others' experiences, particularly as they relate to patterns of inequality and discrimination (Laird & Engberg, 2011). This aligns with the wider GE requirement rationale that a holistic education in which students are well-versed in disciplines beyond their field of study encourages in them a sense of social responsibility that will hopefully guide them to practice their professions ethically and with integrity. Finally, DRC topics almost always include critical and historical discussions of race, and sometimes that category is broadened to allow for additional primary or secondary categories like gender identity, sexuality, religion, and ability status (Laird & Engberg, 2011).

Several years ago, our university (a public, R1 university on the Pacific Coast) experienced a series of anti-black incidents on campus, which culminated in overtly racist acts. As a result of these incidents, student and community activists put forth a list of demands to the university's administration. These demands included several campus-wide initiatives to support vulnerable student, faculty, and staff populations and emphasize the importance of diversity in the university's mission statement. One of the changes that were implemented was that all incoming undergraduate students would be required to take two DRCs in order to graduate. To date, there are almost 100 courses that have been designated as a DRC through a proposal, screening, and approval process, with the vast majority being offered in the Social Sciences and Arts and Humanities. For the 63 DRCs that were offered during the 2018–2019 academic year, 10% of the instructors were graduate students, 33% were lecturers, and 57% were ladder rank faculty. The DRC guidelines at our institution require, in part, that courses pay particular attention to historically marginalized racial/ethnic groups in the United States, and that students are given an opportunity to explore their identity both in relation to others and in relation to broader issues of equity and inclusion in society. A common challenge educators face when teaching DRCs is the inherent difficulty of navigating discussions about equity and inclusion with students who are at very different stages of intercultural maturity (King & Magolda, 2005), and who have divergent lived experiences. As instructors, we have both taught DRCs and have first-hand experience with these challenges. As educational developers who support faculty with their teaching at our institution, we heard many stories from DRC instructors of instructional challenges they faced, ranging from a lack of genuine student engagement to outward hostility in the classroom expressed by some students. While we had anecdotal evidence of these issues, in addition to our own experiences, we wanted to formally investigate the challenges educators were facing to target our instructional support resources and professional development opportunities. We wanted to know what knowledge, skills, and/or values did DRC educators want students to develop in their courses? How confident do DRC educators feel in their ability to navigate difficult dialogues that emerge in their courses? What resources do DRC educators need to support their teaching of these courses? While we already offered workshops and resources related to teaching DRCs through a social justice theoretical lens, hearing directly from educators what they hoped students would learn from their courses beyond content knowledge, as well as specific challenges they faced and resources they needed, could inform our work and theoretical approaches to the humanistic goals of DRCs.

EDUCATOR EXPERIENCES

The first phase of our Institutional Research Board-approved investigation involved the creation and distribution of an electronic survey to all DRC instructors (faculty, lecturers, teaching assistants). Development of the survey questions was a collaborative effort between our unit, the campus teaching and learning resource center, and other DRC stakeholders, including DRC faculty. It included 10 content questions and 1 demographic question. The questions were qualitative in nature and were structured to allow respondents to choose one to three unique answers that best fit their experiences, with space to elaborate. Seventy-one unique respondents in total completed the entire survey, all of them self-identifying either as tenured/tenure-track faculty or adjunct lecturers. Our institution typically employs no more than 80 non-student DRC instructors per academic year, so the response rate for this demographic of instructors exceeded expectations.

Course Goals

The most pertinent results of the survey relate to course learning outcomes. Respondents mostly wanted their students to complete their course with an understanding of how power is distributed and maintained in society (23%); the ability to have meaningful discussions about identity and difference with their peers (19%); and the skills to historicize and contextualize the processes/characteristics of oppression (18%). From these results, we can glean that instructors want their students to meaningfully engage with each other and critically engage with the course content beyond the knowledge level (i.e., beyond memorizing, defining, etc.).

Common Challenges

Related to common challenges DRC instructors face, respondents identified several examples of student resistance, including students being indifferent about the course content, overtly challenging instructor authority, refuting the legitimacy of the course content and denying historic oppression, and being resentful of having to take the course and thus, refusing to engage with the material or others during class. Many instructors attributed a lack of student engagement to students refusing to see the relevance of the course to their lives or to their fields of study. One instructor explained:

> Some students express resistance to the need to take DRC courses, as well as to the material being presented. For example, a student in lecture recently expressed his view that he should not need to take a DEI class since 'my family and ancestors have never done any of this!'

Instructors also attributed the lack of student engagement to the policy that students can take their DRC for Pass/No Pass credit, rather than being assigned a letter grade. One respondent noted the difference between productive and nonproductive resistance:

> Productive resistance is resistance coming from a place of inexperience where students are just not familiar with the concepts and ask questions in the spirit of learning. Unproductive resistance are students who come in with the attitude that [my DRC] is just "liberal brainwashing" and do not listen to the actual nuance embedded in the course. So I don't know what to do there.

Along with student resistance, another common concern instructors reported in the survey was poor student feedback on course evaluations. One instructor's comment best captures this concern:

> They [students] were resentful when I assigned theoretical and historical work that challenged white "common sense" ideas about progress and race. They took it out on me in the evaluations. Since I don't emphasize everyone doing them since it seems to reinforce consumerist ideas of education, a small number of resentful students skewed the results, and damaged my teaching record.

Finally, faculty expressed what they perceived to be the uniqueness of their position as DRC instructors, with some of them invoking the language of *emotional labor*[2] to describe the additional (and sometimes unrecognized) tax they experienced in teaching these courses.

Identified Needs

The primary resources faculty identified that would best meet their support needs were training for graduate student instructional assistants, consultations with education specialists in our unit who have expertise in designing and teaching DRCs, and campus-wide talks/events that included prominent diversity education experts. Graduate student instructor training was the most common support request, which was also reflected in what faculty highlighted in the focus groups (discussed in the following). Faculty also identified opportunities for growth for themselves as instructors, which suggests a willingness to learn about different approaches to facilitating DRCs. This is encouraging because it suggests an openness to learning about diverse pedagogical approaches and theoretical perspectives. In general, faculty were more interested in professional and pedagogical development opportunities than in financial incentives, and the only need that was identified that cannot be directly and immediately addressed by faculty development and support services is the issue of smaller class sizes, which was the second-most identified need. This, however, might be gradually attended to by establishing resources that encourage interdisciplinary collaboration on proposing and teaching DRCs. Currently, only three STEM departments offer DRCs. If we could help foster cooperation between disciplines and divisions, then more DRCs would be offered in total, which might result in smaller class sizes.

Focus Groups

Following the results of the survey, we organized a focus group study that we facilitated during the second half of a DRC luncheon that was held to reflect on and celebrate the success of our diversity requirement and to identify opportunities for moving forward. Our goal for the focus groups was to gather additional information related to specific themes that emerged from the survey and to give students an opportunity to share their experiences as learners in DRCs. Approximately 30 people participated in the focus groups, including undergraduate students, faculty, deans, provosts, and administrators. Facilitators and note-takers were assigned to a table of at least four participants and were tasked with asking 4 questions over an 80-minute period. The questions probed more deeply into the experience of emotional labor, faculty interest in designing and teaching interdisciplinary courses, and effective strategies instructors use to increase engagement, respond to resistance, and/or make the course material more accessible. Immediately relevant data gleaned from the focus groups included: faculty are interested in designing and teaching interdisciplinary DRCs, although there was some concern expressed about the potential for faculty in Arts and Humanities and Social Sciences being required to do the heavy lifting in these collaborations; faculty requested we investigate the possibility of developing a web-based, centralized introductory training and resources pages for DRC instructors and Teaching and Instructional Assistants (TAs); and faculty requested that we investigate the possibility of developing a digital space, such as a Twitter hashtag, or a physical space, such as a message board installation, where DRC students can share their research and experiences.

Some faculty and students were candid about feeling underappreciated in their roles as advocates for diversity with one student observing:

> [in my role as Diversity Advocate for the Student Council in my college], I know that not every college in our university is a [DRC] advocate. My college is widely known as "the white man's college," with students primarily in STEM majors. [...] As the Diversity Advocate, I feel like I have to go out of my way to do things in my position.

This student expressed that widespread apathy toward DRCs made them feel hopeless to change perspectives among their peers in the college, and they admitted that they feel their role is largely symbolic and ignored, and gave evidence to support this:

> When I first started in my position, I was told I didn't have to do anything, so I can see how it isn't viewed as an important role. [...] My position was also close to being cut from the college.

In another focus group, a faculty member in a Social Sciences department acknowledged that the emotional burden of teaching DRCs can sometimes be significant, especially for faculty of color who are targeted with racist comments, and cited an experience their colleague had:

> I wish there was some kind of support in place about dealing with controversial topics. A colleague of mine had a student who kept making racist comments, and they felt that they didn't have the experience to handle that situation.

In the end, this professor identified ways faculty of color can provide personal support networks for one another. On the issue of institutional-level support, another Social Sciences faculty member spoke about the training TAs in their department receive and disclosed the following:

> We struggle preparing students of color to step into the classroom, as there can be hostility, and questions about authority and expertise. To prevent under-training, a [TA] training was prepared, specifically on how race and gender impact the classroom experience. The need was there, this was created ad-hoc, but it would be great if it was offered university-wide.

Positively, faculty did express pride in teaching DRCs and confidence in their ability to facilitate their own classes. Faculty also emphasized their desire to see the university implement systematic and consistent training for DRC instructors and TAs. This training would ideally be tailored to the DRC mission, stressing tools to promote classroom engagement and strategies for responding to common challenges like student apathy and hostility.

Frameworks for Humanizing Learning Outcomes

The broad themes that emerged from the survey and focus groups challenged us to review our existing resources related to teaching DRCs and make any necessary modifications to address the teaching challenges faculty faced. We were also challenged to identify and fill gaps in our resources and workshop offerings. A concern we had prior to the results of the survey and focus groups was whether or not our approach to course design, which is informed by backward design (Wiggins & McTighe, 1998) and Adams & Love's (2009) social justice faculty development framework, aligned with how faculty approached their courses, including their identified learning outcomes. As instructors and educational developers who are personally concerned about social justice and take seriously our institutional commitment to equity, diversity, and inclusion, the Adams and Love framework is particularly salient to our work (and our own humanistic goals) with all educators, not just those who teach DRCs. Their model encourages us (educators) to examine teaching through a social justice lens that includes knowing our students and how their educational experiences and social contexts impact learning; knowing ourselves and how our own biases, privileges, and experiences impact our teaching and relationships with students; and examining our course content and pedagogical choices and the degree to which they challenge dominant paradigms in teaching and in the discipline, and the impact of our choices on student learning. Examining the complexities of teaching and learning through a social justice lens minimizes the possibility of "inclusive" or "active learning" strategies, both which aim to involve students in the learning process. An educator who has good intentions of incorporating active learning into the classroom with a goal improving student learning outcomes, but who does not pay attention to student–student interactions that contribute to classroom climate, or who does not pay attention differential outcomes among different populations of students, may unintentionally reproduce educational inequity. Generally, we found that the goals of DRC faculty are humanistic and social justice oriented; however, course learning outcomes are often absent from syllabi or are not clearly articulated. It is crucial that instructors examine their frameworks and the theoretical lenses that guide the design of their DRC in order to articulate their course learning outcomes. When working with DRC instructors in the past, we identified two commonly used frameworks that informed instructors' approaches to teaching, as well as their course content: multiculturalism and social justice.

Multiculturalism as a teaching philosophy came to prominence – and prominent backlash – in the 1990s. As defined by Seltzer, Frazier, and Ricks (1996, p. 124) multicultural education (MCE) is "an attempt to foster an appreciation for cultural diversity, with the overall goal of developing within students a sense of esteem for different cultures," with the key concepts being *appreciation* and *tolerance*. Tolerance as a teaching tool is non-confrontational and does not intrinsically demand of the student any critical self-reflection. Instead, to tolerate someone is to allow for their presence and their otherness in a public space without harassment. This was a relatively appropriate framing for the historical context; the popular media discourse centered around multiculturalism during the time Seltzer et al. (1996) was written was a direct reaction to the so-called consensus or majority politics of the Reagan era of conservative backlash, which championed assimilation and demonized the abject other as anti-American. This was a time when the model minority thesis had even greater cultural currency than it does today. In contrast to the popular beliefs about identity and citizenship at the time, multiculturalism as a philosophy made transparent the impossibility and irresponsibility of the assimilationist project, which sought to acculturate all Americans to the same beliefs about merit, democracy, and the integral fairness of our sociopolitical and legal systems (Seglow, 2003). For multiculturalists, the status of *other* was something celebrated as an asset in education rather than something to be ignored or overcome. Therefore, multicultural learning objectives tend to champion the respectful discussion of others over critical contexts that force dialogues which center the self within a hegemony.

In a DRC that is framed with multiculturalism, one of the learning outcomes might be that students should be able to articulate some of the vital contributions of Black American scientists. This approach frames Black Americans as the *other*, a subject to be learned and memorized for the explicit purpose of being able to pass a course assessment like a final exam. A more critical and humanized learning outcome would encourage students to contextualize how systemic racism has contributed Black Americans' compromised and limited access to education and equal employment opportunities, and then articulate the ways in which certain individuals were able to succeed despite these barriers, and reflect on how this can inform systemic changes to contemporary systems to make them more equal. This challenges the student to stop thinking about examples of achievement as rewards for merit, or as instances of *overcoming* by individuals with great will, but instead as case studies to explore the complex ways in which the hegemonies that dictate American society are in a constant state of flux.

Advocating for multiculturalism at first appears to make sense for DRCs designed for traditional pedagogies, where students are expected to primarily passively receive information in the lecture model about "the histories of racial and ethnic groups as well as their contemporary behaviors and beliefs" which should ideally lead to "prejudice reduction" (Seltzer et al., 1996, p. 125). The emphasis on tolerance and co-existence reflects a desire to encourage a high percentage of "buy-in" because as Seglow (2003) explains, "multiculturalism cannot be avoided. Whether [it is] endorsed as a policy (cultural diversity is good), it cannot be circumvented as a social fact." That is, given the society in which diversity across a range of identities exist, multiculturalism demands an authentic response which first involves the acknowledgement of its existence. This is the ethos that appears to drive most diversity requirements, which privilege a recognition in difference-of-equality between students and groups in society at large, above consciousness-raising with regard to oneself (Lee, 2015).

The de-emphasis on pushing boundaries led to some educators and activists even in the 1990s to levy charges of racial obliviousness against MCE philosophies (Lee, 2015) as students come away from these courses without the tools to mitigate or even necessarily investigate white supremacy, exploitative capitalism, and systemic oppression. This is partially informed by a desire to respect the founding rationale for offering courses which center the marginalized, which originated from a movement that has roots in Black community action and the subsequent (limited) recognition of the discipline of Black Studies on college campuses (Biondi, 2012). Black Studies emerged from the Civil Rights Movement, as part of the empowerment initiatives that sought to tie Blackness to a history of dignity and excellence, rather than accepting the narrow framing of Black history as the history of slavery. Some of the very first Black Studies and Ethnic Studies departments emerged here on the Pacific coast, and that legacy of student activism was felt at our institution in the aftermath of the racist incidents that led to the implementation of the diversity requirement. So, that many DRCs should be taught by

Ethnic Studies and related departments goes without saying, but the burden of the expectation that these courses are taught *by* those departments (solely) has become outsized and perhaps counterintuitive to the spirit of the DRC, which seeks to fully integrate diversity into the culture and climate of the campus, which cannot be achieved if the expectation that the work of diversity education is only relevant in certain disciplines. The subject of DRCs (underrepresented racial populations) can easily become subsumed under the weight of the identities of those majority students in the classroom, especially when those DRCs are taught by faculty of color in relatively marginalized and underfunded departments. On the other hand, the mission statements of many R1 universities are explicit in the neo-liberal (Goldin & Katz 1998) purpose of their institution (i.e., to train students to succeed in their careers in a transactional process that results in the eventual financial enrichment of both parties), so the introduction of anything that might be considered controversial into the GE curriculum is now uncommon.

Social justice is the new multiculturalism in many ways – it has become a buzzword in the media signaling the alleged excesses of so-called political correctness on college campuses and the challenging of traditional narratives about power and difference. Those who identify themselves as opposed to social justice in education often cite the alleged inappropriateness of encouraging student activism, or of instructors promoting any particular political view. Renault (2019) writes that Frederich Hayek's conceptualization of the alleged ills of social justice is quite influential, quoting Hayek as saying:

> What we have to deal with in the case of 'social justice' is simply a quasi-religious superstition of the kind which we should respectfully leave in peace so long as it merely makes those happy who hold it, but which we must fight when it becomes the pretext of coercing other men. And the prevailing belief in 'social justice' is at present probably the gravest threat to most other values of a free civilization. (p. 66)

Arguments based upon Hayek's defense of classical liberalism and his related suspicion of collectivism and egalitarianism tend to misrepresent both the structure and purpose of modern social justice education (SJE), which is less about tutoring students in the procedures of political activism than it is in centering intersectionality and making students aware of their own positionality within the various hegemonies that they do and will operate in as members of society. SJE pushes the instructor to collaborate with their students in a learning process that mutually empowers and challenges all parties to consider their intersectional identities through practicing vulnerability, empathy, and consciousness-raising toward a common goal. Intersectionality, too, has become a hotly debated topic in the popular (mis)understanding of Crenshaw's (1989) original legal concept. Just as with multiculturalism in the 1990s, opponents of SJE claim that examining power dynamics within social hierarchies will lead to a balkanization of education (Laird & Engberg, 2011), where individuals are judged based solely upon their identities, and those with a more marginalized identity status will be placed at the top of a new hierarchy that values difference above all else (i.e., identity politics). This perspective on intersectionality is transparently inaccurate, as the reasoning behind acknowledging intersectionalities in power systems is not to displace traditional hierarchies by creating new ones, but instead to abolish unequal distributions of power by making their inherent non-sensicality and unfairness apparent. Intersectionality's centrality to SJE can also prevent educators who fear backlash from students, parents, or administrators from implementing the principles of SJE in their own classrooms.

Some measure of hesitancy from a classroom management perspective when utilizing SJE is understandable, as it does make demands of the student and instructor that MCE does not. Adams, Bell, Goodman, and Joshi (2016) describe these demands by citing educator and philosopher Paulo Freire. Freire argued that ultimate goal of teaching students within a social justice framework, broadly, is to provide them with the tools to "awaken" them from their subordinated status into a consciousness of their oppression, with the intention being that they will seek out making change. Encouraging students to reflect on their own position in society challenges them to become aware of their own oppression, thereby motivating them to advocate for the reduction of artificial barriers to equity in education and society for all. Utilizing the universal human tendency toward selfishness and relating the way one experiences the world to how one *feels* in order to allow students to understand how systems of oppression affect others is a powerful redistribution of empathy. Since SJE is an experiential pedagogy that demands vulnerability, a support system for students engaging in the emotional labor of this work is essential. The formation of a learning community within the classroom is a key to encouraging not only an environment conducive to critical inquiry and complex thinking but also a safe space in which students can take risks as they explore the complexities of their own and others' identities, and the impact of their identities within a society that maintains structural inequality. Despite these logistical and practical difficulties, SJE as a framework and praxis should not be disregarded as too impractical or advanced for a general student audience, or watered-down to appease the neo-liberal and transactional philosophy some individuals and R1 institutions take to college education. SJE requires engaging the whole student, which aligns with the humanistic goals of higher education.

Teaching Beyond Disciplinary Content

Given that most instructors surveyed identified students' ability to have meaningful dialogue around issues of power, identity, and oppression, course learning outcomes should include human dimension and caring goals (Fink, 2013), as well as discipline-specific goals (Nilson, 2016). This humanistic approach can help the instructor articulate a framework in which students can do more than grapple with foundational knowledge and concept application, which makes this approach well suited to DRCs. Making human dimension and caring goals explicit in a course also encourage instructors to think more deeply about where their students might be developmentally and how they (instructors) can help students develop important skills (e.g., listening and questioning for understanding) for productive dialogue around difficult topics. Discussions of equity, power, privilege, and oppression cannot be approached without an explicit emphasis on social justice. Freire's conceptualization of the classroom as a space for dialogue (1970) is crucial – if universities are mandating that their students enroll in courses about identity and difference, then the expectation of critical self-reflection is explicit.

Students must engage in the study of theory, the art of thinking and reflecting critically, and the praxis of intergroup dialogue. Zúñiga and Sevig (2000, p. 9) define intergroup dialogue as encouraging the "direct encounter and exchange about contentious issues, especially those associated with issues of social identity and social stratification." Students must empathize with one another, and come to understand their own identity as intersectional. A major component of this praxis is teasing out "the dynamics of privilege and oppression that shape relationships between social groups" (Zúñiga & Sevig, 2000, p. 11), which of course includes the interactional social group of the college classroom. This is not passive work; it demands vulnerability and honesty, and the classroom culture it requires cannot be developed through a model of tolerance alone, as acknowledging power dynamics can be controversial. Again, the myth of meritocracy explicitly teaches students that the very best will find success independent of extenuating social factors. The idea that outside forces can be social actors is accepted by those who champion the invisible hand of free market capitalism, but that same logic is not extended to systemic discrimination. The contemporary political climate is one in which individuals find themselves essentially arguing for or against empathy. That dichotomy must be challenged and dismantled by cultivating a critical social awareness that highlights for each student that they cannot invalidate the experiences of their peers simply because they *believe in* meritocracy or racial colorblindness. The lived experience (Freire, 1970) of each student is of great consequence and anecdotal evidence must be tempered by theory and research.

This is challenging work for anyone, and especially for young undergraduates who might not have experience with those whose identities are very different from their own. Therefore, classroom intergroup dialogue needs to be facilitated rather than forced, based upon terms that are understood and agreed upon by every student. Counterproductive modes of interaction like debate (although there is a place for structured debate) should be discouraged in favor of first discussion and eventually dialogue, where emotions and especially empathy help students understand "personal, group, and intergroup relationship issues" (Zuniga, Nagda, Chelser, Cytron-Walker, 2007). It is crucial that instructors also practice empathy by regularly acknowledging the hard work students are doing, and reminding them that their intellectual and emotional labor are in service of their learning and development as scholars, and the wider SJE goal of dialogue that allows them to "recognize, question, and analyze prevailing beliefs and behaviors that maintain systems of stratification and perpetuate estranged and oppressive relations between groups" (Zúñiga & Sevig, 2000, p. 10). If done well, students come away from their DRCs with so much more than having simply learned to appreciate and tolerate; they learn to collaborate, to practice humility, and to seek out making social change that results in a net good for the society in which they live and work.

REFLECTION AND FUTURE DIRECTIONS

Our work as educational developers is to assist DRC instructors in helping their students achieve a critical social conscience by articulating holistic, humanizing learning outcomes and fully aligned assessments and activities that support the goals of SJE. Williams (2013) articulates several models for how we might successfully approach framing diversity on college campuses that have a history of bias and discrimination, and some of these are of particular use for instructors teaching DRCs. First, framing the purpose of DRCs as aligning with institutional missions can be particularly powerful, and students might (correctly) interpret the purpose of the courses as aligned with the professional development skills they expect to learn. For this, the language of *leadership* can be effective – Williams (2013) outlines a rubric of "Five essential leadership skills of the new economy," which include communication abilities and cultural competence. This language may at first appear antithetical to that of SJE, but when framed with intention, students can come to understand that the only way to achieve some of the goals they need to become leaders in their field and to tackle the world's complex problems is through collaboration and intergroup dialogue, to which empathy is key. Williams (2013) offers language that is quite direct about this, and might resonate with faculty who are struggling with why they should commit to the admittedly difficult and at times labor-intensive work of SJE. He states:

> The changing demographics of the American population have been and will be increasingly reflected in our classrooms, as the presence of women and historically underrepresented groups pursue higher learning. Yet discrimination and injustice continue to persist, and we will continue to struggle with transforming our [classrooms] in ways that nurture diversity. (p. 78)

And what is more transformational than a praxis which champions personal growth (critical self-reflection) as integral to the goals of a course?

The MCE approach might indeed work for some instructors, depending upon their course-level student learning outcomes and the university-level DRC language. For example, an instructor might have as one of their course-level learning outcomes that students should be able to, "articulate how the practice of redlining has negatively impacted access to education, food, and healthcare majority-Black neighborhoods." Answering this question fully requires connection making with ambiguous-to-implicit relationships, and the assessment tools to successfully meeting this outcome are not inherent within the outcome itself (i.e., "demonstrate knowledge of how literary analysis functions by writing a literary analysis paper"). A student could conceivably approach *articulating* this outcome in multiple ways, perhaps with a podcast or a video project, a short piece of fiction, or a series of film reviews, in addition to the traditional research paper. If it is the instructor's intent to teach students how to write essays, then having essay writing as an assessment is clearly necessary, but DRC instructors would be well advised if they considered the university-level language around diversity and the purpose of the DRC within the context of their institution when crafting learning outcomes. Being realistic about course engagement limitations as made inherent by the structure of the DRCs is frustrating, but can also liberate the instructor from the constraints of traditional methodology.

The DRC guidelines (currently under review by a workgroup who are charged with making recommendations for improvement) at our institution are explicit in the requirement that DRC's must focus on a historically marginalized ethnic group in order to be approved for GE credit. Several of the survey respondents expressed confusion or concern about this relatively inflexible language and proposed that additional marginalized identities be included within the acceptable central framework. One respondent suggested that race and class are inextricable in America, so foregrounding socioeconomic status rather than a protected racial or ethnic group category would be just as appropriate at approaching the subject from a single racial perspective alone. Three respondents expressed dissatisfaction with what they perceive as the erasure of sexuality and gender identity from the DRC proposal guidelines, and presented an intersectional argument for why the university should consider broadening the acceptable parameters to include these categories as well as additional non-racial identities, such as disability status. These arguments make sense within the praxis of intersectionality, as any one person can and does contain a multitude of identities, some of them subordinated and some of them dominant, which can dictate their access to power in society. Proponents of changing the DRC guideline language persuasively argue that grouping individuals based upon just or even primarily race leads to replicating and perhaps even implicitly endorsing silences in the literature/historiography.

Yet defenders of the current DRC guideline language make a persuasive argument – that the DRC initiative was implemented due to a specific, race-based hate incident on campus and the group of activists and administrators who convened to discuss how to best address the issue emphasized the necessity of race-based community support. The concern, then, is that the history of the institution and the purpose of the DRC mandate will become lost if the language of the requirement is expanded significantly. It is the legacy and the contemporary reality of the United States that unequal access and outright exclusion are more often than not predicated on one's racial identity, so making explicit to students that they will be working in a society that is often inequitable for some races by design is paramount. What students are trained to do with this knowledge remains the decision of the instructor, and should be made explicit in the learning outcomes. Lee (2015) describes his opposition to emphasizing multiculturalism over radical action, and specifically of comparing the Asian American experience to the Black experience as a "case study" of multiculturalism by stating, "Thus we see the deep problematic of multiculturalism, a discourse that ostensibly allows for the incorporation of new *subjects*, but subjects enabled consistently and persistently on antiblack grounds" (p. 172) [emphasis added]. The introduction of new, not necessarily racial identity subjects into the DRC guidelines could result in students favoring those classes over race-based courses because critical race theory does not align with their "colorblind" philosophies, or because they do not want to be confronted with the difficult realities of racism in the United States.

The tensions here should be obvious; depending upon an instructor's subjectivity and views on the language of the DRC guidelines, they might decide to approach crafting their course learning outcomes to encourage students to participate actively in social justice. To demonstrate how learning outcomes differ depending upon the perspective of the instructor, let us revisit Nilson's (2016) outcomes related to human dimension and caring goals (Fink, 2013). MCE, with its primary emphasis on recognizing that cultures are valuable and distinct (Seglow, 2003), would prioritize that students come away from their courses with

(1) foundational knowledge and that their newfound awareness of these key figures, facts, and events, (2) will give them the skills to successfully and compellingly complete the required final assessment, and (3) they will apply what they learned to their lives in the form of bias reduction and acknowledgement of difference. Students in MCE-aligned courses might be required to (1) define a variety of key terms and memorize and recall historically significant figures and events, (2) write either an original research paper or a literature review/historiography, and (3) tolerate – and hopefully celebrate – difference. Of course, internal states or values-based learning outcomes are difficult to measure, and teaching DRCs can be emotionally draining because some students are diametrically opposed to diversity measures, so a reliance on learning outcomes that are clearly evaluative makes sense for instructors who believe that their courses will not be approached with the same seriousness as other classes. Indeed, since completing DRCs for credit is required of every student, these classes can subsequently become very large and difficult from a classroom management perspective. Consequently, a desire for uncomplicated learning outcomes and similarly straightforward assessments built to measure them is perhaps even a way the instructor might protect herself from undue emotional labor.

This is where the issue becomes difficult to discuss. Based upon the responses of instructors and students at our institution, most people do recognize that teaching these courses is burdensome, but are also passionate about supporting the original intent of the DRC, which is to support marginalized and underrepresented racial groups on campus with consciousness-raising efforts. This does require working with values-based outcomes, which complicates the course design process. Human dimension and caring outcomes require that students "demonstrate they have gained a new understanding of themselves or others," that they "obtain new interests, feelings, or values" with regard to the course subject matter, as well as the "motivation to learn more about the subject" after the course has completed; and that students meta-cognitively reflect on the process of learning and their own positionality as a learner (Fink, 2013; Nilson, 2016, p. 30). Measuring any one of these outcome types is difficult and often reliant on indirect (self-reported) measures, which complicates common grading practices that claim to be more objective. Nilson (2016) herself provides a "Rubric for Evaluating and Revising Student Learning Outcomes" that places values-based outcomes as part of the lowest order on the rubric (missed the point), valuing high levels of cognition (application, analysis, synthesis, evaluation) over low-level internal states (know, understand, appreciate). Yet critical inquiry can take place within the context of values-based learning, and should, because the goal of SJE is for the student to leave the classroom with the tools and the will to improve the world in which they live.

So what do SJE learning outcomes look like, and how might they be assessed? Perhaps the most promising way to frame values-based outcomes is to allow students to demonstrate their growth as critical thinkers, because it is difficult to be dishonest about one's true feelings under sustained inquiry. Paul and Elder (2013) outline a model of measuring the development of critical thinking in students. This model employs the practice of questioning for understanding, or a version of the Socratic method that allows the instructor to confront the student with their own logic and push them to make connections between the course material and their own lives by asking them to elaborate. For example, a student might speak up in class to answer a question, and the instructor instead of praising them and moving on might consider gently guiding the student to *clarify* (e.g., asking students to elaborate on a point or to provide examples). For students who are having difficulty connecting with the material, it might be useful to encourage them to expand the *depth* and *breadth* of their answers, asking them to persuasively argue that their answers address the complexities of the question successfully, and pushing them to make connections with other arguments they have heard in the class by asking "What might another person say about your answer? Can you envision a counter-argument, or different perspective?" And for those students who are resisting the course material actively, instructors can stress the validity of the course by demanding that the student engage with the methods of the discipline and the presented evidence in good faith. This might look like pressing those students to be more *accurate* in their answers (e.g., asking students how they validate the accuracy of a statement), to be more *precise*, and to answer to the relevance of their evidence (Paul & Elder, 2013). Additionally, consistently encouraging students to assess the *logic* ("How does this follow from the evidence?") and *fairness* ("What stakes do you have in this argument?") of either their own answers or those of the scholars under consideration is an excellent strategy to develop critical thinking skills.

If critical thinking is the model for values-based learning outcomes, then the instructor should also invest time into helping their students develop a process of epistemological reflection (i.e., metacognitive self-inquiry.) Magolda (2004) offers a framework to assess "levels of knowing," which can help students evaluate their growth. The four levels of knowing are *absolute, transitional, independent*, and *contextual*. Students in the absolute level of knowing display black-and-white thinking, where there are right or wrong answers. Students in the transitional stage of knowing begin to experience uncertainty, and independent students accept that uncertainty. Finally, students in the contextual stage of knowing show more "correct" patterns of thinking, allowing for uncertainty, consistently contextualizing, and supporting answers with empirical evidence. Creating a reference resource for students to continually check how they are interacting with the knowledge they have can be a powerful tool; if a student takes something for granted, be it an idea they had before entering the classroom or something they picked up along the way, it can be helpful to push them to categorize how well they *know* what they know. For example, Magolda (2004) describes encountering first-year college students with what she describes as a tremendous respect for authority – the authority of the instructors, scholars, and what they had come to believe are "cut-and-dried" facts about the world, which resulted in inflexible thinking patterns that closed off critical inquiry because there was, seemingly, nothing ambiguous about the subject (Magolda, 2004). Students tend to approach STEM disciplines with this high level of esteem for authority, and that leads to reductive thinking patterns where students are unable or unwilling to interrogate certain things they *know* because these things seem so absolutely true that questioning them would be counterintuitive at best.

It is the goal to move students away from absolute knowing and toward contextual knowing that prioritizes the position of the subject to the self – you only know what you know within the context of your subjective positionality. This work is not simple, but if courses are designed within an SJE framework around values-based critical and self-inquiry, then teaching DRCs becomes an opportunity to help students mature as people, and possibly impact the way they solve problems and react to unfamiliar or uncomfortable information. This work can change lives. And that is SJE – a transformative approach to teaching and learning. Social justice theory helps clarify intentions, and challenges unproductive and counterproductive practices in the classroom, because SJE stems from the same philosophy that created the diversity requirement on our campus and so many others: that oppression has consequences for everyone, and both marginalized and advantaged groups are dehumanized by oppression (Adams et al., 2016). Students should care about their DRCs because completing these courses successfully should not only help them *tolerate* and *appreciate* those who are different from themselves, but can actually change their perspective on who they are as people, and what they want to make of their place in society.

NOTES

1. R1 universities are institutions that meet the criteria of the highest levels of research activity, according to the Carnegie Classification of Institutions of Higher Education.

2. To learn more about the concept of emotional labor as it relates to teaching and identity, see Schueths, Gladney, Crawford, Bass, and Moore (2013), Bellas (1999), and Mahoney, Buboltz, Buckner, and Doverspike (2011).

REFERENCES

Adams, M., Bell, L. A., Goodman, D. J., & Joshi, K. Y. (2016). *Teaching for diversity and social justice*. New York, NY: Routledge.

Adams, M., & Love, B. J. (2009). A social justice education faculty development framework for a post-Grutter era. In K. Skubikowsji, C. Wright, & R. Graf (Eds.), Social justice education: Inviting faculty to transform their institution.

Bellas, M. L. (1999). Emotional labor in academia: The case of professors. *The Annals of the American Academy of Political and Social Science, 561*(1), 96–110. https://doi.org/10.1177/000271629956100107

Biondi, M. (2012). What happened to Black Studies? In M. Biondi (Ed.), *Black revolution on campus* (pp. 241–267). Berkeley, CA: University of California Press.

Crenshaw, K. (1989). Demarginalizing the intersection of race and sex: A Black feminist critique of antidiscrimiation doctrine, feminist theory and antiracist policies. *The University of Chicago Legal Forum, 140*, 139–167.

Espinosa, L. L., Turk, J. M., Taylor, M., & Chessman H. M. (2019). *Race and ethnicity in higher education: A status report*. Washington, DC: American Council on Education.

Fink, D. L. (2013). *Creating significant learning experiences: An integrated approach to designing college courses*. San Francisco, CA: Jossey-Bass.

Freire, P. (1970). *Pedagogy of the oppressed*. New York, NY: Continuum Publishing.

Goldin, C., & Katz, L. (1998). The shaping of higher education: The formative years in the United States, 1890 to 1940. *Journal of Economic Perspectives, 12*(1), 37–62.

King, P. M., & Magolda, M. B. (2005). A developmental model of intercultural maturity. *Journal of College Student Development, 46*(6), 571–592.

Koopman, G. (1987). The thread of humanism in the history of American education. *Journal of Curriculum and Supervision, 2*(3), 233–247.

Laird, T. F., & Engberg, M. E. (2011). Establishing differences between diversity requirements and other courses with varying degrees of diversity inclusivity. *The Journal of General Education, 60*(2), 117–137.

Lee, J. K. (2015). Multiculturalism. In C. J. Schlund-Vials, L. Trinh Võ, & S. Wong (Eds.), *Keywords for Asian American studies* (pp. 169–173). New York, NY: NYU Press.

Magolda, M. B. (2004). Evolution of a constructivist conceptualization of epistemological reflection. *Educational Psychologist, 39*(1), 31–42.

Mahoney, K. T., Buboltz, W. C., Jr, Buckner V, J. E., & Doverspike, D. (2011). *Emotional labor in American professors. Journal of Occupational Health Psychology, 16*(4), 406–423. https://doi.org/10.1037/a0025099

Nilson, L. B. (2016). *Teaching at its best: A research-based resource for college instructors.* San Francisco, CA: Jossey-Bass.

Paul, R., & Elder, L. (2013). Critical thinking: Intellectual standards essential to reasoning well within every domain of human thought. *Journal of Developmental Education, 37*(1), 32–35.

Renault, E. (2019). The aporias of social justice. In E. Renault (Ed.), *The experience of injustice: A theory of recognition* (pp. 65–93). New York, NY: Columbia University Press.

Schueths, A. M., Gladney, T., Crawford, D. M., Bass, K. L., & Moore, H. A. (2013). Passionate pedagogy and emotional labor: Students' responses to learning diversity from diverse instructors. *International Journal of Qualitative Studies in Education, 26*(10), 1259–1276, doi:10.1080/09518398.2012.731532

Seglow, J. (2003). Multiculturalism. In R. Bellamy & A. Mason (Eds.), *Political concepts* (pp. 156–168). Manchester: Manchester University Press.

Seltzer, R., Frazier, M., & Ricks, I. (1996). Multiculturalism, race, and education. *The Journal of Negro Education, 64*(2), 124–140.

Wiggins, G. P., & McTighe, J. (1998). *Understanding by design.* Upper Saddle River, NJ: Merrill/Prentice Hall.

Williams, D. A. (2013). *Strategic diversity leadership.* Sterling, VA: Stylus Pub.

Zuniga, X., Nagda, B., Chesler, M., & Cytron-Walker, A. (2007). Intergroup dialogue in higher education: Meaningful learning about social justice. *ASHE Higher Education Report, 32*, 1–128.

Zúñiga, X., & Sevig, T. D. (2000). Bridging the us/them divide: Intergroup dialogue and peer leadership. In M. Adams, W. J. Blumenfeld, R. Castadñeda, H. W. Hackman, M. L. Peters, & X. Zúñiga (Eds.), *Readings for diversity and social justice* (pp. 488–493). New York, NY: Routledge.

CHAPTER 3

IMPROVING CLASSROOM ENGAGEMENT AND LEARNING: ADAPTABLE TOOLS, STRATEGIES, AND RESOURCES FOR NURTURING DIVERSITY APPRECIATION AND A MINDFULLY MULTICULTURAL ENVIRONMENT IN THE ONLINE CLASSROOM

Jennifer Schneider

ABSTRACT

This chapter seeks to help and support online educators in their efforts to improve tomorrow. Specifically, the chapter shares practical strategies and tools that online educators can easily apply, adapt, and/or personalize in order to help promote a mindfully multicultural classroom in their online classrooms and programs. The chapter includes a wide range of actionable tools and exercises to help online instructors optimize the learning experience for all students by building upon the unique strengths and diverse cultural backgrounds of all students in their online classrooms. The strategies help instructors leverage diversity as a means to promote equity and social justice in online programs and, ultimately, the world as a whole. The chapter relies upon Gollnick and Chinn's (2017) six beliefs that are fundamental to multicultural education

Developing and Supporting Multiculturalism and Leadership Development:
International Perspectives on Humanizing Higher Education
Innovations in Higher Education Teaching and Learning, Volume 30, 33–61
Copyright © 2020 by Emerald Publishing Limited
All rights of reproduction in any form reserved
ISSN: 2055-3641/doi:10.1108/S2055-364120200000030005

and presents strategies from two perspectives or lenses (student-focused and faculty-focused). Approaching the issue from a dual-sided lens is intended to best support the ultimate goal of improving the student learning experience. Emphasis is placed on both public and private interactions between faculty and students. Public interactions include all discussion board and announcement communications. Public interactions also include resources that are shared in the online classroom for all students' benefit.

Keywords: Multicultural education; diversity; online learning; online education; instructional strategies, pedagogy; student communications; intentional instruction; critical analysis; awareness

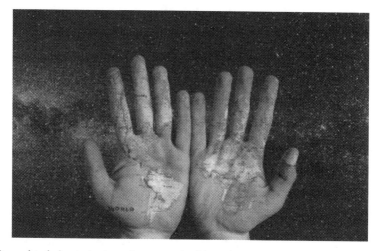

We need to help students and parents cherish and preserve the ethnic and cultural diversity that nourishes and strengthens this community.... – Cesar Chavez

Chapter outcomes:

- *Summarize and describe increasingly diverse online learners.*
- *Define and describe multicultural education.*
- *Analyze the importance of multicultural education in online classrooms.*
- *Generate strategies to promote mindfully multicultural environments in online classrooms.*

1. INTRODUCTION

Online programs have become an increasingly common method of learning for an increasingly diverse population of students (Allen & Seaman, 2017). A *recent study* found that the number of students taking online courses has risen to more than 6 million nationally (Online Learning Consortium, 2017). Additional research finds *millions of K-12 students* learning online (Herold, 2017).

However, this trend (and opportunity) is not without challenges. Access to post-secondary online learning is not in and of itself sufficient to ensure a student's educational success. Related research shares some of the "'promises and limits' of online" learning and describes a variety of practices that can improve online learning experiences (Xu & Xu, 2019, p. 1). Xu and Xu (2019) note that "online courses without strong support to students may exacerbate educational inequities" (American Enterprise Institute, 2019, para. 4). Culturally diverse groups of learners both need and deserve personalized support in order to succeed in the online learning environment. Relatedly, Bettina Love (2019) reminds readers that teachers "*will* hurt a [student] whose culture is viewed as an after-thought" (para. 7). Parallel arguments persist and present in all disciplines, educational levels, and online classrooms.

Gollnick and Chinn (2017) write that "[m]ulticultural education is a construct that acknowledges the diversity of students and their families and builds on the diversity to promote equality and social justice in education" (p. 19). For multicultural education "to become a reality in the formal school situation, the total environment must reflect a commitment to multicultural education" (Gollnick & Chinn, 2017, p. 25). Online learning environments are no exception.

Nurturing online learning environments committed to multicultural education promote long-term goals related to diversity, tolerance, inclusion, and social justice in all disciplines and fields. As one prepares to teach a course online, there are a variety of steps and strategies that can help support a goal of increased reflection and respect in all thinking. As online learning grows in popularity, developing, managing, and contributing to online classrooms in a manner that supports the type of respect and tolerance we hope to see in the world more broadly is critical. Successfully removing barriers for women, minorities, and other under-represented groups in the workplace originates, in part, in the nature of relationships and interactions we promote and encourage through our online classrooms.

Diversity: the art of thinking independently together. – Malcolm Forbes

Daily, we encounter persistent and challenging questions of how best to create true and meaningful opportunities for conversation, dialogue, and growth (Barnes & Souza, 2019). The future of our communities and our places of work are in today's online classrooms. It is our collective responsibility to ensure we create a classroom environment that is representative of the type of future we both deserve and desire. Doing so is not without challenges, especially in online learning environments. For the online instructor who connects with students remotely, nurturing and sustaining an inclusive learning environment can feel daunting. For online educators, the challenge of promoting a mindfully multicultural environment is complex. Online educators often do not have easy access to student backgrounds. Such educators also often lack easy access to peers. Isolation is a concern for both educators and students. Similarly, information and communication can often feel one-sided, limited, and incomplete (from both the perspective of the instructor and the students).

The future of the world is in my classroom today, a future with the potential for good or bad … I must be vigilant every day, lest I lose one fragile opportunity to improve tomorrow – Ivan Welton Fitzwater

2. OVERVIEW

This chapter seeks to help and support online educators in their efforts to improve tomorrow. Specifically, the chapter shares practical strategies and tools that online educators can easily apply, adapt, and/or personalize in order to help promote a mindfully multicultural classroom in their online classrooms and programs. The chapter includes a wide range of actionable tools and exercises to help online instructors optimize the learning experience for all students by building upon the unique strengths and diverse cultural backgrounds of all students in their online classrooms. The strategies help instructors leverage diversity as a means to promote equity and social justice in online programs and, ultimately, the world as a whole. The chapter relies upon Gollnick and Chinn's (2017) six beliefs that are fundamental to multicultural education and presents strategies from two perspectives or lenses (student-focused and faculty-focused). Approaching the issue from a dual-sided lens is intended to best support the ultimate goal of improving the student learning experience. Emphasis is placed on both public and private interactions between faculty and students. Public interactions include all discussion board and announcement communications. Public interactions also include resources that are shared in the online classroom for all students' benefit.

3. ORGANIZATION

The work is broken down in sections that align with elements of an online classroom (including discussion boards, announcements, grading feedback, email communications, and applications beyond an individual course session). The chapter also includes interactive exercises and activities designed to raise awareness and understanding of the meaning and importance of multicultural education in the online learning environment. Case-based scenarios are incorporated in order to provide practical illustrations of the presented tools and strategies. The chapter concludes with a list of recommended resources and additional reading.

3.1. Discussion Boards

A quality education involves much more than "simply a course of study or textbooks" (Schramm-Pate, n.d., p. 1). Rather, curriculum includes subject matter content, pedagogy, co-curricular activities, and areas of diversity (Schramm-Pate, n.d.). In online classrooms, discussion boards offer excellent opportunities to celebrate diversity and model the values inherent to, and a critical component of, a multicultural education.

Values are generally "the intangible forces that guide and influence" decisions and that provide "a frame of reference for evaluating information and options" (Sukiennik & Raufman, p. 37). According to Seligman (2002), there are fundamental values and virtues that emerge across cultures and time. These values and virtues include wisdom, courage, love and humanity, temperance, justice, and transcendence (Seligman, 2002).

Education provides a source of strength (both content and non-content based), and that strength (originating with every student) can transform the lives of infinitely more (families, communities, towns, and generations to come). Online discussion boards offer excellent opportunities to model interactions that are heavily influenced by values (and virtues) based on equity, social justice, and fairness. Illustrative values include wisdom (quality learning experiences, and empowered learners), justice and fairness (all individuals deserve quality education), and love and humanity (resisting violence against girls and others).

The following strategies offer options for supporting a multiculturally sensitive and supportive approach in all online discussion forums.

3.1.1. Qualitative Discussion Reviews

Approach discussion prompts in ways that support and encourage student choice. Share personally relevant and meaningful resources that relate to course content and have personal relevance for students and a wide range of possible career aspirations. Read all students posts (both text and subtext) and proactively address any insensitive posts and issues of possible cultural insensitivity.

Open all posts with a personalized greeting using the student's preferred name and/or pronoun. Prioritize warmth, support, and authenticity in all interactions. Pause and review all emails and posts for *tone and clarity*. Actively ensure all sides of a topic are explored. When prompts encourage discussion on controversial topics, consider all sides of an issue. Read opposing perspectives carefully and deeply. Ask thoughtful, respectful questions to deepen understanding. When a discussion prompt requires students to take a position, encourage all learners to take a counter position in peer responses. Use *questions intentionally* and in a *learner-focused manner*. Actively reflect on explicit and implicit issues of culture, diversity, and inclusivity as they relate to discussion topics. These acts take courage. Remember that courage leads to positive change, in the classroom and in the field.

Demonstrate curiosity and get to know your students and their perspectives

Curiosity in discussion posts:

- Ask probing questions to encourage reflection and additional conversation
- Share observations, not judgements

Inspire confidence, cultural sensitivity, and capacity in students.

- *Example openings:*

  - What experiences have you had that might help others appreciate this challenge in more depth?
  - How might we ensure all are comfortable discussing this topic?
  - What resources might help us explore this topic from additional perspectives and sides?
  - What additional challenges might individuals from different cultures face when presented with this issue?

  A lot of different flowers make a bouquet. – Muslim Origin

  Reflection activity:

- How might intentionally working with the above suggested activities promote greater ability to interact with others?
- Identify two career scenarios where the skills developed and nurtured in the above suggested activities will be relevant and valuable.

  Ice-breaker ideas:

- Variations on "three truths and a lie":

  o Personal facts/statements.
  o Fears.
  o Hopes/dreams.
  o Cultural characteristics.

- A question for another student.
- An image that represents something important about your culture.

- A list of objects and/or traditions that are important to you and why.
- Post a selection of quotations sharing varying perspectives on a key course theme.
- Share a favorite book, movie, author. Explain why.
- Share a favorite quotation and why.
- Who am I? Five clues.
- Where am I from? Five clues.
- What countries have you visited?
- If you could visit any country in the world, what would it be and why?
- What languages do you speak?
- If you could learn a new language, what would it be and why?

3.1.2. Individual and Quantitative Self-Checks

Keep track of your weekly discussion board responses. Strive for consistency and equity in replies shared with other students over the course of a term. Merryfield (2003) reminds us to be watchful for "the lesson of isolates" *in student responses* (p. 154). Respond to different peers each week and/or posts with no replies.
Exercises and activities:

- After a class or module ends, reflect on your contributions from a content and tone perspective. How, if at all, might a receiver have misinterpreted your writing? How might you proactively work to minimize the potential for misinterpretations going forward (in educational and professional contexts)?
- Assign students to sides of a topic by the first letter of their last name, first name, etc.
- Ask students to respond to posts with no replies before responding to others.
- Before a course module opens, consider which students you have not yet had a chance to connect with on a 1:1 level. Work to engage them in conversation by responding to their posts. Email them to touch base and see how their course experience has been to date.
- Complete study skills checklists to continuously self-evaluate and reflect:

    o See: *https://www.educationcorner.com/study-skills-checklist.html*
    o See: *https://ucc.vt.edu/academic_support/study_skills_information/study_ skills_checklist.html*
    o See: *https://www.educationcorner.com/study-skills.html*
    o See: *https://www.mansfield.edu/trio/online-modules/upload/Study-Skills-Checklist.pdf*

- Reflect: How might the above-referenced study skills checklists improve the way you approach career-related events and interactions?
- Identify two career scenarios where the skills developed and nurtured in the above suggested activities will be relevant and valuable. Reflect on how students with different cultural background might respond differently.

3.1.3. Personalization

> Good teaching cannot be reduced to technique; good teaching comes from the identity and integrity of the teacher. – Parker Palmer

Celebrate diversity through warm, inclusive, and supportive responses. You may enter a new course feeling vulnerable and unsure. Others will surely feel the same way. This is, in many ways, similar to what you (and others) will encounter out in the field.

There are many ways we can help other students feel that they belong. Just like there are many ways we can help all individuals feel that they belong in the communities they are a part of. When greeting other students in an online forum, make note of preferred names/pronouns. Digital tools like Excel, Google Sheets, and Word all work well. Actively seek out what makes students unique and what makes them curious. Share personal anecdotes and narratives to humanize inter-actions. Model safe sharing. Express interest in cultural backgrounds and the etymology of unusual names. Merryfield (2003) writes about making the most of access to *insider discourse* throughout learning communities. Read all student and instructor posts, even if you do not formally respond.

At the end of a session, consider opening up a discussion thread where students can celebrate each other and those students who might have impacted their think-ing. You might include a discussion forum where students thank other students for impacting their thinking in a positive way. Ask students to include the name of the referenced student in the subject line of their post. Include guidelines such that once a student is "tagged," new posts must acknowledge another student so that every-one is "tagged" and celebrated at least once. If we hope to support a future world where respect, diversity, and appreciation for all cultures is the norm, we also need to ensure we build the habits that are critical if such a world is ever to be.

People don't decide their future. They decide their habits and their habits decide their futures
– F. M. Alexander

Guiding reminders:

- Share your language, your culture, your traditions.
- Work toward a norm of open sharing.
- Use names in all posts.

   o See: Sharing Preferred Names

- Address peers and instructors with intentionality.
- Celebrate diversity through warm, inclusive, and supportive responses.
- Sign all posts with your preferred name.
- Upload images of yourself.
- Utilize digital tools to establish your personality

   o Bitmoji: *https://www.bitmoji.com/*
   o Voki: *https://voki.com/*
   o Screencastify: *https://www.screencastify.com/*
   o "Digital You: Tech Tools to Help You Create Amazing Avatars for the Online Classroom," see: *http://www.codlearningtech.org/2018/03/01/ digital-you-tech-tools-to-help-you-create-amazing-avatars-for-the-online-classroom/*

Share a document that collects all students' preferred names. At many institutions, students cannot always get names changed in the system. Consider asking for preferred pronouns, as well. For a piece cautioning against asking for preferred pronouns, see: *https://www.insidehighered.com/views/2018/09/19/why-asking-students-their-preferred-pronoun-not-good-idea-opinion*

Reflection:

- What approach do you prefer and why?

3.2. Announcements and Other Public Communications

Arthur Dobrin (2013) writes about *the power of first impressions and the "halo effect"*. As we begin an online course, we can actively evaluate course shells from the lens and perspective of all entering students. Consider:

- As a student in this course, what might seem unclear or confusing?
- How might the instructor more intentionally welcome all students upon entry?
- Does the course layout model inclusivity at all times?
- Are all components of the course accessible to all students?
- Are many different voices represented?
- Are many different faces represented?
- Are many different genders, races, ethnicities, cultures, etc., represented?
- Are all documents accessible to all students?

Review all communications for clarity. Consider:

- What is my primary message?
- Is my intended message clear?
- Where might confusion present and how can I proactively address it?
- Do I include any unnecessary text?
- Does my subject line align with my intended message?

Instructors often teach how they were taught. We often fail to recognize the diversity that we do not see. Thus, it is up to each of us to work to make diversity visible in our online classrooms. We can do this by sharing our backgrounds, incorporating our experiences, and demonstrating respect and intellectual curiosity for others at all times – both in our online classrooms and in our work in the field.

Enlist student help – building a community of awareness

- Continuously seek questions.
- Ask students to reach out when concerns present.
- Remain humble and be proactive.

3.3. Assessment and Grading Feedback

3.3.1. Feedback

Student assessment and associated reporting practices have been a fundamental component of educational practices for centuries (O'Connor, 2010). Grading and grading practices, in contrast, have a long but more recent history, dating back to the early 1900s (O'Connor, 2010). Mary Lovett Smallwood (1935) documents early grading practices at Yale University early in the twentieth century. Despite the longstanding use of both assessment and grading, the grading process remains a complicated and contentious endeavor. The issue is so complex that even John Hattie (2008), a scholar with decades of research focusing on feedback, admits that he has "struggled to understand the concept" (p. 173).

It is no secret that grading is a powerful impact and influence on how well and whether one learns. According to John Hattie (2012), grading feedback is one of the most powerful influences on what, and how, a student learns. Many articles and professional development sessions focus on the qualities of valuable feedback. Feedback, for example, should be timely, detailed, personalized, and student specific (Hattie, 2012). However, the topic of equity and grading feedback is less often discussed. Questions of how race and ethnicity influence, often in implicit ways, the equity and nature (tone, quality, content) of grading feedback are important and worthy of further study.

Equity challenges associated with the grading feedback process are complex and persistent. In "A History of Grading," Mark Durm provides both a history of grading as a process and as a form of potential discrimination. Durm (1993) describes an unstandardized and persistently uncalibrated grading system and writes that "[d]ifferentiating between students in the very earliest days of American colleges and universities seemed to center around social class" (p. 1). Challenges persist to the current day. Kohn (1999), for example, questions the entire premise and purpose of grading and writes that "the most impressive teachers are those who despise the whole process of giving grades" (p. 1).

Issues of bias also arise when evaluating grading feedback. It is important to note that instructors often bring biases (some unconscious, some conscious) to the grading processes. Biases can result from a variety of factors, including prior knowledge of student grades and scores, race, class, ethnicity, gender, and other factors (Malouff, 2008; Malouff, Emmerton, & Schutte, 2013).

The following resources explore how concerns for equity, bias, and discrimination are endemic throughout all levels of education, including higher education, and including the grading feedback process. The resources also pose opportunities for reflection and growth in this area. The collection of resources takes both a summary and a critical approach, identifying themes and sharing reflections and potential interventions to help mitigate and minimize the potential for bias in higher education and the grading feedback process.

Collection of Related Articles/Studies

Article 1.

Students' race and teachers' social support affect the positive feedback bias in public schools	Kent D. Harber, Jamie L. Gorman, Frank P. Gengara, Samantha Butishingh, Willian Tsang, Rebecca Ouellette	2012

Reference: Harber, K. D., Gorman, J. L., Gengaro, F. P., Butisingh, S., Tsang, W., & Ouellette, R. (2012). Students' race and teachers' social support affect the positive feedback bias in public schools. *Journal of Educational Psychology, 104*(4), 1149–1161. *http://dx.doi.org/10.1037/a0028110*

Purpose of study: This study tested whether White public-school teachers demonstrate positive feedback bias. Positive feedback bias describes evaluation scenarios where White teachers provide more praise and less criticism to minority students than to White students for equivalent work. In general, minority students often suffer from a "challenge deficit" in which they are deprived of the expectations that generate intellectual growth and academic achievement (Steele, 1995). The study also tested whether teachers who lack school-based social supports (whether from fellow teachers and/or school administrators) are more likely to display a positive feedback bias and whether the positive feedback bias applies to Latinos as well as to Blacks.

Results/findings: Teachers in the Black student condition showed the positive bias, but only if they lacked school-based social support. Teachers in the Latino student condition showed the positive bias regardless of the presence of school-based support. Results suggest that a positive feedback bias may contribute to the challenge deficit that undermines minority students' academic achievement.

Related articles:

Harber, K. D. (1998). Feedback to minorities: Evidence of a positive bias. *Journal of Personality and Social Psychology, 74,* 622–628. doi:10.1037/0022-3514.74.3.622

Harber, K. D. (2004). The positive feedback bias as a response to out-group unfriendliness. *Journal of Applied Social Psychology, 34,* 2272–2297. doi:10.1111/j.1559-1816.2004.tb01977.x

Harber, K. D., Stafford, R., & Kennedy, K. A. (2010). The positive feedback bias as a response to self-image threat. *British Journal of Social Psychology, 49,* 207–218. doi:10.1348/014466609X473956

Steele, C. M. (1995). Black students live down to expectations. *New York Times,* August 31, p. A15.

Article 2.

Bias in the classroom: Types, frequencies, and responses	Guy A. Boysen (SUNY Fredonia) and David L. Vogel (Iowa State University)	2009

Reference: Boysen, G. A., & Vogel, D. L. (2009). Bias in the classroom: Types, frequencies, and responses. *Teaching of Psychology, 36*(1), 12–17.

Purpose of study: Incidents of bias still occur in college classrooms. Explicit bias is overt and intentional. Implicit bias is subtle, automatic, and often occurs without the perpetrator's intention or awareness (Greenwald & Banaji, 1995). Limited research has specifically explored the presence of incidences of such bias in the college classroom. This study sought to address this gap in the literature. The study documented the frequency with which professors perceive bias in their classrooms, the methods used to respond to that bias, and the perceived effectiveness of those responses. Study results suggested that 38% of professors perceived an incident of bias in the classroom in the last year, and that they perceived overt (explicit) and subtle (implicit) bias with similar frequency. Explicit (27%) and implicit bias (30%) occurred with similar frequency. Professors generally believed their responses to bias were successful, but many could not assess success.

Related articles:

Greenwald, A. G., & Banaji, M. R. (1995). Implicit social cognition: Attitudes, self-esteem, and stereotypes. *Psychological Review, 102,* 4–27.

Harlow, R. (2003). "Race doesn't matter, but . . .": The effect of race on professors' experience and emotion management in the undergraduate classroom. *Social Psychology Quarterly, 66,* 348–363.

Lawrence, S. M. (1998). Unveiling positions of privilege: A hands-on approach to understanding racism. *Teaching of Psychology, 25,* 198–200.

Sol'orzano, D., Ceja, M., & Yosso, T. (2000). Critical race theory, racial micro-aggressions, and campus racial climate: The experiences of African American college students. *The Journal of Negro Education, 69,* 60–73

Sue, D. W., Capodilupo, C. M., Torino, G. C., Bucceri, J. M., Holder, A. M. B., Nadal, K. L., et al. (2007). Racial microaggressions in everyday life: Implications for clinical practice. *American Psychologist, 62,* 271–286.

Article 3.

Written in Black and White: Exploring confirmation bias in racialized perceptions of writing skills	Arin Reeves	2014

Reference: Reeves, A. N. (2014). *Written in Black & White: Exploring confirmation bias in racialized perceptions of writing skills.* Chicago, IL: Nextions.

Purpose of study: The authors followed up on an earlier study on unconscious bias (conducted 10 years prior) that showed supervising lawyers were more likely than not to perceive African American lawyers as having subpar writing skills in comparison with their Caucasian counterparts. In the current study, the researchers focused on the specific bias of writing skills and asked if confirmation bias unconsciously causes supervising lawyers to more negatively evaluate legal writing by an African American lawyer. Confirmation bias refers to a mental shortcut by the brain that makes one actively seek information that affirms established beliefs while missing data that contradicts established beliefs. The same memo averaged a rating of 3.2/5.0 under a hypothetical "African American" Thomas Meyer and a rating of 4.1/5.0 under hypothetical "Caucasian" Thomas Meyer. Qualitative comments on memos, consistently, were more positive for the "Caucasian" Thomas Meyer than our "African American" Thomas Meyer. There was no significant correlation between a partner's race/ethnicity and the differentiated patterns of errors found between the two memos. There was also no significant correlation between a partner's gender and the differentiated patterns of errors found between the two memos. Researchers found that female partners generally found more errors and wrote longer narratives than the male partners.

Data findings affirmed the researcher's hypothesis, namely, when expecting to find fewer errors, we find fewer errors (unconscious confirmation bias). Findings also illustrated that the evaluators' confirmation bias occurred in the data collection phase of their evaluation processes when they evaluated errors, and not the final analysis phase. Evaluators unconsciously found more of the errors in the "African American" Thomas Meyer's memo, but the final rating process was a conscious and unbiased analysis based on the number of errors found.

Related articles:

Blascovich, J., Mendes, W. B., Hunter, S. B., Lickel, B., & Kowai-Bell, N. (2001). Perceiver threat in social interactions with stigmatized others. *Journal of Personality and Social Psychology, 80,* 253–267. doi:10.1037/0022-3514.80.2.253

Cohen, G. L., Steele, C. M., & Ross, L. D. (1999). The mentor's dilemma: Providing critical feedback across the racial divide. *Personality and Social Psychology Bulletin, 25*, 1302–1318. doi:10.1177/0146167299258011

Steele, C. M. (1995). Black students live down to expectations. *New York Times*, August 31, p. A15.

Article 4.

Preventing halo bias in grading the work of university students	John M. Malouff, Sarah J. Stein, Lodewicka N. Bothma, Kimberley Coulter, Ashley J. Emmerton	2014

Reference: Malouff, J. M., Stein, S. J., Bothma, L. N., Coulter, K., & Emmerton, A. J. (2014). Preventing halo bias in grading the work of university students. *Cogent Psychology, 1*, 988937.

Purpose of study: Explored the use of anonymous marking as a strategy for minimizing the presence and impact of bias when assessing subjective student work. Sought to fill identified gaps in the literature associated with the impact of halo bias (where prior knowledge of a person can create a positive or negative view of the individual) when grading subjective work. Findings suggest that keeping students anonymous, as in the condition with no knowledge of the student's performance in the oral presentation, helps prevent bias in grading.

Related article:

Brennan, D. J. (2008). University student anonymity in the summative assessment of written work. *Higher Education Research & Development, 27*, 43–54, doi:10.1080/07294360701658724

Article 5.

Race and ethnicity: Views from inside the unconscious mind	Cheryl Staats, Kelly Capatosto, Lena Tenney, and Sarah Mamo	2017

Reference: Staats, C., Capatosto, K., Tenney, L., & Mamo, S. (2017). State of the science: Implicit bias review. Retrieved from *http://kirwaninstitute.osu.edu/implicit-bias-training/resources/2017-implicit-bias-review.pdf*

Purpose of study: Focused on highlighting the wide variety of ways that unconscious associations can create unintended outcomes. Presents a curated collection of selected pieces from the academic literature (published in 2016) addressing the topic of implicit bias across the domains of criminal justice, health and health care, employment, education, and housing. Shares implicit bias mitigation strategies.

Related articles:

Carbado, D. W., Turetsky, K. M., & Purdie-Vaughns, V. (2016). Privileged or mismatched: The lose–lose position of African Americans in the affirmative action debate. *UCLA Law Review Discourse, 64*, 174.

Fridell, L. A. (2017). *Producing bias-free policing: A science-based approach.* Springer Briefs in Criminology: Translational Criminology. Springer.

Knips, A. (2019). 6 Steps to equitable data analysis. Retrieved from *https://www.edutopia.org/article/6-steps-equitable-data-analysis*

Article 6.

Breaking the cycle of mistrust: Wise interventions to provide critical feedback across the racial divide	David Scott Yeager, Julio Garcia, Patti Brzustoski, William T. Hessert, Valerie Purdie-Vaughns, Nancy Apfel, Allison Master, Matthew E. Williams, Geoffrey L. Cohen	2014

Reference: Yeager, D. S., Purdie-Vaughns, V., Garcia, J., Apfel, N., Brzustoski, P., Master, A., ... Cohen, G. L. (2014). Breaking the cycle of mistrust: Wise interventions to provide critical feedback across the racial divide. *Journal of Experimental Psychology: General* (2), 804.

Purpose of study: Research based on the assumption that *trust* is the crucial component for successfully delivering critical feedback. Study looks at critical feedback given by a White teacher to an African American student. Three double-blind randomized field experiments examined the effects of a strategy to restore trust on minority adolescents' responses to critical feedback. Tested a method of fostering minority adolescents' trust during feedback interactions.

Related articles:

Brophy, J. E. (1981). Teacher praise: A functional analysis. *Review of Educational Research, 51*, 5–32. doi:10.3102/00346543051001005

Cohen, G. L., & Steele, C. M. (2002). A barrier of mistrust: How negative stereotypes affect cross-race mentoring. In J. Aronson (Ed.), *Improving academic achievement: Impact of psychological factors on education* (pp. 303–327). San Diego, CA: Academic Press. doi:10.1016/B978-012064455-1/50018-X

Cohen, G. L., Steele, C. M., & Ross, L. D. (1999). The mentor's dilemma: Providing critical feedback across the racial divide. *Personality and Social Psychology Bulletin, 25*, 1302–1318. doi:10.1177/0146167299258011

Harber, K. D. (1998). Feedback to minorities: Evidence of a positive bias. *Journal of Personality and Social Psychology, 74*, 622–628. doi:10.1037/0022-3514.74.3.622

Harber, K. D. (2004). The positive feedback bias as a response to out-group unfriendliness. *Journal of Applied Social Psychology, 34*, 2272–2297. doi:10.1111/j.1559-1816.2004.tb01977.x

Article 7.

Bias in **online** classes: Evidence from a field experiment. CEPA Working Paper No. 18-03	Rachel Baker, Thomas Dee, Brent Evans, June John, Stanford Center for Education Policy Analysis (CEPA)	**2018**

Reference: Baker, R., Dee, T., Evans, B., John, J., & Stanford Center for Education Policy Analysis (CEPA). (2018). *Bias in online classes: Evidence from a field experiment.* CEPA Working Paper No. 18-03. Stanford Center for Education Policy Analysis.

Purpose of study: While online learning environments are increasingly common, relatively little is known about issues of equity in these settings. There is experimental evidence that these biases exist even in settings that lack face-to-face interactions. College students with racially or gender-connotative names may receive different responses from instructors when asking for a face-to-face meeting or when asking to discuss research opportunities as a prelude to applying for a doctoral program (Milkman, Akinola, & Chugh, 2012, 2015). Study sought to add more to existing literature exploring issues of equity in online learning environments.

Related articles:

Bertrand, M., & Mullainathan, S. (2004). Are Emily and Greg more employable than Lakisha and Jamal? A field experiment on labor market discrimination. *American Economic Review, 94,* 991–1013.

Milkman, K. L., Akinola, M., & Chugh, D. (2015). What happens before? A field experiment exploring how pay and representation differentially shape bias on the pathway into organizations. *Journal of Applied Psychology, 100,* 1678–1712.

Oreopoulos, P. (2011). Why do skilled immigrants struggle in the labor market? A field experiment with thirteen thousand resumes. *American Economic Journal: Economic Policy, 3,* 148–171.

Article 8.

Turkish Science Teacher Candidates Understandings of Equitable Assessment and Their Plans about It	Kemal Izci	2018

Reference: Izci, K. (2018). Turkish science teacher candidates understandings of equitable assessment and their plans about it. *Journal of Education in Science, Environment and Health (JESEH), 4*(2), 193–205. doi:10.21891/jeseh.436744

Purpose of study: Investigated how Turkish science teacher candidates understand equitable assessment (EA) and in what ways they work to provide EA practices for their students. Results showed that science teacher candidates mostly equated EA with fairness including fairness in grading. However, most of the teacher candidates did not consider that providing equal opportunities for students to display their levels of understanding about the related concepts was not an important characteristic of EA.

Related articles:

Darling-Hammond, L. (2006). Constructing 21st-century teacher education. *Journal of Teacher Education, 57*(3), 300–314.

Siegel, M. A. (2014). Developing preservice teachers' expertise in equitable assessment for English learners. *Journal of Science Teacher Education, 25*(3), 289–308.

Article 9.

Relationship Between Minority Students Online Learning Experiences and Academic Performance	Alex Kumi Yebeoh, Patriann Smith	2016

Reference: Yeboah, A. K., & Smith, P. (2016). Relationships between minority students online learning experiences and academic performance. *Online Learning, 20*(4).

Purpose of study: Investigated the relationship between minority students' use of technology, social media, the number of online courses, program of study, satisfaction, and academic performance (measured by grade point average). Mixed-method study that examines the relationship between minority students' online learning experiences and academic performance.

Related articles:

Adeoye, B., & Wentling, R. M. (2007). The relationship between national culture and the usability of an e-learning system. *International Journal of E-Learning, 6*(1), 119–146.

Hughes, H., & Bruce, C. (2006). Cultural diversity and educational inclusivity: International students' use of online information. *International Journal of Learning, 12*(9), 33–40.

Article 10.

Same work, lover grade? Student ethnicity and teachers' subjective assessments	Reyn van Ewijk	2011

Reference: van Ewijk, R. (2011). Same work, lower grade? Student ethnicity and teachers' subjective assessments. *Economics of Education Review, 30*(5), 1045–1058.

Purpose of study: Previous research shows that ethnic minority students perform poorer in school when they are taught by teachers belonging to the ethnic majority. Study focused on one potential explanation: whether ethnic majority teachers *grade* minority and majority students differently for the *same work*. Focused on the question whether and how ethnicity, independently of any of its correlates, affects students' grades; a question that is particularly relevant in light of the persisting achievement gaps in school between ethnic groups that exist in many countries.

Related articles:

Bertrand, M., & Mullainathan, S. (2004). Are Emily and Greg more employable than Lakisha and Jamal? A field experiment on labor market discrimination. *American Economic Review, 94*(4), 991–1013.

Dee, T. S. (2005). A teacher like me: Does race, ethnicity, or gender matter? *American Economic Review, 95*(2), 158–165.

Seraydarian, L., & Busse, T. V. (1981). First-name stereotypes and essay grading. *Journal of Psychology, 108*(2), 253–257.

Article 11.

From Degrading to De-Grading	Alfie Kohn	1999

Reference: Kohn, A. (1999). From degrading to de-grading. Retrieved from *https://www.alfiekohn.org/article/degrading-de-grading/?print=pdf*

Purpose of study: Explore the effects, intended and unintended, of grading (including letter and/or number grades). Highlights a variety of negative outcomes associated with grades.

Related articles:

De Zouche, D. (1945). 'The Wound Is Mortal': Marks, honors, unsound activities. *The Clearing House, 19*, 339–344.

Kirschenbaum, H., Simon, S. B., & Napier, R. W. (1971). *Wad-Ja-Get?: The grading game in American education.* New York, NY: Hart.

Krumboltz, J. D., & Yeh, C. J. (1996). Competitive grading sabotages good teaching. *Phi Delta Kappan*, December, 324–326.

Salili, F., Maehr, M. L., Sorensen, R. L., & Fyans, L. J., Jr. (1976). A further consideration of the effects of evaluation on motivation. *American Educational Research Journal, 13*, 85–102.

Article 12.

Grading for equity: What it is, why it matters, and how it can transform schools and classrooms	Joe Feldman	2019

Reference: Feldman, J. (2019). *Grading for equity: What it is, why it matters, and how it can transform schools and classrooms.* Thousand Oaks, CA: Corwin.

Purpose of study: Shares a variety of research, strategies, and practical tools that are designed to address the prevalence of inconsistent grading practices in schools. Resources are intended to help address the achievement and opportunity gaps that persist among a diverse student population.

Related articles:

Close, D. (2009). Fair grades. *Teaching Philosophy, 32*(4), 361–398.

Skiba, R. J., Michael, R. S., Nardo, A. C., & Peterson, R. L. (2002). The color of discipline: Sources of racial and gender disproportionality in school punishment. *The Urban Review, 34*(4), 317–342.

Article 13.

A lesson in bias: The relationship between implicit racial bias and performance in pedagogical contexts	D. S. Jacoby-Senghor,, S. Sinclair,, and J. N. Shelton,	2016

Reference: Jacoby-Senghor, D. S., Sinclair, S., & Shelton, J. N. (2016). A lesson in bias: The relationship between implicit racial bias and performance in pedagogical contexts. *Journal of Experimental Social Psychology, 63*(3), 60–65. *https://doi.org/10.1016/j.jesp.2015.10.010*

Purpose of study: Researchers posited that instructors' implicit racial bias serves as a factor in racial disparities in academic achievement. Study tested the relationship between this factor, instructor lesson quality, and learners' subsequent test performance.

Related articles:

Holroyd, J. (2015). Implicit bias, awareness, and imperfect cognitions. *Consciousness and Cognition, 33*, 511–523.

Blanchard, S., & Muller, C. (2015). Gatekeepers of the American dream: How teachers' perceptions shape the academic outcomes of immigrant and language-minority students. *Social Science Research, 51*, 262–275.

Glock, S. Kneer, J., & Kovacs, C. (2013). Preservice teachers' implicit attitudes toward students with and without immigration background: A pilot study. *Studies in Educational Evaluation, 39*(4), 204–210.

Grading feedback checklist:

- Have I included a greeting?
- Have I addressed the student with a preferred name?
- Have I included my own name and contact information in my closing?

3.3.2. Assignment Assessment

Whenever possible, request room for student choice and voice in assignments (topics, prompts, format). Meaningful choice is empowering, strengthens assignment relevance, and conveys respect for students. Proactively offer alternatives when appropriate. Articulate a desire that supplemental resources represent a wide range of gender, ethnic, and racial groups. Share your voice, actively seek different perspectives, and work to bring in your own resources to supplement discussions.

If we teach today's students as we taught yesterday's, we rob them of tomorrow – John Dewey

3.4. Supporting Long-Term Learning

If we want students to be able to apply the work we do in the classroom, with respect to both content and diversity of thought, we need to ensure students understand how long-term learning works. We can also share resources that support long-term learning.

Suggest active learning, effective learning strategies such as retrieval practice, spaced repetition, and interleaving.

See: *https://www.remnote.io/*

3.5. Self-Checks and Reflection

Every word has consequences, every silence too. – Jean-Paul Sartre

What we do not say or do can be just as powerful as our speech and our actions. It is important to acknowledge that we all bring our own biases, many unrecognized, to our classrooms and our work. Whether a student or an instructor, we have our own set of biases, many of which are often unrecognized.

Continuously search for your own implicit biases that may unintentionally and unknowingly impact and influence classroom dynamics and learning. Address student and instructor responses to your classroom posts. Respond to all emails. Share thorough, well-supported responses to peer and instructor questions and posts.

Personal bias, awareness, and action resources and tools:

- See: *https://www.tolerance.org/professional-development/test-yourself-for-hidden-bias*
- See: *https://www.adl.org/sites/default/files/documents/assets/pdf/education-outreach/Personal-Self-Assessment-of-Anti-Bias-Behavior.pdf*
- See: *https://www.viacharacter.org/survey/account/register*

Next, we can ask how to proactively address these implicit biases, in order to promote a multicultural, inclusive environment – both in the online classroom and beyond.

Exercises and reflection:

- Reflect: How might the above referenced survey tools impact the way you approach career-related events and interactions?
- Identify two career scenarios where the above referenced survey tools might be relevant and valuable.

Start small, and take intentional steps to support a more inclusive classroom with the long-term goal of supporting a more inclusive world.

- Take small steps to promote inclusivity.
  - o List three to five small steps you might take to promote inclusivity in your current online course.
  - o List three to five small steps you might take to promote inclusivity in your current work.
- Work to visualize the composition of your most recent class and participants.
  - o How attuned were you to the cultural diversity in the classroom?
  - o Do you believe everyone felt welcome? Spoken to?
  - o For how many students in your class was English not their first or only language?
  - o How might this experience impact the way you interact with others when working in the field?

3.5.1. Reflection

A well educated mind will always have more questions than answers – Helen Keller

Questions are powerful tools that can spark *curiosity*, awareness, and action. As prompts for intentional and ongoing reflection consider the following questions:

- What types of messages might my language and choice of content convey?
- How well do my actions model and support a mindfully multicultural environment for my peers?
- How might I more deliberately acknowledge, embrace, and celebrate unique backgrounds and experiences of others in my classroom?

Effective Questions for Maximizing Learning/Decreasing Assumptions

Do I address all students by name?	Do I adopt a professional, respectful tone?
Have I included scholarly support for my responses?	Do I acknowledge opposing arguments?
Are my responses based on scholarly research?	Have I reviewed my arguments for logical errors?
Have I considered alternative perspectives?	Do I use grammatically correct sentences?
Is my writing clear?	Do I pose thoughtful questions in response to students' shared perspectives?
Are my positions fully developed?	Do I ask sincere and genuine questions to better understand counter-arguments and examples?

For more on "Effective Questions for Leading Discussions," see: *https://serc. carleton.edu/onramps/leading_compelling_discussions.html*
For more on "Criteria for Evaluating Multicultural Literature," see:
http://www.pages.drexel.edu/~dea22/multicultural.html

Success doesn't come to you. You go to it. – Marva Collins

3.5.2. Evaluation

Each course interaction and course assignment provides an opportunity for evaluation and an associated chance to improve equity in our classrooms. Ongoing evaluation and reflection are critical components of growth, fairness, and multiculturism.

Resources help students and educators evaluate written text and websites for multiculturalism. Tools help us evaluate our course frameworks, content, and ourselves for inclusivity and multicultural competency. For sample assessment tools, see *Engaging Diversity – Assessment Tools* (*https://blogs.lanecc.edu/engaging-diversity/*

assessment-tools/), *Criteria for Evaluating Multicultural Literature* (*http://www.pages. drexel.edu/~dea22/multicultural.html*), and *Racial Equity – Multicultural Competency* (*https://www.racialequitytools.org/act/strategies/multicultural-competency*). For accessibility, see *Accessibility in Online Courses – Trends, Tips, and Tools* (*https://wcet. wiche.edu/sites/default/files/Accessibility-Online-Courses-TrendsTipsTools.pdf*).

Approach all readings and course content critically, with considerations for characteristics well beyond content alone. Approach your learning intentionally, whether by asking questions, reaching out for more specific, actionable, and timely feedback, or inquiring about additional support resources. Develop, nurture, and model the types of mindful, inclusive, and multicultural behaviors you hope to see in the workplace and the world more broadly.

> If you are neutral in situations of injustice, you have chosen the side of the oppressor. If an elephant has its foot on the tail of a mouse and you say that you are neutral, the mouse will not appreciate your neutrality. – Desmond Tutu

CARE

Guiding principal – CARE
    Collect: Curate resources from a wide range of voices and perspectives.
    Assess: Evaluate all course content for objectivity and bias.
    Reflect: Pause and reassess, often. Are all students' voices, cultures, and diversity being heard and celebrated?
    Evaluate: Constantly evaluate all aspects of a course's design and instruction for opportunities to improve.

3.5.3. Collaboration and Feedback Improvement Cycles

> Do the best you can until you know better. Then when you know better, do better.
>
> – Maya Angelou

Share course design feedback to raise awareness of potential oversights and opportunities for more representative curriculum. Students are often closest to course

content and design teams rely upon your insights regarding curricular relevance, inclusivity, and impact. Ask students for their feedback and their suggestions.

Encourage students to watch for emails sharing end of term (and/or midterm) evaluations. Encourage students to complete them honestly, fully, and thoroughly. Remind students of the importance of sharing their voice, their experiences, and providing feedback. Look to these communication opportunities and responses as additional opportunities to build more multicultural sensitivity into your course design and content.

In general, we tend to connect most easily and readily to people "like us." Doing so builds a barrier, often unintended, to the value of diversity and diverse perspectives and experiences. Use your online course experience as an opportunity to encourage students to connect with people who have very different backgrounds and experiences from one another.

Consider steps you can take to actively, intentionally, and purposefully build in course opportunities for students to collaborate and work with people from backgrounds, cultures, and experiences very different from themselves.

Exercise:

View: *https://whyy.pbslearningmedia.org/collection/the-ways/?utm_source=&utm_medium=internal&utm_content=community&utm_campaign=community_2019*

(a) Reflect. How might you encourage students to share their culture in the online classroom?
(b) What elements of your own culture might you share?

Student exercises:

Who am I?

Name:	Professional Experiences:
Educational Background:	Aspirations:
Geographic Background:	Educational Goals:
Ethnic Background:	Family:
Cultural Background:	Hobbies & Interests:
Gender:	Anything Else!:

What Can I Learn from Peers Different from Myself?

Questions:
Observations:
Reflections:
New ways of thinking about the world:
Anything Else!:
Anything Else!:
Anything Else!:

Exercise:

See David Logan's TED Talk on Tribal Leadership at: *https://www.ted.com/talks/david_logan_on_tribal_leadership*

Reflection question:

- How might you expand your interactions in your online classrooms?
- How might you apply these efforts to your future work?

Commit and pledge to adopt strategies that support respect for all people:

- Demonstrate honesty and transparency in all communications
- Make connections. Look to optional forums to share personal background, experiences, questions
- Practice nonjudgmental behaviors
- Listen and read with purpose
- Pause and review emails and posts before sending/submitting
- Wait several hours before responding to an upsetting email
- Express appreciation for well done work
- Be reliable. In groups and team assignments, meet deadlines. Do what you say you will do.
- Use humor with caution

We are all different, which is great because we are all unique. Without diversity life would be very boring. – *Catherine Pulsifer*

See: Donovan Livingston: Lift Off, at: *https://www.youtube.com/watch?v=9XGUpKITeJM*

Reflection questions:

- How does this video relate to your own experiences in your online coursework?
- How might you apply the lessons from this video to your future work?

3.5.4. Private Interactions

Never doubt that a small group of thoughtful committed people can change the world. Indeed, it is the only thing that ever has. – Margaret Mead

Private communications with others are just as critical as our class-wide (and other public) communications. In emails, be careful not to assume preferred gender pronouns. Address other students and instructors by name. Phone conversations can often help personalize instruction, build relationships, and clarify misunderstandings. Consider sharing *audio recordings* for name pronunciations.

In all email communications, practice professionalism.

For strategies, see:

https://www.thebalancecareers.com/how-to-write-and-send-professional-email-messages-2061892

https://www.grammarly.com/blog/professional-email-in-english/

3.6. Resources

The remainder of this chapter shares a variety of resources that help achieve our goals for more inclusive, intentional, and supportive teaching for all students..

Recommended Books

Bajaj, M. (Ed.). (2017). *Human rights education: Theory, research, praxis.* Philadelphia, PA: University of Pennsylvania Press, 2017.

Boutte, G. S. (2016). *Education African American Students: And How Are The Children?.*

New York, NY: Routledge. 217 pp. $45.55. ISBN: 978-1-138-89232-3

Schooling diaspora: Women, education, and the overseas Chinese in British Malaya and Singapore, 1850s-1960s, by Karen M. Teoh, New York, Oxford University Press, 2018, xi + 210 pp., $74.00 (hardback), ISBN 978-0-19-049561-9

Sperling, G. B. (2016). *What works in girls' education: evidence for the world's best investment.* Brookings Institution Press.

Yousafzai, M., McCormick, P., & Gilkes, J. (2018). *I am Malala: How one girl stood up for education and changed the world.* Waterville, ME: Thorndike Press, a part of Gale, a Cengage Company

Recommended TED Talks

"The danger of a single story | Chimamanda Ngozi Adichie." See: *https://www. youtube.com/watch?v=D9Ihs24Izeg*

"A Tale of Two Teachers | Melissa Crum | TEDxColumbusWomen". See: *https://www.youtube.com/watch?v=sgtinODaW78*

"Valerie Purdie-Vaughns on Unintentional Bias". See: *https://www.youtube. com/watch?v=EzsuWkskU88&feature=youtu.be&list=PLrMqXQ2J_13ubw2OiT y9FdkAYHm_y2IIy*

"Expanding Teacher Self Knowledge". See: *https://www.youtube.com/watc h?v=S977Lz6Bfs0&feature=youtu.be&list=PLrMqXQ2J_13ubw2OiTy9FdkA YHm_y2IIy*

"Cultural difference in business | Valerie Hoeks | TEDxHaarlem" See: *https:// www.youtube.com/watch?v=VMwjscSCcf0*

"Bettina Love: On Black Girls, Discipline, and Schools". See: *https://youtu. be/_HCqUClUWlc*

Your Name is the Key! | Huda Essa | TEDxUofM. See: *https://www.youtube. com/watch?v=TuGL9_Isfyg*

Recommended Web-based Resources

(i) Assessment tools

Engaging Diversity – Assessment Tools, Criteria for Evaluating Multicultural Literature

For accessibility, see Accessibility in Online Courses – Trends, Tips, and Tools. See: https://wcet.wiche.edu/sites/default/files/Accessibility-Online-Courses-Trends TipsTools.pdf.

Engaging Diversity – Assessment Tools. See: https://blogs.lanecc.edu/engaging-diversity/assessment-tools/

Criteria for Evaluating Multicultural Literature. See: http://www.pages.drexel.edu/~dea22/multicultural.html

Racial Equity – Multicultural Competency. See: https://www.racialequitytools.org/act/strategies/multicultural-competency

Accessibility: Accessibility in Online Courses – Trends, Tips, and Tools

(ii) Personalization resources

Sharing Preferred Names (Google Doc)
Response Tracker (Google Doc)
Bitmoji
Voki
Vocaroo (new version is in beta testing, can subscribe for updates)
Screencastify
https://www.remnote.io/homepage (personalized note-taking tool that generates spaced repetition flashcards that support long-term learning; input course content with professional applications and relevance to support the transfer of course material to the field and practice)

(iii) Diversity in our classrooms (articles)

"Tips and Rewards of Teaching Seniors". See: *https://owlcation.com/academia/Difficulties-and-Rewards-of-Teaching-Seniors*

"How Demographic Change is Transforming the Higher Ed Landscape". See: *https://www.higheredjobs.com/blog/postDisplay.cfm?post=1843&blog=25&utm_source=03_13_2019&utm_medium=email&utm_campaign=InsiderUpdate*

"How education will change to support lifelong learning". See: *http://www.mininggazette.com/opinion/columns/2019/03/how-education-will-change-to-support-lifelong-learning/*

"Going back to school after 50". See: *https://hechingerreport.org/going-back-to-school-after-50/*

"Dear White Teachers: You Can't Love Your Black Students If You Don't Know Them". See: *https://www.edweek.org/ew/articles/2019/03/20/dear-white-teachers-you-cant-love-your.html?cmp=eml-enl-eu-news2-rm&M=58779536&U=1804327&UUID=d24c7e3146a8a0190e93181947ee8398*

"Edutopia, Todd Finley - A Look at Implicit Bias and Microaggressions". See: *https://www.edutopia.org/article/look-implicit-bias-and-microaggressions*

"How To Pronounce Chinese Names". See: *http://www.cs.cmu.edu/~zhuxj/readpinyin.html*

"NCTE Position Statements". See: *http://www2.ncte.org/statement/genderfair-useoflang/*

"My name, My Identity". See: *https://www.mynamemyidentity.org/*

"Ending the Perpetuation of Stigma", HigherEd Jobs (July 17, 2017). See: *https://www.higheredjobs.com/articles/articleDisplay.cfm?ID=1360*

Please add to the collection and the conversation:

Consider sharing additional resources for inclusion, here: Resources for Supporting All Students

I can see myself in all things and all people around me. – Sanskrit Phrase

Continue to reflect and further the conversation, as these strategies are only small steps in an ongoing journey.

If you talk to a man in a language he understands, that goes to his head. If you talk to him in his language, that goes to his heart. – Nelson Mandela

REFERENCES

Allen, I. E., & Seaman, J. (2017). Digital learning compass: Distance education report enrollment report 2017. Retrieved from https://onlinelearningsurvey.com/reports/digtiallearningcompassenrollment2017.pdf

American Enterprise Institute. (2019). The promises and limits of online higher education: Understanding how distance education affects access, cost, and quality. Retrieved from https://www.aei.org/research-products/report/the-promises-and-limits-of-online-higher-education/

Baker, R., Dee, T., Evans, B., John, J., & Stanford Center for Education Policy Analysis (CEPA). (2018). *Bias in online classes: Evidence from a field experiment*. CEPA Working Paper No. 18-03. Stanford Center for Education Policy Analysis.

Barnes, E., & Souza, T. (2019). Intercultural dialogue partners: Creating space for difference and dialogue. Retrieved from https://www.facultyfocus.com/articles/teaching-and-learning/intercultural-dialogue-partners-creating-space-for-difference-and-dialogue/

Boysen, G. A., & Vogel, D. L. (2009). Bias in the classroom: Types, frequencies, and responses. *Teaching of Psychology, 36*(1), 12–17.

Dobrin, A. (2013). The power of first impressions. Retrieved from https://www.psychologytoday.com/us/blog/am-i-right/201302/the-power-first-impressions

Durm, M. (1993). An A is not an A is not an A: A history of grading. *Educational Forum, 57*, 294–297.

Feldman, J. (2019). *Grading for equity: What it is, why it matters, and how it can transform schools and classrooms*. Thousand Oaks, CA: Corwin.

Gollnick, D. M., & Chinn, P. C. (2017). *Multicultural education in a pluralistic society* (10th ed.). Boston, MA: Pearson Education.

Harber, K. D., Gorman, J. L., Gengaro, F. P., Butisingh, S., Tsang, W., & Ouellette, R. (2012). Students' race and teachers' social support affect the positive feedback bias in public schools. *Journal of Educational Psychology, 104*(4), 1149–1161. http://dx.doi.org/10.1037/a0028110

Hattie, J. (2008). *Visible learning: A synthesis of over 800 meta-analyses relating to achievement*. New York, NY: Routledge.

Hattie, J. (2012). *Visible learning for teachers: Maximizing impact on learning*. New York, NY: Routledge.

Herold, B. (2017). Online classes for K-12 students: An overview. Retrieved from https://www.edweek. org/ew/issues/online-classes/index.html

Izci, K. (2018). Turkish science teacher candidates understandings of equitable assessment and their plans about it. *Journal of Education in Science, Environment and Health (JESEH)*, *4*(2), 193–205. doi:10.21891/jeseh.436744

Jacoby-Senghor, D. S., Sinclair, S., & Shelton, J. N. (2016). A lesson in bias: The relationship between implicit racial bias and performance in pedagogical contexts. *Journal of Experimental Social Psychology*, *63*, 50–55.

Kohn, A. (1999). From degrading to de-grading. Retrieved from https://www.alfiekohn.org/article/ degrading-de-grading/?print=pdf

Love, B. (2019). Dear white teachers: You can't love your black students if you don't know them. Retrieved from https://www.edweek.org/ew/articles/2019/03/20/dear-white-teachers-you-cant-love-your.html?cmp=eml-enl-eu-news2-rm&M=58779536&U=1804327&UUID=d24c7e3146 a8a0190e93181947ee8398

Malouff, J. M. (2008). Bias in grading. *College Teaching*, *56*(3), 191–192.

Malouff, J. M., Emmerton, A. J., & Schutte, N. S. (2013). The risk of halo bias as a reason to keep students anonymous during grading. Teaching of psychology, *40*(3), 233–237.

Malouff, J. M., Stein, S. J., Bothma, L. N., Coulter, K., & Emmerton, A. J. (2014). Preventing halo bias in grading the work of university students. *Cogent Psychology*, *1*, 988937.

Merryfield, M. (2003). Like a veil: Cross-cultural experiential learning online. *Contemporary Issues in Technology and Teacher Education*, 3(2), 146–171.

O'Connor, K. (2010). Grades--When, why, what impact, and how? *Education Canada*, *50*(2), 38–41.

Online Learning Consortium. (2017). New study: Over six million students now enrolled in distance education. Retrieved from https://onlinelearningconsortium.org/news_item/new-study-six-million-students-now-enrolled-distance-education/

Reeves, A. N. (2014). *Written in Black & White: Exploring confirmation bias in racialized perceptions of writing skills*. Chicago, IL: Nextions.

Schramm-Pate, S. (n.d.). *EDCS J725 principles of curriculum construction, basic theories of curriculum [Class handout]*. Lecture.

Seligman, M. (2002). *Authentic happiness: Using the new positive psychology to realize your potential for lasting fulfillment*. New York, NY: The Free Press.

Smallwood, M. L. (1935). *Examinations and grading systems in early American universities*. Cambridge: Harvard University Press.

Staats, C., Capatosto, K., Tenney, L., & Mamo, S. (2017). State of the science: Implicit bias review. Retrieved from http://kirwaninstitute.osu.edu/implicit-bias-training/resources/2017-implicit-bias-review.pdf

van Ewijk, R. (2011). Same work, lower grade? Student ethnicity and teachers' subjective assessments. *Economics of Education Review*, *30*(5), 1045–1058.

Xu, D., & Xu, Y. (2019). The promises and limits of online higher education: Understanding how distance education affects access, cost, and quality. Retrieved from https://www.aei.org/publication/the-promises-and-limits-of-online-higher-education/

Yeager, D. S., Purdie-Vaughns, V., Garcia, J., Apfel, N., Brzustoski, P., Master, A., … Cohen, G. L. (2014). Breaking the cycle of mistrust: Wise interventions to provide critical feedback across the racial divide. *Journal of Experimental Psychology: General*, *2*, 804.

Yeboah, A. K., & Smith, P. (2016). Relationships between minority students online learning experiences and academic performance. *Online Learning*, *20*(4). Retrieved from https://files.eric.ed.gov/fulltext/EJ1124650.pdf

CHAPTER 4

ADVANCING INCLUSIVITY AND CITIZENSHIP: ADAPTING THEORY, CHANGING PRACTICE

Alison Robinson Canham and Luisa Bunescu

ABSTRACT

The European Forum for Enhanced Collaboration in Teaching (EFFECT, 2015–2019) (EFFECT, 2019), a project co-financed by the European Commission, through its Erasmus+ programme, has been exploring effective methods for university teachers' development at the European level, including pedagogical staff development "modules" to support inclusivity and citizenship in teaching and learning practice. Throughout the project and in this chapter, the authors have taken "inclusivity" to convey an attitude and appreciation for principles which inform "inclusion" as a practice – in the context of reflective and reflexive practice the words become largely interchangeable.

The way academic staff teach is of critical importance in any reform designed to enhance inclusion and citizenship in higher education. Conveying these values-related topics in an academic context hardly lends itself to a traditional pedagogical training model. Promoting inclusion means stimulating discussion, challenging stereotypes and unconscious biases, as well as improving educational and social frameworks. The Change Laboratory methodology (Engeström, 2001) was chosen for the pedagogical staff development workshops under EFFECT, with a view to engaging teaching staff in a deeper reflection about the topics and about their teaching practice. Change Laboratory is an intervention-research methodology that aims at reconceptualizing activity: it intends to provoke authentic reactions, responses and disagreements among the participants and provides opportunity for them to work together

Developing and Supporting Multiculturalism and Leadership Development:
International Perspectives on Humanizing Higher Education
Innovations in Higher Education Teaching and Learning, Volume 30, 63–83
Copyright © 2020 by Emerald Publishing Limited
ISSN: 2055-3641/doi:10.1108/S2055-364120200000030006

to reimagine their activities and to identify "concrete" solutions that address persisting issues in their practice. The theory takes a broad conceptualization of "activity" and "practice," which is not specific to the education sector or the "classroom." The Change Laboratory is a methodology designed to support the "expansive learning cycle" described by Engeström and as such can be understood as a theory of change which the EFFECT project team applied to a pan-European higher education learning and teaching context.

In 2017, the project team designed and implemented four physical, face-to-face pedagogical staff development workshops on inclusivity and citizenship skills based on this methodology, attended by over 100 participants from across Europe. In 2018, the workshop model was adapted to a virtual learning environment and three online sessions on inclusivity and citizenship skills for higher education teaching staff were offered.

The pedagogical staff development workshops enabled participants to use open reflective questions to provoke discussion about the challenges faced in their own learning and teaching contexts, think about their pedagogical practices and identify their unconscious biases. Most of the participants rated the workshops as very good and innovative, and considered the methodology an effective vehicle for promoting meaningful open discussion.

In this chapter, the authors reflect on the design, implementation and lessons learnt from the pedagogical staff development workshops on inclusivity and citizenship skills. The authors propose a set of recommendations for individual teaching staff and institutional leadership to consider when addressing continuous professional development for inclusivity and citizenship.

Keywords: Pedagogical staff development; inclusivity; citizenship; learning and teaching; change laboratory methodology; reflection; pedagogical practice; workshop; theory of change; student centered; mirror data

THE PROJECT AND THE METHOD

The European Forum for Enhanced Collaboration in Teaching (EFFECT, 2015–2019) project worked to facilitate European collaboration on teaching enhancement. The project was coordinated by the European University Association (EUA) and co-funded by the Erasmus+ programme of the European Commission. EFFECT involved active participation and collaboration by strategic leaders in higher education, educators and staff and student representative bodies. The project pursued two interconnected strands of activity: a strategic dimension which identified and promoted high-level principles for higher education learning and teaching, and a practice element focused on how education could address inclusion and citizenship as two of society's "grand challenges."

Ten European Principles for the Enhancement of Learning and Teaching (EFFECT, 2018) were developed through the strategic strand of the EFFECT project, and the first Principle directly speaks to a humanizing agenda for higher education:

The higher education learning experience nurtures and enables the development of learners as active and responsible citizens, critical thinkers, problem solvers, equipped for life-long learning. Higher education equips people with the confidence and skills to live and learn in a changing world, able to proactively address their own and the world's grand challenges. (EFFECT, 2018)

This Principle is also a call to action, for students and educators alike, to apply education to address the "grand challenges" of our time. This chapter presents and reflects on the pan-European initiative pursued by the practice strand of the EFFECT project to address the challenge of advancing inclusivity and citizenship through pedagogic staff development based on the expansive learning theory of change proposed by Engeström (2001) in what we have called an "adapted Change Laboratory" methodology.

Defining the Challenges

Academic Staff Development and Variation across Europe

The terminology used in the area of learning and teaching varies across Europe, sometimes with the same concepts being understood in different ways. Here, "pedagogical staff development" refers to any kind of formal teacher training, such as initial teacher training and continuous professional development.

The quality of an education system is often judged through perceptions of the quality of its teachers. Pedagogical development for academic teaching staff continues to be implemented against a background lacking consensus on what makes quality university teaching and how teachers can be efficiently and effectively prepared for it. Not only is the definition of quality teacher training problematic, but there is also an ongoing debate about how to target enhancement initiatives: at the micro (individual level), the meso level (the department, the discipline) or the macro level (the higher education institution, the regional and national authorities) (Roxå & Mårtensson, 2012). This lack of clarity and coherence has been described as a "pretty" yet ineffective model of policy development, the so-called "Christmas tree": "plenty of pretty lights and shiny baubles, but they don't last long, have little relationship to each other and don't have any lasting effect on normal daily life" (Trowler & Bamber, 2005). While the UK, Scandinavia, North America and Australasia enjoy a well-established track record of reflective staff development, the EFFECT project through the adapted Change Laboratory initiative particularly, aimed at promoting this reflective approach to universities and academic staff across Europe. According to Trends 2015 report (Sursock, 2015), staff development is being regarded by universities in Europe as pivotal in improving learning and teaching, with the professionalization of academic work emerging as a major theme. The EFFECT project consortium estimated that the reflective element in staff development opportunities is still not being encouraged at many universities in Europe, although several authors (Boud, Keogh, & Walker, 1996; Keough & Walker, 1985; Zeichner & Liston, 1996) have discussed the importance of reflection in teachers' intellectual and professional growth. As a pan-European initiative, the EFFECT consortium had to be particularly mindful of potential incongruences arising from the diversity of higher education systems and cultures across Europe.

Staff Development for Change

Throughout our experience of working in learning and teaching enhancement over a number of years and during the workshops, we observed that academic staff development is often based on a deficit assumption about teaching capability. The inclusivity and citizenship work undertaken through our adapted Change Laboratory methodology indicates there is considerable potential to re-engage with the fundamental humanity of education by shifting away from traditional knowledge transmission and didactic methods and toward psycho-social experiential development which encourages educators to connect with all their learners in thoughtful and empowering ways.

Arguably all initial and continuous professional development for academic teaching staff is predicated on a theory of change, a broad ambition that teacher training leads to new insights and behavioral change among the academics, which in turn will lead to a cultural shift across the entire higher education institution and system, eventually enhancing the educational experience for students. Thus enhancing the teaching competences of academic staff aims to facilitate and increase student learning. We have taken Engeström's expansive learning cycle as a theory of change particularly relevant to this ambition (Fig. 1).

Evidencing and measuring the impact remains challenging. In general, although there is anecdotal evidence for the benefits, it proves extremely hard to compare between various teaching enhancement programs implemented in different national and institutional contexts and delivered through different modalities. The relationship between student success and teaching competences is therefore analyzed through the proxies of:

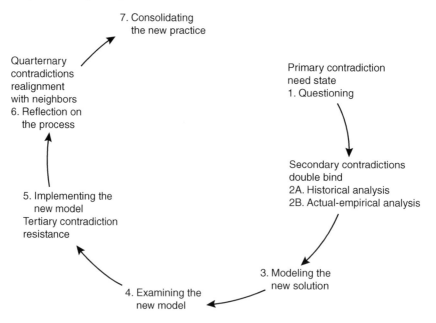

Fig. 1.   The Cycle of Expansive Learning as Designed by Engeström
(Engeström (2001), p. 152).

- Reflective practitioners' accounts of their experiences of adapting learning processes to improve the quality of student learning (such as classroom inter-actions, moderating discussion forums, providing feedback, etc.), sometimes augmented by accounts of peer observation.
- Established theories of pedagogical perspective based on "good practice" in facilitating learning and teaching.

Gibbs and Coffey (2004) demonstrated that pedagogical staff development leads to a more student-focused approach, which encourages a deeper approach to learning by the students – students adopting deep learning attempt to make sense of the content, compared to those students who adopt a surface approach to learning by trying to memorize and remember content, and thereby achieve superior learning outcomes, especially in terms of understanding and develop-ing new and more sophisticated conceptions of the subject. Hence, changing the teachers' approach to teaching, for instance by encouraging collaboration with colleagues, external partners like employers or professional associations, or by co-creation between students and lecturers, can lead to positive learning out-comes for students (Asikainen & Gijbels, 2017) The student-centered approach also appreciates and considers the diverse needs that can be found within a given group of students (Ödalen, Brommesson, Erlingsson, Schaffer, & Fogelgren, 2019). Student-centeredness is helpfully defined:

> Student-centred learning is based on the philosophy that the student [...] is at the heart of the learning process. [...] By its very nature, student-centred learning allows students to shape their own learning paths and places upon them the responsibility to actively participate in making their educational process a meaningful one. (Attard, Di Ioio, Geven, & Santa, 2010)

Impact on Individual Practice and Institutional Culture
The impact of pedagogical staff development is similarly difficult to evaluate or prove. In the UK Advance HE (previously Higher Education Academy) main-tains the UK Professional Standards Framework for Teaching and Supporting Learning in Higher Education (The UKPSF) on behalf of the HE sector (UKPSF, 2011). Advance HE fulfills a range of functions similar to those of a profes-sional association: accrediting institutions' courses and development schemes, and awarding individual recognition through Fellowships and Awards. A series of annual reports (Pilkington, 2018; Smith, 2019) notes that the introduction of continuous professional development schemes (schemes which are supported and facilitated by HEIs that enable their staff to undertake and record formal and informal development activities which meet the expectations of the UKPSF) have had significant impact on the education culture within these institutions. Although the report authors are hesitant about pointing to concrete and defini-tive correlations between activity of these schemes and the quality of teaching, their evaluation shows cumulative positive impacts on the teaching and learning culture and practice fostered by systematic support provided through the schemes. In the 2016–2017 review, 73% of the respondents stated that schemes impacted teaching and learning, especially by encouraging critical reflection on one's prac-tice, which was shifting staff's attention:

onto the students' experience of teaching and improving their capacity to enhance and develop
their practice in the longer term. [...] There was an acceptance across reports that by changing
and rethinking how staff practice as a result of engagement in Fellowship/scheme activity, there
is a cumulative transformative impact upon the student experience.(Pilkington, 2018)

The benefit of sustaining and embedding pedagogical development over time
is born out elsewhere. Levinson-Rose and Menges concluded that seminars and
workshops, lasting from half-day to weeklong or longer, are useful to raise awareness and motivate teachers, but are the least likely to "produce lasting changes
in teaching behavior or lasting impact on students" (Levinson-Rose & Menges,
1981). Weimer and Lenze (1997) and Prebble et al. (2004) reached a similar conclusion about the reduced impact of short courses, workshops and seminars on
changing teachers' behavior and attitudes. A systematic approach in teacher
training is recommended instead, rather than interventions that have no conti-
nuity and are independent of one another. EUA's 2018 thematic peer group on
continuous development of teaching competences came to the same conclusion
and recommended that continuous professional development should be seen as
a process with which academics engage throughout their career in higher education. This process should include activities that support the enhancement of the
quality of learning and teaching as well as research and academic career development (McIntyre-Bhatty & Bunescu, 2019).

Department and discipline-based initiatives might amplify the impact of individual teacher training. An individual approach alone is insufficient to have significant impact on teaching enhancement in universities. It is therefore important
to consider the meso level to check if and to what extent the effects of pedagogical
staff development go beyond the individual level and have the potential to turn
into an institutional culture. The meso level arguably reflects the institutional culture, which is:

not something an organization has, but rather what it is. It refers to ways of doing, talking, and
thinking about things, about patterns that make up a group visible against the backdrop of
other groups. (Alvesson, 2002)

The "Grand Challenges" of Inclusivity and Citizenship

A question arises of how well individual educators are equipped to address the
"grand challenges" alluded to in the first European Principle for the Enhancement
of Learning and Teaching. If our students are to be equipped "with the confidence and skills to live and learn in a changing world, able to proactively address
their own and the world's grand challenges" by virtue of their higher education,
our teachers need to be equipped and confident to facilitate that learning. Thus,
the challenge for developers becomes how to support educators to prepare students for a future radically different from their own past. From this perspective an
educator's ability and agility to work with and adapt to factors inherent in inclusivity and citizenship become a litmus test for our education systems' capacity to
respond to otherness, difference and change.

Promoting inclusion means stimulating discussion, challenging stereotypes and
unconscious biases, as well as improving educational and social frameworks within

HEIs, for example, student/staff interactions, involvement of different communities within the university, consultation activity, student councils, the governance structures, the dynamics of physical and virtual learning environments (VLEs). Herein lies the dilemma the EFFECT consortium had to address, that having defined pedagogic staff development as a formal process the group realized that the fundamental challenge of addressing inclusivity and citizenship required educators to harness and channel the learning derived from the "being" and "doing" of their lived lives, an essentially informal and humanized development process. As Dirkx (2006) states, "we in higher education often minimize or ignore the potent emotional context in which our work is embedded." Essentially, teaching about/for inclusion and citizenship requires that educators reflect on their own experiences, beliefs and values and how they impact teaching practices.

UNESCO defines inclusion as:

> a process of addressing and responding to the diversity of needs of all children, youth and adults through increasing participation in learning, cultures and communities, and reducing and eliminating exclusion within and from education. (UNESCO, 2009)

The EFFECT project adopted this broad interpretation, rather than focusing on particular groups identified by a single characteristic. Inclusivity was therefore tackled in terms of addressing any factors other than intellectual capability which inhibit academic performance and attainment. Inclusive learning and teaching in higher education was defined as referring to:

> the ways in which pedagogy, curricula and assessment are designed and delivered to engage students in learning that is meaningful, relevant and accessible to all. It embraces a view of the individual and individual difference as the source of diversity that can enrich the lives and learning of others. (Hockings, 2010)

Citizenship skills were understood as pertaining to the concept of active citizenship, which could be defined as: "Participation in civil society, community and/or political life, characterized by mutual respect and non-violence in accordance with human rights and democracy" (Hoskins, 2006).

Citizenship and inclusivity topics have many aspects in common. Neither issue is considered a "hot topic" for the majority of higher education teachers, who are rarely receptive to staff development events and resources explicitly labeled as "inclusivity/citizenship teacher training." Furthermore, for some countries and higher education institutions, the challenge is how to "cope" with diversity, while for others the challenge is how to foster and increase diversity. Both angles impact the notions of inclusion and citizenship, and at the time of writing are playing out against a backdrop of populist nationalism in many parts of Europe.

ADAPTING THE CHANGE LABORATORY METHOD

As observed above, a fundamental paradox arises from seeking to formalize informal learning and yet if psycho-social change is to be achieved deeply reflective social learning needs to be deployed in the domain of academic staff development.

As discussed previously the project was heavily informed by Engeström's expansive learning model, itself part of the "social theories of learning" family of theories which explore and structure thinking about learning through "being" and "doing" in the lives we live. By applying a theoretical framework to the project the work has been formalized to some degree, while retaining the reflective approach of informal learning. The project team considered a conservative training model poorly suited to conveying values-based topics such as inclusion and citizenship in an academic context. A "how to" training approach would be ineffective as it would not engage teachers in a deeper reflection about the topic and about their personal agency in addressing specific circumstances they experience with their students.

The Change Laboratory methodology appeared to reconcile formal staff development with informal social learning. By deploying a highly systematic model to a behavioral change agenda (e.g., changing attitudes of educators to diverse students) and by acknowledging the established structures, habits and histories of traditional approaches to education these norms and assumptions could be respectfully challenged with the deliberate intent of achieving change in the individual and collective practices of educators. As an intervention-research methodology, Change Laboratory offered an opportunity for people to work together in a structured and cyclical way to provoke discussion and to envisage new activity in their own practices and in their organizations.

The project team drew heavily on the work of Bligh and Flood (2015) to frame and execute the project. However, the nature of the EFFECT project and the pan-European context demanded some significant modifications to the established model. A detailed account of the EFFECT process can be found in a suite of reports and resources published on the EUA's website (EFFECT, 2019), so here we reflect on the adaptations which enabled meaningful development activity to emerge from a distributed multi-national, trans-cultural setting.

Normally, Change Laboratory presupposes that the implementation team works with the same group of participants over a period of 9–12 months. The group would meet several times during this period, with tasks in between the sessions:

> A Change Laboratory is typically conducted in an activity system that is facing a major transformation. [...] Working practitioners and managers of the unit, together with a small group of interventionist researchers, conduct five to ten successive Change Laboratory sessions, often with follow-up sessions after some months. (Engeström, Rantavuori, & Kerosuo, 2013)

The time and funding constraints imposed on the EFFECT project made this impractical, but in addition, the team was committed to developing and testing an academic staff development intervention that could be adapted to a range of different cultural and practical contexts, and potentially adapted for distance delivery. The requirement to test adaptability in different countries led the team to look for the most universal and widely applicable principles and practices – in essence a fundamentally humanizing endeavor. By adopting processes which transcended cultural difference, and focusing on themes of inclusivity we sought to create situations in which participants could articulate, explore and challenge their own human emotional responses to difference and discomfort. The Change Laboratory method appeared particularly pertinent to this mission: group discussion is stimulated by "mirror data" which reflects aspects of the situation under scrutiny; activity systems recognize and accommodate both individual and collective histories; and change is provoked through exploration of contradictions emerging from the structures and cultures inherent in the activity systems.

Rather than attempting to implement the full cycle of Change Laboratory the team adapted the method, organizing a series of face-to-face and online staff development workshops, so that the approach could be tested in both face-to-face and virtual environments. For the four face-to-face workshops, the implementation team worked each time with a different group of participants, in different national and international contexts, with the mirror data evolving for each successive meeting from the insights and discussion captured in the previous sessions. This approach required careful facilitation so that each fresh group was enabled to comfortably enter the "expansive cycle of learning actions" without starting the conversation afresh. For the online workshops, a pilot group of 10 participants all followed a series of 3 webinars following a similar format to the modified face-to-face model.

The project consortium envisaged that the physical and online workshops would be both research (for the implementation team, into the adapted method and into inclusivity/citizenship attitudes and practice) and development activity (for those participating in roundtable discussions and in the online pilot group). The workshops, face-to-face and online, were designed to:

- use open reflective questions to provoke discussion about the challenges teachers faced in their own learning and teaching contexts;
- identify possible solutions and approaches;
- act as catalysts for change, even if no specific change project was discussed;
- foster discussions which would help academic staff recognize the "problem" even when it may not appear to be the most pressing issue in their context;
- lead to the design of a customizable workshop prototype for local and digital adaptation, and which could lend itself to a range of topics and themes, in addition to inclusivity and pedagogic practice for academic teaching and learning support staff; and
- lead to the development of supplementary resources specifically derived from the discussions about inclusivity and citizenship (Table 1).

The face-to-face workshops were delivered in different European locations. The venues were pragmatically selected to coincide with scheduled events during 2017 while also representing a diversity of local cultures within the broader European context. Two of the workshops (in Porto, Portugal and Joensuu, Finland) were offered in culturally and institutionally homogenous environments, whereas the workshops in Budapest (Hungary) and Paris (France) attracted a wider European audience. During the workshops, the team used scenarios and videos as stimulus material/mirror data to trigger discussions and help academic teaching staff address real life/work problems. The stimulus material was initially based on short, single-sentence extracts from student feedback, becoming progressively more complex and nuanced to reflect issues and attitudes arising in the

Table 1.   Summary of the Face-to-Face Workshops.

Location	Date	Number of Participants	Workshop Audience	Facilitation Language	Data Capture
University of Porto, Porto, Portugal	January 31, 2017	71	Local (Porto)	Mostly Portuguese, with some feedback in English	Facilitated feedback on flipcharts Video recording Written feedback from facilitators
Eötvös Loránd University, Budapest, Hungary	March 20, 2017	33	Regional/ pan-European	English	Facilitated feedback on flipcharts Written feedback from facilitators
University of Eastern Finland, Joensuu, Finland	August 22, 2017	12	Local	English	Facilitated feedback on flipcharts
University Pierre and Marie Curie, Paris, France	September 27, 2017	7	Regional/pan-European	English	Facilitated feedback on flipcharts

workshops. A full repository of all the stimulus material generated and used in the project is available on the EFFECT website. Each of the workshops was of different duration ranging from 90 minutes to 4 hours and structured to allow for two or three cycles of discussion, carefully facilitated by well-briefed table scribes who in addition to capturing contributions also helped the discussion move through the stages of the expansive learning cycle (Fig. 1).

To test the viability of the model in a VLE, the team modified the approach in slightly different ways. Volunteers were recruited to participate in a series of three webinars over a four-month period, so that the cumulative discussion and learning envisaged in the original Change Laboratory method could be more closely replicated. In the face-to-face environment, three hours appeared to offer a good balance of discussion time and participants' concentration capacity; in the virtual environment 60–90 minutes worked better. Group size was limited to a maximum of 10 participants in the virtual webinar facilitated by a single facilitator with additional technical support, whereas face-to-face the workshop could accommodate a much higher number (70 participants at the workshop in Porto) as long as the table groups were limited to between six and eight participants with each table supported by a facilitating scribe. For this project, webinar participants were fast-tracked through the earlier stages of the process based on the learning and stimulus material developed from the face-to-face series. The online group then moved through the expansive cycle to the point where they produced their own scenarios for the group to work with rather than the facilitator crafting the material (Fig. 2). To make best use of the online time participants were set homework tasks based on issues arising

I was expecting some help or words of wisdom from the director to progress the project or give me useful feedback.

Instead he brought me a box of chocolate.

I kindly told him that I would not accept the chocolate. He got furious. At his reaction I told him that I would not accept anything from anybody, not just him. It was not true but I wanted to calm him down by providing a somehow acceptable justification which was not personal. I was shocked by his reaction.

Once alone, I found the real subconscious reason of my refusal. He would have never given a box of sweets to a male colleague. With a male colleague he would have discussed the workload, how to better manage the situation and eventually also advise him about future career pogression. A box of chocolate was a kind gift - enough for a woman.

Very interesting to examine how the artefact (the box of chocolates) is seen differently by the two parties. The narrator of the story - she sees the box of chocolates as inappropriate as she is expecting something different, a discussion.
The director - the box of chocolates is the director's peace-offering. He is not willing to discuss the situation. The box of chocolates is to placate the narrator hoping she will go away.

XYZ Thurs, 26th 3.57 PM

In terms of the director's history it would be interesting to know if this tactic had been an acceptable form of feedback previously

helen Thurs, 26th 3.58 PM

there might be that director had a unconsious bia for at giving box of and assumed that situation is solved by that way.

lo Thurs, 26th 4.01 PM

At first glance, this may be seen as a gender issue but could there be other factors at play here?

XYZ Thurs, 26th 4.01 PM

how would he know why the chocolates were considered inappropriate?

Fig. 2. Mirror Data Generated by a Participant. This example shows how participant generated material is used to stimulate discussion during the third cycle. It illustrates how the participant has internalized the concepts and applied them to events in their professional life, and how the material continues to stimulate a range of responses.

in the sessions, for example, completing and reflecting on unconscious bias questionnaires (*https://implicit.harvard.edu/implicit/* and *https://secure.understandingprejudice.org/*) or applying the model to issues they experienced in their own work. Working with the same group of participants, even over a relatively short period, allowed the team to identify small changes to attitudes and practice which might yield high impact on student/learning outcomes. In both face-to-face and online workshops, the team attempted to reflect a diversity of stakeholders: lecturers, students and other staff (technical, library, support).

As identified above, the EFFECT project was responding to perceptions of inadequate and patchy academic staff development opportunities across Europe. The potential to deliver a standardized intervention which could nonetheless be customized to local culture and practice made the online option attractive. Progress in video technology has promised to turn such online exchanges into easy, accessible and comfortable methods for interaction, coupled with a widespread predisposition and willingness to explore the world of VLEs that have already become part of many higher education institutions and systems around Europe, especially through blended learning. The online approach has become feasible because of technological advances, and necessary to address the potential to deliver pan-European staff development at high scale and low cost. Although the current European student population is a highly mobile youth cohort – between 2014 and 2016 1.8 million individuals took part in mobility activities under Erasmus+ (Commission, 2018) – international peer learning and professional development opportunities for academic teaching staff across Europe still remain limited due to a variety of financial, socio-economic, time and personal circumstances. Online-facilitated discussions have the potential to address these barriers, being a feasible alternative for academic staff unable to participate in physical peer learning or continuous professional development activities.

By encouraging academic staff to pursue their own development through online tools the project team also sought to normalize this mode of learning and explore how it could support deeply reflective approaches to sensitive, sometimes contentious, topics. Covid-19 has increased the urgency of this agenda. For this project no unique technology was developed. Instead, the VLE of one of the EFFECT project partners (Advance HE) was used with the intention that the workshop prototype could be adopted and hosted with locally available tools.

One of the strengths of the face-to-face workshop model was the ability to create a safe space for participants to reveal and explore authentic, rather than "politically correct," responses to situations. The project team was concerned that the online environment would compromise this, so we used supplementary web based collaborative tools to promote discussion. In addition to the VLE platform, the team used free real-time collaboration applications (*https://padlet.com/* and *https://dotstorming.com/*) so participants could comment and exchange views to promote collaboration while minimizing the financial barriers to participation or subsequent adoption by universities.

EVALUATING THE PROJECT

The scale of the EFFECT project has been modest, and the claims made on the basis of this work must be proportionate. However, the team did conduct comprehensive evaluation with participants and while not statistically significant has derived some compelling qualitative insights. A first round of follow-up surveys was launched among all the participants, immediately after the workshops, with very positive overall feedback. For instance, from the largest workshop in Porto (c. 70 participants), 71% of the participants rated the event as very good and 29% as excellent. Across all the workshops and webinars participants credited the EFFECT workshop as leading to: increased interest in being personally more culturally adaptive; interest in issues concerning students and their difficulties; proactivity; increased awareness of enacting inclusivity through academic practice; empathy; greater attention to group dynamics; and increased interest in flexible learning paths to better accommodate a diversity of students.

One workshop/facilitator/scribe noted that:

> The participants appreciated the opportunity to be heard and valued reflection spaces like this one. There were no difficulties in conducting the discussion, as people were willing to talk.

Interestingly, a majority of the respondents said that they had not attended other similar teaching enhancement workshops or initiatives, which points to both the systemic need for such initiatives all over Europe, but also to the innovative aspect of the approach. Having conducted the workshops in Central, Western and Nordic European locations it is pertinent to make an observation about the variability of academic staff development cultures, and as mentioned earlier, to reinforce the overall rationale for the EFFECT consortium's commitment to addressing the issues of pan-European academic staff development. Even in places where a development culture is apparently well established it is worth questioning and scrutinizing the extent to which personal reflection has evolved into a purposeful collective endeavor and whether systemic change has yet occurred as a result. In reflecting on how interaction varied between the workshops the facilitators observed a spike in interest which could be associated with novelty of the approach and topic in contexts where neither inclusivity nor access to similar workshops were established, compared to the apathy or complacency that was observed where such topics are routinely addressed and training is well established.

To see if and how workshop discussions impacted the professional practice of the attendees, the implementation team prepared and launched a second follow-up survey four to seven months after the workshops. The main questions raised in the survey were:

- Did you organize any kind of follow-up activity after this workshop? If yes, please briefly describe it.
- Did the discussions raised during the workshop influence your activity afterwards? If yes, please mention which aspects have had the most impact on your practice.
- Which aspects of the workshop would you like to discuss again?
- Have you attended other similar teaching enhancement workshops or initiatives? If yes, which ones?

Sixty percent (9) of the 15 respondents to this second survey confirmed that the discussions raised during the workshop influenced their professional activity afterwards by helping them to:

- reflect on how to integrate different cultures into their societies;
- develop methods and tools to better integrate migrants into local and higher education communities;
- develop inclusion strategies in higher education and classroom activities to promote collaboration and more exchanges between students; and
- some respondents stated that it was also comforting to see that lecturers face similar problems all over Europe and that this workshop proposed a new methodology mostly based on self-reflection, which enabled participants to think about their pedagogical practice and change the design of their lectures to respond more to students' needs.

Seven of the online workshop participants (10 in total) offered feedback and identified the benefits:

- The methodology used was a different method of reflection on the teaching practice, which helped to identify one's own assumption and biases.
- To think, describe and analyze situations taken from everyday life at work that can potentially be troublesome and frustrating.
- Interacting with others and seeing how other higher education practitioners react to the same problem.

All seven respondents believed that the Change Laboratory methodology, as it was applied during the online sessions, would be useful for discussing themes other than inclusion and citizenship. They perceived it as a transversal thought-provoking method, the added value of which is to facilitate discussion and bring to light unconscious thinking.

Five of the seven respondents had never attended similar teaching enhance-ment workshops or initiatives. One of the respondents believes that this was because:

focus is mostly on innovative teaching methods or on quality assurance measures rather than on issues related to inclusiveness or citizenship which might be understood by teachers as issues for elementary or high schools (teachers at HEIs understand their job as delivering skills and knowledge).

OBSERVATIONS AND REFLECTIONS FROM THE PROJECT

The materials available on the EUA website (EFFECT, 2019) give a detailed account of practical lessons learnt from the project and offer sufficient resources for colleagues to adopt and adapt the method in their own contexts to foster dis-cussion and changes in practice or attitudes around inclusivity and citizenship, or indeed to adapt the approach to address their own grand challenges. Here we reflect on some of the major insights derived from the work.

Mirror Data as Stimulus Material

The quality and relevance of the stimulus material is critical to the effectiveness of a Change Laboratory. Referred to by Engeström (2001) as "mirror data" it quite literally reflects aspects of the situation under discussion which might otherwise remain invisible or marginalized. As the cycle of discussion progresses, the mirror data becomes more sophisticated and indicative of the hidden issues at play in the situation. The workshops themselves provide a safe forum for saying what might otherwise stay unspoken. The mirror data is developed to reflect these attitudes or behaviors back to the discussion group, and acts as the catalyst for challenging and working through the contradictory or contentious issues represented in the material.

The EFFEECT team identified this as one of the most powerful aspects of the process and considered the development of an archive of stimulus mirror data to be a useful outcome of the project, especially if the archive was augmented over time by contributions from teams subsequently adopting the approach. A repository was created comprising all the stimulus material that was used in the EFFECT workshops and can be accessed from the project webpage (EFFECT, 2019). During the course of the project, the team identified some specific features and considerations which ensured the stimulus material fulfilled its role in the process:

- The material should be contextualized, based on cultural and social issues specific to a certain region/state. During the project, the team sourced videos and questionnaires from Australia and North America. While some of these served a universal purpose, like the unconscious bias questionnaires, other material was considered too culturally divergent to be relevant to a European audience. If the workshop is organized in a national/institutional setting, the stimulus material should be adapted to the local higher education culture, so that the attendees identify themselves with the challenges raised.
- Stimulus material should be carefully prepared, as this is the main element that steers the conversation in the direction intended by the facilitator. Provocative stimulus material summarizing challenges in terms of inclusivity and citizenship worked very well, as not only did it stimulate more energized debate, but also counterbalanced the tendency toward a fast (yet at times superficial) achievement of consensus. The Change Laboratory methodology is intended to be provocative. The transformational learning and changes to practice arise from the cumulative impact of reflection on increasingly complex, contextualized and relevant stimulus material, so the stimulus material should be disruptive and lead to disagreement. Therefore, it is crucial to repeat such workshops with the same group of people, allowing adequate time for the discussions.
- Stimulus material should be a combination of written case studies and visual materials like images and videos. As the cycle of discussions progresses the materials can be generated by participants based on the real challenges and

experiences of their lived professional and personal lives. As well as being critical to the success of the Change Laboratory as a crucible of provocation and change, it is also the aspect of the model which harnesses fundamental human experience in the pursuit of educational transformation.

Structure and Conduct of the Workshops

In general, the experience of the workshops showed that conversations and disagreement are powerful tools for understanding specific challenges and advancing toward the identification of possible solutions, and this resonates with much earlier work by Moustakas (1967) who discussed the importance of confrontation: "Paradoxical as this seems, only when persons can openly disagree, if this is the reality of their experience, is it possible for them to establish genuine bonds" (p. 23). During the project, the team observed a tendency for participants to rush to bland consensus around the safe space of familiar (but not necessarily effective) solutions rather than pushing for novel solutions and changed practice. There is a link here with the composition of the discussion groups addressed below, as a self-selecting group of inclusivity champions or experts, for example, will fast-track to solutionizing the challenges based on existing practice, rather than systematically unpacking the status quo to identify genuinely novel approaches. The provocative challenge is that if existing approaches were effective the education sector would no longer need these discussions as universal inclusivity would have been achieved. In this project, we observed a courtesy phenomenon which inhibited robust challenge, although it is possible that over a longer period this would start to occur. The challenge for Change Laboratory facilitators is to achieve and maintain momentum through all stages of the expansive learning cycle, moving beyond the academic tendency to get stuck in "analysis paralysis" around the identified problem.

This is an aspect to challenge and pursue in later cycles of the Change Laboratory process until changed perceptions and practices have been observed. At the end of each workshop, the facilitators should invite the participants to reflect on their individual practice and on how to take the impressions/lessons from the workshop further in their activities. As with any development intervention, reflection should be purposeful and lead to action. The reflection process is not an end in itself and is enacted through teaching behaviors which are then experienced by students (McAlpine & Weston, 2002).

The project team observed some very practical enablers during the face-to-face sessions, for example, that smaller tables, despite appearing cramped, actually encouraged participants to "lean into" the conversation, literally and figuratively, whereas large tables made it easier for individuals to be marginalized or disengage. People were better equipped to engage quickly with the process if they were prepared in advance with some briefing about the theory and practice of the model and definitions of the challenge, either as problem or aspiration. The facilitators can create conditions for energetic debate with deliberately provocative materials from the outset, but should be mindful that their role is to stir not "lead" or monopolize the discussion.

During the workshops, face-to-face and virtual, a set of reflective questions evolved and were increasingly deployed to shape the conversations and challenge the assumptions and practices that emerged from the discussions. They are broadly applicable to a wide range of topics, not just inclusivity and citizenship. Together with authentic mirror stimulus materials, and a commitment to moving discussion and challenge into new ways of working, these questions represent the essence of the model adopted and adapted by the EFFECT team:

- What are the artifacts, rules and organizational structures at play in your institution and which directly affect your teaching practice?
- What different perspectives, points of view and traditions are at play in your teaching practice?
- What is the history or histories that are influencing your situation as academic teaching staff?
- What is the source or nature of the dissatisfaction with your current teaching practice? Why does it matter?
- What is your motivation for seeking change? What will/could be different? What difference will it make?
- What can you personally do about it? Who else would work with you? How disruptive are you prepared to be?

Recognition of Academic Staff Development

There is a widespread acknowledgement that teaching as a professional activity in academia, and the associated development activity, is poorly recognized in most European systems (Bunescu & Gaebel, 2018). This both perpetuates and reflects a fundamental barrier to individuals' engagement in development opportunities. More importantly in the context of fostering personal responsibility for transformational approaches to inclusion in higher education, we potentially dehumanize education by diminishing or marginalizing the personal agency of individual educators or learners. Arguably it is only through acknowledging personal agency, and with it responsibility and accountability, that education avoids being reduced to a transactional exchange of information, and becomes a transformational dimension of human life. Recognition for such pedagogical staff development workshops (for instance, through open badges and certificates that celebrate teaching and learning and help with career progression) could have a significant role in raising profile and encouraging engagement in these kinds of intervention. During the workshops and webinars delivered through the EFFECT project it became increasingly clear that the higher education workforce across Europe is experiencing increasing workload and competing demands on time and intellectual energy. If we are collectively committed to reconnecting teachers with the broadest purposes and ambitions of higher education we should surely work toward more ubiquitous opportunities for developing and rewarding staff who engage with their own holistic development. For some of our participating countries and institutions systematic staff development, especially around inclusivity and diversity, was an almost entirely novel experience which was enthusiastically embraced; in others familiarity inspired apathy or complacency. During the course of the project, it became clear that senior encouragement and expectation made a difference to staff engagement, partly by creating a sense of obligation, but also by sending a signal that senior leaders cared about the agenda. Another EUA report identified that the main success factor for diversity, equity and inclusion is the commitment and support of the institutional leadership (Claeys-Kulik, Jørgensen, & Stöber, 2019).

Composition and Motivation of Workshop Groups

Participants in Porto particularly identified the benefit of bringing together different stakeholders of the university for open and informal discussions. This heterogeneity was critical for identifying sustainable and effective solutions. A key benefit from the methodology is to move participants from a position of "blaming" other groups, often "management," to thinking about what they could do themselves. The previously mentioned need for facilitators to purposefully move participants through the complete expansive learning cycle is essential if the discussion is to move from a "moan and blame" tendency in the early stages of the Change Laboratory cycle to a more productive and innovative focus on changed perceptions and practices, and greater individual ownership of the problems and their solutions.

It is worth observing that group size and senior leadership impacted significantly on the nature of the issues raised and potential for significant changes to occur – where the group was small and self-selecting the project team observed the phenomenon of the "usual suspects" talking about issues already familiar to them, whereas in a larger more diverse group where a degree of senior encouragement had been exercised the team felt they were potentially reaching more colleagues who neither routinely discussed the issues of inclusivity and citizenship nor had access to reflective development interventions. Although the main target group was academic teaching staff the discussions were more meaningful and inclusive with a combination of teachers, students and support staff. A homogenous group (e.g., only teachers) tended to keep the discussions "politically correct" and often identified solutions outside their influence, for instance by referring to the university management or to the "right" kind of students, rather than recognizing their own agency in the teaching interaction. Student representation in training events was observed to have a very positive impact as long as the student perspective was presented in a way that encourages academic teaching staff to reflect on their own personal role in addressing the challenges. It appeared important that discussion groups included participants from different cultural and disciplinary backgrounds so that peer learning could take place in an intercultural and interdisciplinary context, congruent with the inclusive motivation of the project overall.

The presence of institutional leaders as participants did not appear to inhibit the discussion, especially when they appeared well engaged themselves. Indeed, having influencers in senior positions seen to actively and authentically participate was observed to foster enhanced credibility with academic peers, although in a project of this scale it is difficult to judge whether the senior staff participating in these activities already enjoyed established personal credibility which itself encouraged participation by the university community.

CONCLUSIONS

The timescale of the project was sufficient to see early indications of changing attitudes, especially in the webinar version where the same group engaged several times. However, although we were able to see levels of engagement and evidence of fresh interest in professional development, and the topics of inclusivity and citizenship, the project timescale was too short to make confident assertions that sustained change had been initiated, continued, or embedded.

The EFFECT project's aim to explore an innovative, scalable and cost-effective academic staff intervention model, adaptable to a range of cultures, contexts and "grand challenges" was ambitious in its vision despite being constrained by time and resources. Our conclusions are necessarily proportionate to the scale of the project.

The importance and complexity of embedding inclusion and citizenship skills in pedagogy requires a whole organization approach, beyond the EFFECT project's focus on empowering personal agency and accountability, and beyond the benefits of senior stakeholder participation discussed above. In this regard, a consideration of the meso level – the squeezed middle of department, work group, networks and the like – should not be overlooked. There is considerable evidence, for example, from the annual CPD reports of Advance HE, that Heads of Department, Deans and similar have significant influence to either promote or inhibit particular initiatives, both through the authority they have over their teams and influence they have on their own superiors. Thus any initiative to embed inclusivity and citizenship, or any other theme, should be mindful of the role of these mediators between the strategic and the grass roots contexts of an organization. The evidence of the workshops and the tendency to "blame" management for letting the "wrong" students in on one hand and "diverse" students for being "different" on the other, emphasizes the need to foster personal agency but also suggests that without a whole organization approach historic tensions will inhibit genuine change.

The experience of the EFFECT project speaks to a systematic effort that embraces and fosters student and staff engagement, considering that:

- Both students and staff can encourage or inhibit inclusion, individually or collectively, by taking personal responsibility for their actions and reactions to situations in which they experience discomfort. All parts of the higher education community – student, academic, technical and support staff – should work respectfully, collaboratively and openly to explore and resolve the contradictions and tensions in their experiences of each other.
- Educators need to understand more about how students learn, while students need to understand their own learning approach and take ownership of their learning experience – both need to acknowledge their human vulnerability and the parts they play in each other's learning.
- It is helpful to think about how to harness new technology to support learning, as technology and social media are increasingly ubiquitous and natural environments for learners. There is also a pressing need to equip graduates and faculty to adapt to, function in and shape a fast-moving technology-mediated world beyond what can be anticipated during the period of formal education.

The power of the model rests not in slavishly analyzing every situation through the lenses of Engeströmian Activity Systems, nor in a step-by-step adherence to the expansive cycle of learning actions (although both of these are useful in framing the process), but rather in its fundamentally human concern with the lived experiences of all those encompassed by the "activity system" of higher education, whether student, academic, technical or support staff. Focusing on "Mirror" data requires participants to confront, challenge and move beyond the tensions and contradictions which inhibit a genuinely transformative educational experience. And finally, the model demands that reflection is harnessed, assumptions and habits challenged and real commitments to action made. By combining these elements our work suggests the model has potential to support the development of a genuinely humanized and humanizing educational mission.

ACKNOWLEDGMENTS

The EFFECT (2015–2019) project was intended to facilitate European collaboration on teaching enhancement, identifying and developing innovative practices, supporting higher education institutions in developing strategic approaches and assessing the feasibility of a sustainable structure for the enhancement of learning and teaching at the European level. The project consortium was led by the EUA, and brought together experts, dedicated networks, organizations, national rectors' conferences and higher education institutions from different parts of Europe. EFFECT was co-funded by the Erasmus+ programme of the European Commission.

REFERENCES

Alvesson, M. (2002). *Understanding organizational culture*. Thousand Oaks, CA: SAGE.
Asikainen, H., & Gijbels, D. (2017). Do students develop towards more deep approaches to learning during studies? A systematic review on the development of students' deep and surface approaches to learning in higher education. *Educational Psychology Review, 29*(2), 205–234.
Attard, A., Di Ioio, E., Geven, K., & Santa, R. (2010). *Student centered learning: An insight into theory and practice*. Bucharest: European Student Association.
Bligh, B., & Flood, M. (2015). The change laboratory in higher education: Research-intervention using activity theory. *Theory and Method in Higher Education Research, 1*, 141–168.
Boud, D., Keogh, R., & Walker, D. (1996). Promoting reflection in learning: A model. *Boundaries of Adult Learning, 1*, 32–56.
Bunescu, L., & Gaebel, M. (2018). *National initiatives in learning and teaching in Europe*. Brussels: European University Association.
Claeys-Kulik, A.-L., Jørgensen, T., & Stöber, H. (2019). *Diversity, equity and inclusion in European higher education institutions: Results from the INVITED project*. Brussels: European University Association.
Commission, E. (2018). *Report from the Commission to the European Parliament, The Council, the European Economic and Social Committee of the Regions: Mid-term evaluation of the Erasmus+ programme (2014–2010)*. Brussels: European Commission.
Dirkx, J. M. (2006). Authenticity and imagination. *New Directions for Adult and Continuing Education, 2006*(111), 27–39.

EFFECT. (2018). Ten European principles for the enhancement of learning and teaching. Retrieved from https://eua.eu/downloads/content/ten%20european%20principles%20for%20the%20 enhancement%20of%20learning%20and%20teaching16102017.pdf

EFFECT. (2019). Project page and resource repository. Retrieved from https://eua.eu/101-projects/560-effect.html

Engeström, Y. (2001). Expansive learning at work: Toward an activity theoretical reconceptualization. *Journal of Education and Work, 14*(1), 133–156. doi:10.1080/13639080020028747

Engeström, Y., Rantavuori, J., & Kerosuo, H. (2013). Expansive learning in a library: Actions, cycles and deviations from instructional intentions. *Vocations and Learning, 6*(1), 81–106.

Gibbs, G., & Coffey, M. (2004). The impact of training of university teachers on their teaching skills, their approach to teaching and the approach to learning of their students. *Active Learning in Higher Education, 5*(1), 87–100.

Hockings, C. (2010). Inclusive learning and teaching in higher education. *Higher Education Academy Online Assets.* Retrieved from https://www.advance-he.ac.uk/knowledge-hub/inclusive-learning-and-teaching-higher-education-synthesis-research

Hoskins, B. (2006). *Draft framework on indicators for active citizenship.* Ispra: CRELL, July 31.

Keough, B. D., & Walker, D. (1985). *Promoting reflection in learning: A model.* Oxford: Routledge.

Levinson-Rose, J., & Menges, R. J. (1981). Improving college teaching: A critical review of research. *Review of Educational Research, 51*(3), 403–434.

McAlpine, L., & Weston, C. (2002). Reflection: Issues related to improving professors' teaching and students' learning. In N. Hativa & P. Goodyear (Eds.), *Teacher thinking, beliefs and knowledge in higher education* (pp. 59–78). Dordrecht: Springer.

McIntyre-Bhatty, T., & Bunescu, L. (2019). *Continuous development of teaching competence: A thematic peer group report.* Brussels: European University Association.

Moustakas, C. (1967). *The authentic leader:sensitivity and awareness in the classroom.* Cambridge, MA: Howard A Doyle Publishing.

Ödalen, J., Brommesson, D., Erlingsson, G. Ó., Schaffer, J. K., & Fogelgren, M. (2019). Teaching university teachers to become better teachers: The effects of pedagogical training courses at six Swedish universities. *Higher Education Research & Development, 38*(2), 339–353.

Pilkington, R. (2018). *Annual review of HEA accredited CPD schemes 2016–17.* York: Advance HE.

Prebble, T., Hargraves, H., Leach, L., Naidoo, K., Suddaby, G., & Zepke, N. (2004). *Impact of student support services and academic development programmes on student outcomes in undergraduate tertiary study: A synthesis of the research: Report to the Ministry of Education*: Wellington: Ministry of Education.

Roxå, T., & Mårtensson, K. (2012). *How effects from teacher-training of academic teachers propagate into the meso level and beyond.* Retrived from https://www.researchgate.net/publication/285489579_ How_effects_from_teacher-training_of_academic_teachers_propagate_into_the_meso_level_ and_beyond

Smith, L. (2019). *Annual review of Advance HE accredited CPD schemes 2017–2018.* York: Advance HE.

Sursock, A. (2015). *Trends 2015: Learning and teaching in European universities.* Brussels: European University Association.

Trowler, P., & Bamber, R. (2005). Compulsory higher education teacher training: Joined-up policies, institutional architectures and enhancement cultures. *International Journal for Academic Development, 10*(2), 79–93. doi:10.1080/13601440500281708

UKPSF. (2011). *UK Professional Standards Framework for teaching and supporting learning in higher education.* York: Higher Education Academy/Advance HE.

UNESCO. (2009). *Policy guidelines on inclusion in education.* Paris: UNESCO.

Weimer, M., & Lenze, L. F. (1997). Instructional interventions: A review of the literature on efforts to improve instruction. In R. P. Perry & J. C. Smart (Eds.), *Effective teaching in higher education: Research and practice* (pp. 154–168). New York, NY: Agathon Press.

Zeichner, K. M., & Liston, D. P. (1996). *Reflective teaching: An introduction.* Mahwah, NJ: Lawrence Erlbaum.

CHAPTER 5

INCLUSIVE AND MULTICULTURAL EDUCATION: THE DYNAMICS OF HIGHER EDUCATION INSTITUTIONS IN BOTSWANA – INEQUALITY AND EXCLUSION OF STUDENTS

Veronica Margaret Makwinja

ABSTRACT

Higher education in Botswana is believed to transform life through the provision of job opportunities for those with the privilege to access it. Parents believe that when their children graduate with degrees, this will alleviate them from poverty, and hence encourage their children to work hard and perform to their best ability. Higher education is viewed as the pinnacle a good life – an assurance of a better future for the extended family kinship.

Unfortunately, access to higher education institutions is a prerogative of those who can attain high marks in their last national or international examinations. When students do well, they receive full scholarship from the Botswana Government to attend any institution of higher learning of their choice. However, most students from the marginalized or minority groups tend to fail to access higher education due to various socio-economic challenges they face.

Developing and Supporting Multiculturalism and Leadership Development:
International Perspectives on Humanizing Higher Education
Innovations in Higher Education Teaching and Learning, Volume 30, 85–99
Copyright © 2020 by Emerald Publishing Limited
All rights of reproduction in any form reserved
ISSN: 2055-3641/doi:10.1108/S2055-364120200000030007

Keywords: Higher education institutions; transform; poverty; marginalized; semi-desert; livestock; farming; peaceful co-existence; humanizing education; exclusion; development; unity; self-reliance

BOTSWANA'S HISTORY

Botswana is in Southern Africa located between South Africa, Namibia, Zambia, Zimbabwe and Angola. It is a former British colony that was one of the poorest countries in the world when it attained its independence in 1966. Botswana is about 581,730 km^2 (224,610 square miles), of which 566,730 km^2 (218,820 square miles) are land of which two-third of the country is covered by a semi-arid desert known as the Kgalagadi desert.

According to the 2011 population census, there were about 2.2 million people (Statistics Botswana, 2015). Most of Botswana's fertile land, settlement and economic activities are concentrated on the eastern strip of the country. Despite that the country has a total land area of 566,700 km^2, most of it is semi-desert and has not been explored whether it has any economic value. Arable and livestock farming is extremely limited in a fragile ecosystem, coupled with harsh climatic conditions (Botswana Government, n.d.-a).

Botswana, for a long time has been an epitome of peace, a shining example of democracy in Africa despite its recent insecurity due to escalating rates of crime has made everyone from all walks of life uncomfortable when visiting touring. The country is a tourist hub with a variety of wildlife especially the big five – the lion, leopard, rhino, elephant and African buffalo. Botswana has a unique inland Okavango river delta with its sprawling grassy plains, which flood seasonally, from the rivers of Angola and Namibia.

BOTSWANA'S ECONOMIC DEVELOPMENT

In the 1960s, when the country was among the poorest in the world, Botswana discovered diamonds which greatly changed Botswana's economic landscape. Botswana gained its independence in 1966 and with the leadership of the former late presidents, Sir Seretse Khama and Ketumile Masire, the country boomed into one of the present middle-income economies. However, despite its development Botswana has always faced challenges of lack of diversity of the economy, high rates of poverty, youth unemployment, HIV and AIDS infections. HIV/AIDS affects the size of the labor force, the availability of skills and productivity (Bloom & Mahal, 1995). The economy mostly relies on diamond mining and cattle production. The diamond sector accounts for almost one-third of GDP. In the year 2006–2007, the mining sector accounted for 75% of national export earnings, 42% of GDP and 48% of government revenues, mainly in the form of taxes and dividends from mining (Republic of Botswana, 2008b).

Livestock is the primary source of subsistence and income for two-third of rural households. The agricultural industry suffers from bouts of drought from time to time leading to loss of crop and animal production. The rural areas are increasingly becoming more and more of waste lands while the contribution of agriculture to GNP is, at 3.3% (Botswana Government, n.d.-a, n.d.-b). The amount of food produced by farmers is negligible as chain stores are full of imported foodstuffs from South Africa, Europe and all over the world.

Botswana imports its beef to the European Union and recently the EIU has set stringent regulations that only meat produced in enclosed farms will be viewed as healthy beef and this has affected the traditional communal Batswana farmers tremendously. About 70% of land in Botswana is zoned as tribal (or communal), meaning that it has customary grant or lease; state land (parks, research stations, military establishments, large dams, etc.) is 24% while 6% is freehold (private leasehold) (Leepile & Tsopito, 2013). They are unable to send their animals grown in communal land to the country's abattoir for sale because they do not meet the set standards. This exacerbates rural poverty. These changing market requirements improving animal care for beef export, land use patterns, dictated the need for farmers to review the use of communal land and incline more to commercial land (Leepile & Tsopito, 2013).

There are several ethnic groups residing in Botswana peacefully despite their cultural and language differences. The Botswana forefathers and leaders advocated for the concept of unity through the philosophy of Kagisano, which encouraged peaceful co-existence among the Batswana. Kagisano advocated the four national principles of democracy, development, unity and self-reliance, philosophy if well pursued, would have made Botswana one of the richest countries in Africa. Although the country is democratic and unified, it failed to uphold the develop self-reliance individuals through its education. The education system signifies reliance on mental abilities at the expense of various multiple intelligences since the education places an emphasis on the three Rs.

HUMANIZING EDUCATION

Education is a right and prerogative of all children and adult learners and must be treated as a lifelong process. Therefore, educational opportunities must be opened for all despite individuals' academic performance. It is important to re-examine higher education in Botswana and advocate for quality education and support every student to achieve high academic standards. The proponents of humanizing education such as Freire discuss humanizing education in the form of moving away from the one-size-fits all notion to a more inclusive model. He advocates humanizing education through changing pedagogical approaches that would lead to the academic and social resiliency of students (Freire, 2005). Freire's idea was to provide the marginalized with opportunities to be democratic and denounce oppressive structures to give them hope for a better future (Schugurensky, 2011). For Botswana to provide opportunities for its population, the education system must change and focus more on competent and outcome based that remain emphasizing on standardized test. In Botswana standardized tests are the norm hence denying those who cannot conceptualize facts and regurgitate them the right to further their learning.

Botswana's educational systems were set on the foundations of two policies of Education for Kagisano (meaning peaceful co-existence) of 1977 and Revised National Policy of Education (RNPE) of 1994 which, advocated humanizing education through the learner-centered methods. The policy of Kagisano supported the concepts of democracy, development, unity and self-reliance. The first policy intended to build a unified nation through democratic means and education had the responsibility to produce individuals who could learn to co-exist despite ethnic and cultural difference. Its strategy was to give priority to quantitative and qualitative improvements in primary education; the of nine years of basic education and a re-orientation of the curriculum in order to embody the cardinal national principles and to emphasize acquisition of basic knowledge and skills needed for national development (International Bureau of Education, 2001).

The RNPE churned out citizens who could participate in economic development in the global political arena. The philosophy of the policy emphasizes investment in human resources for national development, and the development of moral and social values, cultural identity and self-esteem, good citizenship and desirable work ethics (International Bureau of Education, 2001). The education system operates within the realm of the two national policies.

In addition to the two policies explained above, in 2016 the Botswana Government set up new goals to enhance education by striving to attain an informed and educated nation through the Vision 2016. The intention of this vision was to ensure that there was quality education that would adapt to the changing needs of the country as a world around us changes (Botswana Government, 2016). This vision emphasized improving the quality of education to make it more relevant and accessible to all. The education system was to empower citizens to become innovators, and the best producers of goods and services. It was meant to produce entrepreneurs who would create employment through the establishment of new enterprises; public education was to raise awareness on skills needed for life. All Batswana were to have the opportunity for continued and universal education. There were to be options during and after secondary level to take up vocational or technical training as an alternative to purely academic study. The public and private sectors would develop education in partnership.

This vision had good intentions of providing opportunities for all and an alternative education that would encourage skills and competencies of the twenty-first century. It foresaw the requirements of the industry to develop well-rounded citizen who would fit into the world of work. However, the government failed to develop a suitable curriculum to match the vision's intentions. This vision was followed by Vision 2036 advocates prosperity for all, which was adopted from the world's sustainable development goals of 2030 (Botswana Government Vision 2036, 2016). The vision has 4 pillars and education falls under Pillar 2 that states that, "by 2036 Botswana will be a moral, tolerant and inclusive society that provides opportunities for all" (Botswana Government Vision 2036, 2016). This vision is expected to work collectively with the National Transformation Strategy to direct the nation to the ultimate goals of 2036 – which are an adaptation of vision 2030, and will also help in weighing competing alternatives and make strategic choices, prioritize and manage tradeoffs. The vision is ongoing, and the country has yet to reap its benefits. For the government to transform and humanize education, there is need to change the curriculum to outcome based and reduce the focus on performance in the norm referenced examinations. Higher education institutions must prepare students for the world of work.

An analysis report of Vision 2016 by Lekalake (2016) indicated that 70% of the Batswana felt the government had performed well in its mandate of educating the nation but indicated that there was a lot to do to increase access to tertiary education and internet connectivity. The question remains whether the government has attained its goal if several students are still not enrolled in school, drop out of school and fail to continue with their studies. There was need for a thorough monitoring and evaluation to establish whether the nation is educated and informed.

BOTSWANA'S YOUTHFUL POPULATION

Botswana has a youthful population that requires training in knowledge, skills and competencies to fit into the world of work and be internationally competitive. According to the 2011 Botswana's population census a higher percentage was the youths. This cohort is the one that requires education and training (Botswana Government, 2019). According to the UNFPA report of 2018 Children between 0 and 14 years make up 32.6% while adolescents and youth from 10 to 24 years are at 34.6% (UNFPA, 2018). The youths need more services and educational opportunities with a dependency rate of 49.3%. In Africa generally, the young generation is concerned about their future due to limited economic opportunities, growing corruption, rising unemployment and limited opportunities for political participation (UNICEF, 2007). This trend is reiterated by the AfDB, OECD and UNDP that 9 out of 10 working youth between ages of 15 and 24, including those in urban areas, are either poor or likely to be poor. This has exacerbated poverty and petty crime, among the youths of Botswana and over-burdening families with the responsibility to continue looking after their idle grown-up children with the mentality that the government must provide them with jobs. Thirty percent of the population remains just above the poverty line (World Bank, 2016).

Another challenge facing both graduates and non-graduate students is lack of entrepreneurial skills to set up their own businesses. The trend has been that the government provided job opportunities for the population. The students do not possess innovative or risk-taking skills to explore the outside world for job opportunities hence remain stagnant waiting for jobs from the government. Unemployment is a worldwide problem that affects both developed and developing countries. In a report by the OECD, developed countries are no exceptions to challenges of youth unemployment (Bayrak & Tatli, 2018). According to the British Council Report (2014), in Nigeria the unemployment rate is as high as 23.1% for those with undergraduate degrees while it stands at 5.9% in South Africa. Botswana is no exception to this trend, as emphasized by the *Mmegi* newspaper that referred to the 2009/2010 Botswana Core Welfare Indicators Survey which identified the unemployment level at 17.8% (*Mmegi*, 2019). However, the nation strongly believes the rate is much higher than reported since 47,000 graduates were alleged to be unemployed while a significant number of youths are seen roaming the streets of every village, town and city in the country due to lack of diversity of the economy and developing entrepreneurial skills through education,

Employers in various institutions and organizations doubt the capability, skills and competencies of graduates from universities. Recently some universities have developed collaborations with the industry for curriculum development as an attempt to meet the needs of the industry. This is reiterated by the British Council Report indicated that the graduates lacked IT skills, personal qualities and transferable skills such as teamwork and problem solving (British Council, 2016). Unemployment exclude the youths from gaining, participating or benefitting from the economic activities of the country. As mentioned previously this has led to various social ills that the government has failed to harness. Some unemployed youths are involved in crimes that leave Batswana feeling insecure and vulnerable to attacks.

The government has introduced several "social development policies as intervention instruments to provide for the well-being and social protection of citizens and include actions to prevent social risk or to resolve existing social problems" (Diraditsile, 2017, p. 75). Examples of these policies and program are: the Citizen Entrepreneurial Development Agency (CEDA), Young Farmers Fund, Youth Development Fund and Kick Start Program:

> The CEDA Young Farmer Fund (CYFF) was launched in 2007 to enable young Batswana citizens between the ages of 18 and 40 years to have access to training and funding so as to engage in sustainable agricultural activities and reduce the rate of unemployment. (Lesetedi, 2018, p. 130)

Lesetedi (2018) reiterates that CEDA funding was meant to create sustainable employment, encourage youth enterprises and minimize rural–urban migration among young people.

The government provides agricultural programs such as the Livestock Management and Infrastructure Development, project for animal husbandry and fodder support, water development, cooperative poultry abattoirs for small-scale poultry producers, small stock, guinea fowl and Tswana chickens. Many young people accessed this program to keep small livestock and breed chickens. Most of the youths failed to sustain their projects because they do not own land, were forced to lease land from older farmers and had to pay for it (Diraditsile, 2017). Other issues were that the youths had no experience of agricultural activities and had no skills of how to care for animals. The youths are blamed for neglecting the livestock, sell it while some go astray, are attacked by wild animals or stolen. The education provided in Botswana fails to develop entrepreneurial skills to assist the youths run businesses. Due to the low quality and relevance of education and training, Botswana's workforce has inadequate skills to meet the current labor demands resulting in a shortage of skilled labor.

STAGES OF LEARNING IN BOTSWANA

Basic Education

There were 826 primary schools countrywide in 2015 of which 755 (91.4%) were government schools and 71 (8.6%) were privately owned. However, infrastructure in public schools does not meet the demands of the twenty-first century which requires the use of technology. Students use technology to a limited extent in their learning and depend entirely on the teacher to impart knowledge. The school going age for government schools is 7 years. However, some children may start school at 5 years. For many years, Batswana children were privy to free education for 12 years (grades 1–12) but recently the government requires economically viable parents to share costs. This does not disadvantage children whose parents/guardians are unable to pay, as these children are cared for by the Social welfare department which ensures that they receive all the necessary items for school, such as school uniforms and books. For those who can afford private schools, commonly known as English Medium schools can send their children for standards 1 to 5. Private schools charge high fees and it is usually the middle working class who affords to send their children to learn in these schools.

Educating Batswana

According to Mgadla (1994) during the1880s, most Batswana accessed higher education in South Africa at Tiger Kloof, a missionary higher education institution provided by the London Missionary Society. For those families who could not afford formal education, traditional or indigenous education was still emphasized when young boys and girls went to initiation schools to learn the norms, beliefs and values of the society. Parents sold their livestock, especially cattle to educate mostly boys. According to Mosothwane (2015) initiation schools educated youths under the custody of their seniors in tribal laws, fighting skills, hunting skills, initiation songs, tribal folklore, craft making and many other things. The initiation schools additionally trained initiates to have courage and endurance. Some of those whose parents could not afford school fees were left to look after their parents' livestock or homes and got married.

Educating children then was expensive and most of the Batswana did not value formal education. However, in the 1970s the country discovered diamonds, and the first president of the country, Sir Seretse Khama encouraged formal education. Instead of children learning under the trees, more classrooms were constructed. As society became more modernized indigenous schools disappeared. The popularity and importance of bogwera (initiation schools for boys) and bojale (initiation schools girls) have gone through periods of decline and resurgence, (Mosothwane, 2015). Lately some traditional chiefs have resuscitated indigenous schools due to societal challenges such as high rates of crime (Mosothwane, 2015). These schools teach good behavior, appropriate womanhood and manhood.

Higher Education

Higher education in the world is in demand, and with globalization and internationalization, Botswana is no exception. The country needs advanced knowledge, skills and competencies. Generally, the age groups between 18 and 24 require higher education skills. However, various government ministries, parastatals, non-governmental organizations (NGOs) and other institutions and organization in the country send some of their employees for further studies in higher education institutions to develop their skills and capacity. Higher education has for a long time been the prerogative of those who perform exceptionally well and qualify to receive grants to study at the university of their choice. Brahim (2018) and Essinger, Sengupa, and Makhanya (2019) encourage governments to develop an inclusive curriculum for higher education to enable a large number of students have opportunities to better their lives. Those who excel are given the opportunity to choose regional or overseas universities while most are left behind to attend local universities and other institutions that provide skills for various sectors of the economy. On completion of their studies, the government expects the graduates to work for the country and pay back the grant money. In most cases, the government fails to collect the loans given to the students and some students opt either to work for private institutions or do not return to the country to serve the government. Therefore, it is essential that the Botswana Government put in place appropriate measures to retrieve its money from the graduates.

Funding Education

According to Omona (2012), there are two common models of funding higher education in the context of African higher institutions – the public and the market-based models. Botswana follows the public model whereby the central government funds students fully from the government coffers. Like other African countries, this model has become a burden for Botswana that it can no longer afford to sponsor all qualifying students to study at universities. The education sector receives a higher stake of the country's budget than any other ministries. For example, in the financial year 2019/2020 the highest amount of money went to the Ministry of Basic Education amounting to P8.24 billion or 17.5% of the total Ministerial Recurrent Budget (Ministry of Finance and Economic Development, 2019). The money goes to investment in human capital development, teachers' salaries and allowances, maintenance of existing facilities, provision for textbooks, food supplies, stationery, payment of utilities and replacement of furniture and equipment in schools (Ministry of Finance and Economic Development, 2019).

Despite the amount of money invested in education, the government failing to absorb most of the graduates leading to high rates of unemployment, poverty, leading to various social ills especially crime. Now other institutions, industry and organizations absorb graduates from various institutions but have placed the government under pressure to meet the need of the industry. Industries have raised concerns that skills taught in schools and universities do not match those required at the workplace. This makes it difficult for industries to recruit the graduates they need and expect universities and other training institutions to provide knowledge, skills and competencies. There are skills termed scarce in Botswana such as STEM, Setswana Language were given a grant and when employed they are given an allowance known as scarce skills allowance.

TERTIARY INSTITUTIONS IN BOTSWANA

The University of Botswana

The University of Botswana has been in existence since 1964 as an effort by the High Commission Territories and the Oblate of Mary Immaculate of Pius XII Catholic University, Roma, Lesotho. This partnership led to the inception of the University of Basutoland, Bechuanaland and Swaziland (currently known as Eswatini) (History of UB, n.d.). The three countries came together because students from these countries faced racial problems and restrictions from the University of South Africa (History of UB, n.d.). In 1962, the High Commissioner territories transformed the college to the University of Botswana, Lesotho and Swaziland (History of UB, n.d.). However, as time went by, there was student unrest at the University at Roma in Lesotho in 1975 that led to withdrawal of the Lesotho campus from the tripartite. The students from Botswana and Swaziland were withdrawn from Roma to Botswana and Swaziland (History of UB, n.d.). The infrastructure for the two countries developed was able to host students with the intention of separating into two entities. The two universities (Swaziland and Botswana) separated in 1982, leading to the birth of the University of Botswana (History of UB, n.d.).

During this period the leadership of Botswana respected the concept of "ipelegeng" meaning self-reliance, and encouraged the Batswana to build their own university under the auspices of "motho le motho kgomo," meaning that every individual needed to contribute livestock. Many Batswana contributed anything they owned ranging from cattle, chicken to eggs which were sold to begin the construction of the present University of Botswana. Although the government carried the responsibility to ensure the university was constructed to international standard, Batswana pride themselves of participating in its development.

The University of Botswana became the only university in the country which admitted students with higher grades from first to a good third-class pass. These passes were dictated by the grade the students attained in the Cambridge O' Level grade 12 examinations. Those students who got non-qualifying grades would go to vocational institutions or re-sit for the national examinations in those subjects they performed poorly to enable them to qualify for admission into the university. There were centers set either by individuals, churches or NGOs to assist students who failed to make it to the university either to improve their grades or pursue courses that could open job opportunities for them. Those who failed would be absorbed by the government as police officers, soldiers and receive training on the job. In the 1970s, people without higher education found jobs in various organizations or institutions. There were teacher training and nursing institutions that absorbed those who according to the set standards attained lower grades and did not qualify to enter the university. The university provided students with soft skills or so-called "white collar jobs" and those who performed well were absorbed by government ministries, private companies, NGOs and others. Some students failed to make it through the university and would withdraw. The University of Botswana has for a long time been the country's only public university. Parents who could afford to pay for their children who were rejected by the local university would pay for their children to attend universities in local, regional and international universities.

The Botswana International University of Science and Technology (BIUST)

To break the monopoly of the University of Botswana, the government has established the BIUST specializes in Engineering, Science and Technology to advance intensive research at both undergraduate and graduate (Master's and Doctoral) levels to provide more opportunities for students who attain the best grades in science subjects (BIUST, n.d.). This is where the government hopes to develop researchers.

The Botswana Accountancy College (BAC)

When the government realized the need for accountants in the country and to reduce foreign accountants, it brought together the Ministry of Finance and Development Planning, the Debswana Diamond Company and the Botswana Institute of Accountants to set up BAC as an elite institution to train professionals (History of BAC, n.d. Like the University of Botswana and BUIST, BAC enrolls the best students with good grades in business-related subjects.

Colleges of Education

There were three primary school teacher training institutions based in Serowe, Francistown, Lobatse and later Tlokweng. As time went on, the government established two secondary school colleges of education in Molepolole and Tonota (Botswana Teaching Profession, n. d.). Since 2000, teachers in Botswana are required to complete a three-year diploma course at a primary college of education in order to teach in a primary school, or at a secondary college of education in order to teach in a junior secondary school. Formerly, the minimum qualification for primary school teachers was a two-year Primary Teachers Certificate (Botswana Teaching Profession, n.d.). The last cohort of these teachers graduated in 1999. Students enrolled in these institutions were those who attained lower grades that could not be admitted at the University of Botswana. The government then decided that teachers need to improve their qualifications to either a diploma or a degree level. Some of the students upgraded their studies at the colleges while others went to the university. The main concern was to enroll students with lower grades to teach in primary and secondary schools. This to some extent affected the performance of the children leading to poor academic results in national examinations. Recently, the Ministry of Tertiary Education, Science and Technology has embarked on a mission of absorbing all the colleges of education into the Faculty of Education at the University of Botswana. Similar to colleges of education, there are institutions of health sciences that historically have been admitting candidates with lower grades to train as midwives or general nursing practitioners.

Brigades and Technical Colleges

Students who failed to complete higher education due to poor performance were sent to the Brigades. These are vocational learning centers that admit students with low marks and are more practical based. Students are trained to become builders, carpenters, electrician, etc. Since those enrolled do not qualify to complete high school and proceed to higher education institutions, they are undermined and employed as cheap labor with low salaries and benefits.

Lately, the government after realizing the position of brigades and the perception of the society that brigades are for failures and for lesser skills development, the government introduced technical vocational colleges to change the mindset of the society (Mupimpila & Narayana, 2009). These institutions have state-of-the-art infrastructure, but most students do not apply to the brigades due to negative perceptions about the quality of education offered.

Private Education Institutions

There has been growth in private institutions to close the gap for those who do not qualify to attend the government public universities due to their low performance. The entrance requirements in these institutions have been lowered to afford access to many students. With the mushrooming of some private universities that were providing education to students without quality assurance policies, the Botswana Government developed a framework through the then-Tertiary Education Council that later become the Botswana Qualification Authority (BQA). The intention of this body is to ensure an orderly development of the higher education sector and how it feeds into the human resource requirements of the country. BQA strives to ensure that all learners acquire quality assured awards through implementation of a national quality assurance system.

Botswana Open University

The Former Botswana College of Distance and Online Learning, which has now become the country's open university called Botswana Open University (BOU) was set up to meet the growing local demand for online distance learning at tertiary level and to provide learning opportunities for those who failed to enroll in higher education institutions or who wish to attain more knowledge, skills and competencies in their workplace through in-service training (*Botswana Daily News*, n.d.) This has opened opportunities and access to education for the out-of-school youths and adults who can learn at their own pace and time through flexible learning mode (*Botswana Daily News*, n.d.). However, individuals are required to pay for their tuition and if they cannot, they would not access learning.

Inclusiveness, Exclusiveness and Inequality in Education

Botswana has an Inclusive Education Policy for ensuring that all Batswana have access to a high-quality education system (Revised National Policy on Education, 1994). Despite this policy education is still a prerogative of the so-called "normal child." There are children missing from the system due to either cultural inhibitions, disabilities, lack of knowledge of some communities about the value of education, poor management, monitoring and evaluation of the education system or negligence by society including the government (UNICEF. 2006). Although the government has made efforts to ensure that all children across all ethnic groups access education, some children among the marginalized groups are left behind.

Most of these children can learn but may drop out due to various issues. This leads to exclusion from the education system because they do not enjoy the economic benefit of the country, do not have jobs and remain in poverty for the rest of their lives.

Currently, success and access to all levels of education are based on the dehumanizing factors of how well our young people manage to answer questions. This excludes children with disabilities since some may not possess the capacity to read and write (Klasen, 2002). It is very rare to find many people living with disabilities in Botswana tertiary institutions. Millions of children with disabilities across the world also face far more restricted opportunities than their peers (Watkins, n.d.). In some institutions of higher learning in Botswana attempts have been made to include children living with disabilities but the learning environment is not conducive for the students to learn in. The infrastructure is unsuitable, and the lecturers have no skills to teach these students. Botswana is reported to not have managed to do enough to cater for children living with disabilities (Jonas, 2014).

Botswana's official languages are English and Setswana. Children from other ethnic groups that do not speak Setswana face challenges of language barrier that affects them from accessing basic to tertiary level. Botswana needs to embrace its uniqueness of possessing various languages and attempt to teach children at foundational levels in their languages to enable them to understand the official languages of Setswana and English better. Botswana requires a political readiness to acknowledge the diversity of its population; that no students learn the same and commitment backed by practical policies to reach the marginalized children. The country's curriculum needs to change to meet the needs of the diverse communities and must be relevant, appropriate and meaningful for local, national and continental settings as well as for functioning in a complex, interconnected and unjust world (Helta, 2019). The curriculum is more academic and does not take cognizance of other abilities that children possess. Recently there are efforts made to identify children in school who excel in certain attributes and encourage them to do their best. Attention must be paid to provide equity of opportunities to retain students in higher institutions for quality education and academic achievement as an attempt to humanize higher education and improve social justice conditions have been central to creating a culture of inclusion (Helta, 2019). The government must set review the criteria used for admission of the marginalized and the academically challenged into tertiary institutions and provide remedial where necessary. There should be places set aside in universities to absorb various groups of students.

CONCLUSION

There is inequality and exclusion in the provision of overall education in Botswana and the worst section is in higher education. At the basic level at least, most children are automatically promoted to the next level, from grades 7 to 10 despite their performance in the national examinations. The unfortunate part is when about 50% of them are left behind and cannot proceed to senior school (grades 11–12)

(Makwinja-Morara, 2009). These children do not have any alternative if their parents are unable to pay private institutions to continue with their studies. For those who can access vocational training institutions they do so because they have no other choice. The mindset of the Botswana society is that vocational institutions/brigades are for failures and used as an alternative to avoid staying home idle.

The government formulated educational policies that depict the humanization of education to enable learning institutions provide students with opportunities to be independent learners and reach their potential. However, the curriculum still requires students to memorize factual knowledge and continue to view the teacher as the provider of knowledge and not the facilitator of learning. The teaching in most cases is teacher centered and examination oriented. Students learn through memorization and regurgitation of facts at the end of each level leading to exclusion, inequality and expansion of class differentiation in society.

Although the country encourages lifelong learning, higher education is a privilege for the so-called best performers. The government has a program that identifies the best performers and sends them to best universities internationally. This segregates the students according to class that perpetuates throughout society. After completing their studies, the privileged, academically gifted children enter the market and workplace to become economic, political and social leaders, continue to control the economy and become the elite of country. The gap between the rich and the poor continues to expand as the elite own the best land, receive high salaries as compared to those who barely made it in the education system. The Botswana Government needs to make a conscious effort to provide equity in education to meet the needs of the well thought out educational policies that possess the characteristics of education of the twenty-first century.

REFERENCES

Bayrak, R., & Tatli, H. (2018). The determinants of youth unemployment: A panel data analysis of OECD countries. *European Journal of Comparative Economics, Cattaneo University, 15*(2), 231–248.

Bloom, D. E., & Mahal, A. S., (1995). Does the AIDS epidemic threaten economic growth? Econometrics. *1*(77), 105–124.

Botswana Daily News (n.d.) Parliament passes BOCODOL transformation bill. Retrieved from http://www.dailynews.gov.bw/news-details.php?nid=37084

Botswana Government. (n.d.-a). *National development plan 9 (2003–2009)*. Gaborone: Government Printers.

Botswana Government. (n.d.-b). *National development plan 11 (2017–2023)*. Gaborone: Government Printers.

Botswana Government. (2008). *Botswana mineral investment promotion*. Gaborone: Ministry of Minerals, Energy and Water Resources.

Botswana Government. (2016). *Status at glance across all pillars by key results areas*. Vision 2016 Council. Retrieved from http://www.vision2016.co.bw/vision-content.php?vid=30.

Botswana Government. (2019). *Budget speech*. Gaborone: Government Printing and Publishing Services.

Botswana Government Vision 2036. (2016). *Vision 2036: Achieving prosperity for all*. Gaborone: Lentswe la Lesedi.

Botswana International University of Science & Technology (BIUST). (n.d.). Retrieved from www.buist.ac.bw

Botswana Teaching Profession. (n.d.). Retrieved from https://education.stateuniversity.com/pages/192/Botswana-TEACHING-PROFESSION.html

Brahim, A. (2018). Reshaping Malaysian universities relevance through humanising education and 4IR. *International Journal of Management and Commerce Innovations (Online)*, 6(2), 1106–1113.

British Council. (2014). Can higher education solve Africa's job crisis? Understanding graduate employability in Sub-Saharan Africa. Retrieved from https://www.britishcouncil.org/education/ihe

British Council. (2016). *Unlocking the world of potential: Core skills for learning, work and society*. London: British Council.

Diraditsile, K. (2017). Challenges to social policies: A critical analysis of youth intervention programmes in Botswana. *Asian Journal of Social Science Studies*, 2(1), 74–82.

Essinger, P., Sengupa, E., & Makhanya, M. (2019). Creating inclusive curricula in higher education. Retrieved from https://www.universityworldnews.com/post.php?story=20190422070841869

Freire, P. (2005). *Pedagogy of the oppressed*. New York, NY: Continuum.

Helta, S. (2019). Dismantling colonisation's 'pedagogy of big lies'. Retrieved from https://www.universityworldnews.com/post.php?story=20190107093331500

History of BAC. (n.d.). Retrieved from bac.ac.bw/history

History of UB. (n.d.). Retrieved from https://www.ub.bw/discover/history

International Bureau of Education (2001). The development of education national report of Botswana by Ministry of Education. Retrieved from http://www.ibe.unesco.org/fileadmin/user_upload/archive/International/ICE/natrap/Botswana.pdf

Jonas, O. (2014). The right to inclusive education in Botswana: Present challenges and future prospects. Retrieved from http://www.saflii.org/za/journals/ADRY/2014/1.pdf

Klasen, S. (2002). Social exclusion, children, and education: Conceptual and measurement issues. Retrieved from http://www.oecd.org/education/innovation-education/1855901.pdf

Leepile, M., & Tsopito, C. (2013). *Report on the stakeholders' 'workshop on market facilitation of the dairy and small stock subsectors through partnerships, research, dialogue and discourse'*, Gaborone, Unpublished.

Lekalake, R. (2016). *Evaluating Botswana's performance on National Vision 2016 Public opinion on development pillars*. Afrobarometer Policy Paper No. 33. Retrieved from http://afrobarometer.org/sites/default/files/publications/Policy%20papers/ab_r6_policypaperno33.pdf

Lesetedi, G. (2018). High youth unemployment in Botswana: A case of policy failure or poor research? *Mosenodi Journal*, 21(1), 127–136.

Makwinja-Morara, V. (2009). Female dropouts in Botswana secondary schools. *Educational Studies: A Journal of the American Educational Studies Association (Special Issue): Women and Education*, 45(5), 440–462.

Mgadla, P. T. (1994). The relevance of Tiger Kloof to Bangwato 1904–1916. *Pula Journal of African Studies*, 8(1), 30–52.

Ministry of Finance and Economic Development. (2019). 2019 Budget strategy paper draft. Retrieved from http://www.bb.org.bw/common_up/business-botswana/doc_1538725465.pdf

Mmegi. (2019). Botswana unemployment figures questionable. *Mmegi Online*, June 27. Retrieved from http://www.mmegi.bw/index.php?aid=71398&dir=2017/september/01

Mosothwane, M. N. (2015). An ethnographic study of initiation schools among the Bakgatla ba ga Kgafela at Mochudi (1874–1988). *Pula: Botswana Journal of African Studies*, 15(1), 144–165.

Mupimpila, C., & Narayana, N. (2009). The role of vocational education and technical training in economic growth: A case of Botswana. Retrieved from https://ubrisa.ub.bw/bitstream/handle/10311/785/Mupimpila_IJEED_2009.pdf?sequence=1&isAllowed=y

Omona, J (2012). Funding higher education in Uganda: modalities, challenges and opportunities in the twenty-first century. *Makerere Journal of Higher Education*, 4(1), 11–44.

Republic of Botswana. (1994). *The Revised National Policy on Education April 1994*. Gaborone: Government Printer.

Schugurensky, D. (2011). *Paulo Freire*. New York, NY: Continuum.

The World Bank. (2016). *Poverty and shared prosperity 2016: Taking on equality*. Washington D.C: World Bank Groups.

UNFPA. (2018). *Opportunities and policy actions to maximise the demographic dividend in Botswana*. Demographic Dividend Study Report. Retrieved from https://botswana.unfpa.org/sites/default/files/pub-pdf/Botswana%20DD%20report_For%20Print.pdf

UNICEF. (2006). *A guide to general commnet 7: Implementing child rights in early childhood.* The Hague: Bernard van Leer Foundation.

UNICEF. (2007). *A human rights-based approach to education for all: A framework for the realization of children's right to education and rights within United Nations Children's Fund.* New York, NY: United Nations Educational, Scientific and Cultural Organization.

Watkins, K. (n.d.). Reaching the marginalized – The key to education for all. Retrieved from https://pdfs.semanticscholar.org/01bc/400c071cd5a210eab0416564c9f17299fa77.pdf

PART II

HUMANISTIC PEDAGOGY

CHAPTER 6

HOLISTIC FACULTY DEVELOPMENT: A LEARNER-CENTERED APPROACH

Hope J. Hartman

ABSTRACT

A holistic approach has been applied to teaching the whole student, yet rarely emphasized in faculty development in higher education. Similarly, learner-centered instruction has become more prevalent in higher education as a way of teaching students, but less so as a concept for faculty pedagogy. This chapter examines the psychological underpinnings of holistic, learner-centered instruction and describes strategies and materials for applying these principles to faculty development so that higher education environments are humanized for culturally diverse faculty and students. Conceptual frameworks underlying the approaches emphasize humanistic theories and the needs of adult learners. Topics addressed include: motivation, cooperative learning, culturally responsive teaching, active learning, metacognition, teaching for transfer, nonverbal communication and instructional technology. Faculty development efforts described include both interdisciplinary activities and a special project with the School of Engineering. While modeling holistic, learner-centered teaching in faculty development, university instructors are engaged in their own learning of effective pedagogy and their experiences and knowledge can be used subsequently to enhance student success in their courses.

A holistic, learner-centered approach enables higher education faculty to create stimulating, nurturing, safe and respectful classroom environments

Developing and Supporting Multiculturalism and Leadership Development:
International Perspectives on Humanizing Higher Education
Innovations in Higher Education Teaching and Learning, Volume 30, 103–125
Copyright © 2020 by Emerald Publishing Limited
All rights of reproduction in any form reserved
ISSN: 2055-3641/doi:10.1108/S2055-364120200000030010

which promote student engagement, content mastery, cognitive skill development, intrinsic motivation and attitudes which foster thinking and learning. Consequently, this chapter provides faculty, administrators and policymakers with tools that can be used to help students, especially at graduate and post-graduate levels, learn academic material and become enlightened global citizens with enhanced thinking abilities and affect to meet current and future personal, professional and societal needs.

Keywords: Teaching; learning; humanistic; learner-centered; faculty development; higher education; engineering; active learning; cultural diversity; adult learners

A holistic approach to education has roots in the progressive traditions of Dewey and Piaget, and views education as a living system of interacting forces which impact human learning and development. It prescribes a comprehensive and integrative view of the student, including the totality of factors that affect both education and life. One holistic approach involves implementing a multidisciplinary perspective, making connections between content, skills and attitudes across the curriculum; relating them to everyday life experience; and incorporating educationally relevant contexts such as the home, one's career and culture into the instructional process (Hartman, 1985, 1989). Just as a holistic approach has been applied to teaching the whole student, holistic faculty development focuses on the faculty member as a whole person. Holistic approaches to education typically emphasize the goal of living well in addition to academics. Living well includes the development of the self, pro-social behavior and meeting challenges of everyday life.

A major transformation in higher education has occurred over the past 45 years when there was a tradition of using authoritarian teaching practices (Khatib, Sarem, & Hamidi, 2013) such as lecturing, to maximize content coverage in "sink or swim" classrooms where students rotely regurgitated what they learned on multiple choice tests. This approach has been increasingly modified to emphasize learner-centered, active, meaningful learning; critical and creative thinking; and alternative assessment techniques. One obstacle to improving instruction in higher education has been faculty members' need to attend to their own scholarly work, including obtaining grants, to secure tenure and promotion. Another has been faculty concern about emphasizing students' cognitive development when employers in the real world "… do not always welcome individual initiative, independent moral judgment, and creative thought" (Gruber & Richard, 1989, p. 162).

Learner-centered instruction has become more prevalent in higher education for teaching students, but not for faculty pedagogy. While modeling holistic, learner-centered teaching in faculty development workshops, college instructors are engaged in their own learning of effective pedagogy, so their experiences and knowledge can be used subsequently in their courses. For adult learners, including faculty and graduate students, learner-centered approaches should be tailored to learners' individual interests and needs, providing flexibility and choices in content, methods and environments.

This holistic approach to faculty development is based on a combination of psychological theories which emphasize learner-centered principles and underpin strategies and materials for applying these principles to interdisciplinary faculty development. A key goal is for instruction in higher education to be embedded in environments which are humanized for culturally diverse faculty and students. This approach is also based on the concept that adults and children differ as learners, and these differences should be taken into account to maximize instructional effectiveness.

CONCEPTUAL FRAMEWORKS

Adult Learners

Adult learners have needs which tend to differ from those of children. Whereas children are usually comfortable taking direction from their teachers, adults generally prefer self-directed learning approaches, such as those emphasized by humanistic and many cognitive theories of psychology and education. Adult learning spans several decades and reflects different needs and interests during different stages of life. Lovell (1980) identifies the following stages of learning during adulthood: 16–20 years, 20–25, 25–40, 40–60 and pre-retirement to retirement. He argues that learning approaches should be tailored to the person's age. Lovell also distinguishes between formal and incidental learning. Formal learning occurs in contexts such as classrooms, workshops or laboratories whereas informal learning occurs in everyday life experience. In graduate and post-graduate education, everyday life experience can involve a wide range of professional activities such as creating a blueprint for a bridge, constructing a lesson plan or conducting experiments.

Knowles (1970) argues that adult education has had minimal impact on our civilization because pedagogy is based on teaching children rather than adults, and derives from the archaic conception of knowledge transmission as the purpose of education. Knowles' theory of andragogy makes four assumptions about learners: (1) self-concept develops from dependence on others to self-direction; (2) the learner's experience becomes a key resource for learning; (3) learning readiness increasingly depends on developmental tasks of the learner's social roles; and (4) the learner's perspective shifts from immediate to postponed application of what was learned and from being subject-centered to problem-centered. According to Knowles, the quality of the learning environment can have a major impact on adult students:

> […] when adult learners are first exposed to a learning environment in which they are treated with respect, are involved in mutual inquiry with the teacher, and are given responsibility for their own learning, the initial reaction is usually one of shock and disorganization. Adults typically are not prepared for self-directed learning; they need to go through a process of reorientation to learning as adults – to learn new ways of learning. Once an adult makes the discovery

that he can take responsibility for his learning, as he does other facets of his life, he experiences a sense of release and exhilaration. He then enters into learning with deep ego-involvement, with results that are frequently startling both to himself and to his teachers. Teachers who have helped their adult students to achieve this breakthrough report repeatedly that it is one of the most rewarding experiences of their lives. (p. 57)

This chapter's approaches to faculty development emphasize metacognitive aspects of teaching and learning, which are consistent with Knowles' principle of engaging adult learners in self-diagnosis of their own learning needs. Teachers of graduate and post-graduate students should help them construct a model of the characteristics and competencies to be developed; provide experiences where learners can self-assess their current performance in alignment with that model; recognize and appreciate their inadequacies; and are motivated to develop, implement and evaluate clear directions and plans for self-improvement. To facilitate learning, teachers should model self-evaluation, including articulating criticism about her or his own performance. For theory and research on metacognitive aspects of teaching and learning, see Hartman (2001a).

Knowles emphasizes that the adult learner's experience must be validated and dignified for adults to a much greater degree than children, because: adults generally have more to contribute to other learners, a richer foundation of experience to relate to new learning and are less open-minded, having acquired fixed thought patterns and habits. Consequently, experiential instructional techniques should be emphasized, as should practical applications of what is learned, and "... 'unfreezing' experience, in which the adults are helped to look at themselves more objectively and free their minds from pre-conceptions" (p. 62).

Knowles (1970) specifies 7 "superior conditions" of learning with 15 corresponding principles of teaching. The learning conditions are: (1) Learners feel a need to learn; (2) The learning environment is characterized by physical comfort, mutual trust and respect, mutual helpfulness, freedom of expression and acceptance of differences; (3) Learners connect learning experience goals to their own goals; (4) Learners accept some responsibility for planning and operating a learning experience, thereby feeling commitment toward it; (5) Learners actively engage in the learning process; (6) The learning process relates to and utilizes learners' experiences; and (7) Learners sense progress toward their goals. In some cases, Knowles recommends grouping learners homogeneously while in others, heterogeneously, depending upon the situation.

Wlodkowski (1986) theorizes that positive motivation in adults is influenced by: attitude, stimulation, affect, competence and reinforcement. His model of consistently motivating instruction specifies particular instructional strategies for each of these factors, resulting in 68 motivational strategies. Strategies are based on his four assumptions about adult learners: people are always motivated; people are responsible for their own motivation; if anything can be learned, it can be learned in a motivating manner; and there is no one best way to instruct (Wlodkowski, 1986). According to Wlodkowski, the cornerstones for being a motivating instructor of adult learners are expertise, empathy, enthusiasm and clarity, all of which can be learned, practiced and improved. His emphasis on the emotional climate of instruction and the needs and attitudes of adult learners echoes the positions of other theorists in the holistic, learner-centered and humanistic frameworks.

Humanistic Theories

Several humanistic theories underlie the faculty development goals, strategies, activities and materials described in this chapter. Humanistic theories emphasize the roles of affect, social relations and personal meaningfulness in learning and development. The humanistic perspective was developed in the 1940s as a reaction against behaviorism and psychoanalysis because these theories gave inadequate explanations of human behavior. Humanistic theories of education are rooted in views of human nature where all individuals have internal tendencies to maintain and strengthen themselves and to develop their potential (Jingna, 2012).

Maslow (1956), a founder of humanistic psychology, focuses on the importance of a person's inner nature, which should be nurtured. He views Americans as overly influenced by the opinions of others rather than self-directed by one's own inner voice and argues that the ultimate goal for each person should be self-fulfillment and achieving one's potential, characterizing the phrase most closely associated with him: self-actualization, in his Hierarchy of Needs motivation theory. He argues that a holistic, humanistic educational approach would develop people who are:

> stronger, healthier, and would take their own lives into their hands to a greater extent. With increased personal responsibility for one's personal life, and with a rational set of values to guide one's choosing, people would begin to actively change the society in which they lived. (Maslow, 1971, p. 195)

Erikson, another founder of humanistic psychology, emphasizes the dignity and worth of each human being and the capability of self-realization. He views humanism as a result of socio-genetic evolution which:

> [...] seems to promise a new humanism, the acceptance by man--as an evolved product as well as a producer, and a self-conscious tool of further evolution--of the obligation to be guided in his planned actions and his chosen self-restraints by his knowledge and his insights. (Erikson, 1964 p. 227)

Erikson's theory of psychosocial development claims people confront a new challenge at each of eight stages, spanning infancy through old age. Many students in higher education are in his sixth stage of development, ages 20–39, where the central challenge is intimacy versus isolation, when people need a strong sense of self or identity for successful relationships with others. This dovetails with other theorists' views on the need to treat adult learners holistically, attending to cognitive, affective and social factors, which includes emphasizing positive teacher–student interactions.

Rogers, a pioneer in humanistic psychology and person-centered education, characterizes the instructional approach as follows:

> The structure that occurs in the person-centered classroom is an organic structure that grows out of the situation, not an imposed structure by someone who simply knows the subject matter. And the learning that takes place is significant or experiential learning. It has the quality

of personal involvement with the whole person in both his feeling and cognitive aspects being in the learning event. It is self-initiated. Even when the impetus or stimulus comes from the outside, the sense of discovery, of reaching out, of grasping and comprehending, comes from within. It is pervasive. It makes a difference in the behavior, the attitudes, perhaps even the personality of the learner. It is evaluated by the learner. He knows whether it is meeting his need, whether it leads toward what he wants to know, whether it illuminates the dark area of ignorance he is experiencing. Its essence is meaning. When such learning takes place, the element of meaning-to-the-learner is built into the whole experience. (Rogers, Lyon, & Tausch, 2014, pp. 61–62)

Three core conditions for effective teaching are empathy, caring and genuineness (Rogers et al., 2014). Teachers should be sincere, trusting, sensitive to students' needs, value students and empathize with them. Rogers advocates valuing the learner's experience, trusting them to make decisions, with teachers offering choices in learning activities, and developing insight into the learner's perspective. His goals for the fully functioning student are: being open to experience; having both freedom and responsibility; living with expectations; being creative; and having positive self-esteem, confidence and trust in self (Rogers et al., 2014).

Person-centered education, which began in the 1920s, evolved to a learner-centered approach in the 1990s, however, there is scant recognition of the connection between the two traditions (Cornelius-White, 2006; Cornelius-White, Hoey, Cornelius-White, Pitrik, & Figl, 2003). Cassuto (2013) traces such student-centered approaches to Dewey and Piaget. The key Dewey publication is *Experience and Education* (Dewey, 1938). Dewey is impacting twenty-first century learner-centered instruction globally, as evidenced by approaches ranging from social media technologies to Montessori schools and Philosophy for Children (Williams, 2017). Piaget's key publications are *Science of Education and the Psychology of the Child* (Piaget, 1971) and *To Understand is to Invent* (Piaget, 1973). His student-centered, constructivist pedagogy has impacted educational theory and practice and underlies many educational reform efforts (Bada, 2015). Dewey and Piaget-based constructivist pedagogies overlap with humanistic pedagogies by emphasizing learner-centered instruction and recommending teaching methods such as cooperative learning, and goals, such as self-directed learners. According to Cornelius-White (2006), theorists have used various terms to refer to the same core principles of developing the whole student, as opposed to just focusing on academic achievement. Other commonalities in learner-centered approaches are meeting the learner at her or his current status on a topic and fostering positive and facilitative relationships between teachers and students. They also encourage students to discover their most effective learning approaches and be actively motivated to learn (Jingna, 2012).

Friere's (1968) *Pedagogy of the Oppressed,* which focuses on creating humanization through liberation from oppression, a classic in the history of twentieth century pedagogy, and as evident from Shih (2018) and Firdaus and Mariyat (2017), is still relevant for educational globally today. "The pedagogy of the oppressed is an instrument for their critical discovery that both they and their oppressors are manifestations of dehumanization" (Friere, 1968, p. 33). Friere's "banking" concept of education, where knowledgeable teachers make knowledge deposits into ignorant students' mental receptacles where they simple store the information without appreciating its real meaning, or critically evaluating it, projects an ideology of oppression.

Friere argues that the teacher–student relationship needs to shift to one which the teacher is a humanist who heightens students' consciousness and critical awareness and engages them in problem posing, dialogics (dialogue between teachers and students) and praxis (union of reflection and action), which foster critical and creative thinking about things that are meaningful to the learner and reflect the values of humanity. However, consistent with other holistic, humanistic and learner-centered approaches to education, liberation must be initiated by the oppressed themselves. The educator serves as the facilitator while learners actively develop themselves (Firdaus & Mariyat, 2017). Friere's humanistic approach requires mutuality in the teacher–student relationship as they learn from and with each other, often through dialogic pedagogy. Shih (2018) summarizes the implications of dialogic pedagogy as being based on love, humility, humor and silence; hope-centered, promoting critical thinking and emphasizing the belief that students can make their vocations more fully human. Humanistic education enables learners to be integrated into society rather than merely adapt to it and transforms society in the process (Friere, 1968, 1981). Although much of the work on learner-centered instruction focuses on K-12, Weimer (2013) focuses on it in higher education, advocating five areas for modifying instructional practice: role of the teacher, balance of power, function of content, responsibility for learning and purposes and processes of evaluation. Cassuto (2013) notes that generally, student-centered learning had not yet reached graduate school, but advocated it at the graduate level as a pedagogy for helping students retain and transfer what they learn:

> We expect graduate students to be able to use what they're being taught when the class is over-that's the meaning of 'knowledge transfer'. Indeed, the education scholars Diane F. Halpern and Milton D. Hakel point out [...] that the entire justification for higher education rests on that premise. Your learning benefits your career only if you can draw on it while you work, not just for the brief period of your training. (Cassuto, 2013)

This holistic, humanistic, learner-centered approach to teaching is especially important for graduate and post-graduate students who are on the cusp of becoming professionals in their chosen careers, so understanding and respect by their professors and mentors can be important for enhancing their dignity and confidence as they pursue their goals.

From a humanistic perspective, the teacher's role is to: be a facilitator and a participating member of the group; accept and value students as viable members of society; accept their values and beliefs; make learning student-centered, guide the student in discovering the gap between the real and the ideal self, facilitate the student in bridging this gap; maximize individualized instruction, facilitate independent learning, give students the opportunity to learn on their own, promote open-ended learning and discovery; and to promote creativity, insight and initiative. (University of Wyoming, n.d.). The Humanistic approach to education dovetails with the American Psychological Association's 14 Learner-Centered Principles (Learner-Centered Work Group, 1997), thereby establishing a consensus on best practices for teaching and learning.

All of these conceptual frameworks can fit within the **BACEIS** Model of Improving Thinking (Fig. 1; Hartman & Sternberg, 1993) which has guided the author's work for more than 25 years. The acronym represents Behavior, Affect, Cognition and Environments as Interacting Systems. The theory states that in order to facilitate students' behavior, for example, academic performance,

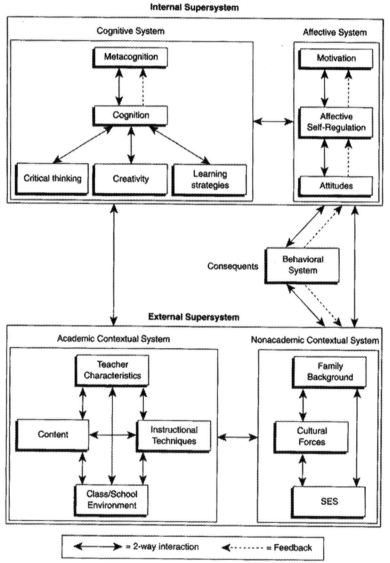

Fig. 1. BACEIS Model of Improving Thinking (Hartman & Sternberg, 1993).

attention should focus on factors internal to the student – cognition and affect, as well as external factors – the academic and nonacademic environments, all of which impact each other.

The rest of the chapter demonstrates how principles of holistic, learner-centered instruction have been applied to faculty development in a diverse, urban, higher education setting. Included are strategies for planning, implementing and evaluating a variety of faculty development activities, both across the curriculum and subject specific.

FACULTY DEVELOPMENT

The faculty development described here provides a case study of how to utilize the referenced conceptual frameworks to model for faculty and help them learn to teach holistically and humanistically, using a learner-centered approach. The articulation between the frameworks and faculty development principles can be summarized as: (1) Holistic: Attend to the whole person including cognition, attitudes, motivation, culture and social relationships. (2) Adult learners: Elicit and build on prior knowledge and experience and apply what is learned to faculty's own teaching and their students' learning in classrooms and beyond. (3) Learner-centered: Enhance self-directed learning – engage faculty in self-evaluation and plans to improve performance, including using a variety of active and meaningful learning, strategies and giving learners choices. (4) Humanized environment: foster pro-social behavior, engage in cooperative and culturally responsive teaching and model respect for faculty's beliefs values and experiences, demonstrating how to do it with their students.

Faculty development was across both the curriculum and subject specific. Activities included series of workshops for faculty college wide; a one-day annual seminar for faculty teaching new students; a year-long City University of New York-wide seminar for diverse faculty and administrators; workshops on assessment while the College was undergoing accreditation review, a summer seminar for engineering faculty; and a nine-year curriculum development collaboration with biology faculty, described elsewhere (Hartman, 2001b). Funding for faculty development was provided by federal and private foundation grants and the college's budget.

Across the Curriculum Workshops

The main purposes of faculty development efforts were to improve students' academic performance, graduation rates and prepare students for their careers. A long-term master plan was developed with the input of full-time senior and junior professors/instructors, department chairs, course coordinators, new faculty, adjuncts and graduate teaching assistance. Input on what faculty would like to see was obtained through a needs-assessment survey.

Participants college wide attended heterogeneous, hands-on, interactive workshops to learn new, learner-centered, active-learning instructional techniques. Videotapes were used for faculty self-evaluation and feedback on their instruction.

The following expected outcomes are consistent with a holistic, humanistic approach to teaching: (1) reduce attrition, (2) improve student performance in targeted courses, (3) improve grade-point averages, (4) give students a sense of greater identification with the college community, (5) empower students with better critical thinking and learning skills and attitudes enabling self-directed learning, (6) promote faculty collegiality, (6) equip faculty with more up-to-date and diversified teaching and assessment strategies, (7) promote mentoring relationships between faculty and students, (8) make the classroom climate more enthusiastic, (9) develop a process for incoming faculty to help them become outstanding teachers and (10) develop models that could be disseminated to other institutions.

One workshop series had topics including: motivation; attitudes; cooperative learning; culturally responsive teaching; active, meaningful learning; questioning; metacognition in learning and instruction; teaching for transfer; nonverbal communication; assessment strategies; and instructional technology. Workshops were conducted by the director of The City College of New York's Center for Excellence in Teaching and Learning (the author) and faculty and administrators from various divisions of the College. Techniques include: activating prior knowledge, questioning, cooperative learning, online learning, role-playing; graphic organizers; questionnaires, self-evaluation and subject-specific examples. One semester 63 full-time faculty from 27 departments or divisions participated in one or more workshops in the series. That semester, 42 adjuncts from 9 departments participated in 1 or more workshops. Nine administrators from seven divisions participated in workshops that semester. Each workshop ended with faculty completing an evaluation of the session to obtain feedback critical for the assessing its impact and making improvements in faculty development activities. This evaluation addressed the extent to which faculty found the material and activities clear, useful and likely to be applied to their own teaching.

A workshop titled "How to Increase Students' Motivation to Learn" began by asking faculty to reflect on: what motivated them as an undergraduate and as a graduate student, what motivated them to attend this workshop, how they define motivation and what increases and decreases their students' motivation to learn. Their responses were recorded on pre-structured graphic organizers and shared with each other in pairs. Faculty were given a booklet on motivation which included the Intrinsic Motivational Framework for Culturally Responsive Teaching (Wlodkowski & Ginsberg, 1995) for teaching multicultural students. The four components of this framework are:

(1) establishing inclusion so students and the instructor feel connected to each other and enjoy mutual respect;
(2) developing attitude by personal relevance and choices creating favorable dispositions;
(3) enhancing meaning by making thoughtful learning experiences which challenge students and include their values and perspectives; and
(4) engendering competence by creating learning experiences in which students succeed and recognize their effectiveness in learning something they consider to be worthwhile.

Faculty were asked, "Do you have activities and/or strategies for each one of these? How might you supplement your lessons to further enhance the incorporation of these principles into your teaching?" Then faculty pairs shared their responses.

To meet the needs of diverse students, faculty should be aware of cultural differences in nonverbal communication to facilitate culturally responsive classrooms and instruction. In one workshop faculty were asked:

> Do you know how and what you communicate nonverbally? How sensitive are you to the nonverbal communication of others? What types of nonverbal cues do you tend to pick up? How do you use this information? How might teachers' smiles and chuckles be used effectively in teaching? How might they interfere with teaching? What do you generally think when you see someone yawn? How do you think a student might feel about seeing her/his teacher yawn? To what extent are you aware of cultural differences in nonverbal communication?

A booklet for faculty included humorous and embarrassing examples of people insulting each other unintentionally through nonverbal miscommunications reported by the *New York Times* (August, 1996). Our culture's "A-O.K." sign of the thumb and index finger making a circle, intended to show "approval," is translated as "worthless" in France, "money" in Japan and recently "white supremacy" and teenage "drug signal" in the United States. Our "V" for victory sign can mean "up yours" in England. When we hold a hand up to mean "stop," someone from West Africa might interpret this as being called a "bastard." Faculty learned about cultural differences in a variety of nonverbal signals including eye contact, posture, facial expressions, hand gestures, vocal characteristics, touch and personal space. They also learned that in contrast, there is remarkable consistency across cultures in some forms of nonverbal communication. For example, sadness is expressed when the corners of the lips are down and eyebrows are raised; warmth is conveyed by a smile, lips turned up and outer corners of eyes crinkled; anger by jaw forward and lips pressed together; and surprise by eyes wide open and eyebrows raised (Hartman, 2010).

A major faculty development theme was using a variety of active learning strategies instead of relying predominantly on lecturing. The cartoons in Fig. 2, "Don't Tell, Elicit," adapted from Honore Daumier (Harris & Harris, 1969), introduced this theme. As a psychologist, the author partnered with subject area experts to develop examples in the various content domains, such as those in Table 1 modeling different types and levels of chemistry questions.

Using technology in teaching included four major, popular, campus-wide initiatives: the Blackboard course management system, student response systems (clickers) to create interactive lectures, podcasting lectures for students to review class content and the anti-plagiarism software Turnitin/iThenticate. These technologies help create a flexible educational environment that responds to learners' needs, preferences and attitudes, promotes meaningful learning and ensures the integrity of student work.

Another popular topic was cooperative learning, which included both pair and small-group methods. Pair methods include Think–Pair–Share (Lyman, 1981), Pair Problem Solving (Whimbey & Lochhead, 1982) and Guided Reciprocal Peer Questioning (King, 1994). Cooperative learning methods include Group

DON'T TELL...

ELICIT!

Fig. 2.   Don't Tell – Elicit.

Investigation (Sharan & Sharan, 1989/1990), Learning Together (Johnson & Johnson, 1992) and Jigsaw (Aronson, Blaney, Stephan, Sikes, & Snapp, 1978). Think–Pair–Share was often used during faculty development workshops regardless of the topic addressed. Jigsaw was especially useful in a workshop on transfer of learning, for helping students to apply what they learned in a variety of settings. Modeling the Jigsaw method, faculty began in "base groups," which broke up with each person going to a different "expert group," where they learned about the specific types of transfer (positive/negative/zero, near/far, high road/low road, lateral/vertical); or area of transfer (within course, across course, professional use, everyday life); or evidence-based guidelines for promoting transfer of learning (Hartman, 2010). Then they returned to teach what they had learned to members of their base group. By engaging faculty in these activities, they acquired personal experiences with the Jigsaw method which they could utilize when using it with their own students, in addition to faculty learning about transfer.

A yearlong seminar on Cognition and Instruction spearheaded by Sigmund Tobias (and assisted by the author), which enabled faculty and administrators to attend irregularly, involved 78 faculty from CCNY and from 12 off-site campuses/offices. At CCNY, colleagues from 23 departments/divisions/offices participated in the seminar. This flexible model reflects a holistic, humanistic approach to faculty development by including a broad range of colleagues from different academic and nonacademic environmental contexts, and allowing participants to choose when to attend based on their personal interests and needs.

Multidisciplinary faculty development activities can facilitate cross-fertilization in academia, which often becomes ensconced in overspecializations. It enables faculty to enjoy learning with and from each other, and can create a campus

Table 1. Types and Levels of Chemistry Questions

Chemistry 104
Sample Questions for Eliciting

Question Levels and Types (Sigel etal 1980)	Example
LOW	
label	In chemical equations, what are the names for the left and right-hand sides?
define/describe	What is the law of chemical equilibrium?
INTERMEDIATE	
sequence	In what order would you execute the steps necessary to solve that problem?
reproduce	How would you paraphrase the definition a reversible reaction in your own words?
describe similarities/ differences	How is a solute in a liquid solution like a gas in a chemical reaction?
estimate	Approximately how long will it be before the esterification reaction takes place?
enumerate	What changes do not cause a shift in equilibrium?
classify	A saturated solution in equilibrium with solute is an instance of which type of equilibrium?
infer similarities/ differences	Compare the following equations: $$\frac{[CH_3COOC_3H_5] \cdot}{[C_2H_5OH]\ [CHC_3OOH]} = K \qquad \frac{[CH_3COOC_3H_5] \chi H_2O}{[C_2H_5OH]\ [CH_3COOH]} = K$$
synthesize	How can you summarize in a single principle the rules regarding change in quantity, volume and temperature?
HIGH	
evaluate	How valuable is the law of chemical equilibrium for each of the following: ideal gases, real gases, liquid solutions?
causal relations	If you change the reaction rate that leads to equilibrium, what will be the effect on reactants and products?
generalization	What usually happens to the number of molecules when the available volume to a mixture decreases?
transform	If the coefficients in the chemical equation are doubled, then what do you do with K?
plan	What equation will you need to solve in order to answer that equilibrium constant problem?
verify	How can you check to make sure your answer is right?
conclude	Based on your examination of Figure 11.1, what would you conclude about the relationship between the percent of HI present and time?
propose alternatives	What other formulas could you use to solve that problem?
resolve conflict	Both times you solved the problem you got a different answer, How can you resolve that discrepancy?
predict outcome	What will happen to the concentration of a substance if you produce more of that substance?

environment with enhanced feelings of belonging and connectedness. However, more homogeneous faculty development can also be quite beneficial, as characterized by the project described next.

Subject Specific: Engineering Faculty Development

Faculty members were homogeneous because all participants were professors in the school of engineering, yet heterogeneous because of a mixture of civil, mechanical, electrical, chemical engineering and computer science. The impetus for this federal grant-funded summer seminar on improving instruction was the dean's and faculty's concern about students not doing as well as expected in their engineering courses. All engineering professors were white men, one of whom was born in a Middle Eastern country. Some had been teaching for decades, while others for fewer than five years. The month-long seminar ran six hours a day, four days a week.

A learner-centered concept is to meet the learner where he or she is, so during the spring semester the author visited each participating professor's classroom to observe and analyze instruction, examining cognition, affect, the academic environment and influences of the nonacademic environment. Classroom observations revealed a wide range of ways the engineering faculty related to students. One senior professor was quite harsh with students, but obviously cared deeply about them and their success. He was methodical about teaching them problem-solving skills and quite enthusiastic about learning new instructional concepts and strategies. He was a "diamond in the gruff"! Another senior professor, who was quite nice when relating to students, despite limited effectiveness as a teacher, had a less open mind and gritted his teeth about participating in this project. The other faculty fell somewhere between these two extremes.

The attitudes and motivations of engineering faculty were surprising, as the author used gender stereotypes to make invalid assumptions about these men and expected them to be less emotional about their teaching than the School of Nursing faculty, all of whom were women, who also participated in a summer faculty development program funded by this grant. One seminar requirement was keeping a reflection diary about each of the classes. Diary entries provided important data on faculty's cognition and affect and the impact of this faculty development effort. Examples include, "Beginning to feel pleasantly inundated with new ideas! Good day!!!"; "Boy do we need counseling! I can't think of any school on the planet with a more diverse cultural make-up. This has been overlooked for too long!"; "Aired a lot of hostility in the morning session. Racism is a hot potato!" and "Feedback is important! Perhaps I've been guilty of not providing enough soon enough. Dialogue is one means to accomplish this."

Faculty members discussed their feelings about teaching, their beliefs about the administration's feelings, their fears about the engineering students and the need for counseling them. One recurrent issue was the implications of students being ethnic and sometimes linguistic minorities, and attending college in an urban, commuter environment. A diary entry which focused on our class discussion about problems associated with student retention in engineering said, "Communication was the main theme of the discussion. Lack of understanding of the student background, culture, etc. may cause problems between the faculty and student, therefore, student will misunderstand." This entry reflects thinking about their students holistically, attending to their cognition, affect and cultural factors. Thinking about students holistically is also reflected by:

> The past four days was a good learning experience and being exposed to the different problems. – use the smart student to explain to the less smart student. – generate discussion about the subject among each other. – questioning is appropriate in American culture some cultures are

opposite. They are told that questioning is an insult. – research has shown that the establishment of ground rules at the beginning of the course has a better impact on the student performance in the course of the course.

To heighten faculty awareness of and to self-evaluate their current status in teaching metacognitively, and to motivate them to improve their instruction, faculty completed and self-scored the Thinking About College Teaching (TACT) questionnaire which provided scores for planning, monitoring and evaluating their teaching (Appendix). Faculty diaries showed this to be valuable for helping them think about teaching differently. For example, "We first answered some questionnaires and we evaluated those questions and answers. It was a productive learning session." Another professor wrote:

discussed hand out of TACT, important points:

– people learn in different ways.
– cultural differences may explain why students do not ask questions.
– make sure you allow enough time for students to answer questions directed at them, rather than insisting on immediate answers.
– important to lay out ground rules of the course and expected performance from students, at the beginning of the course.
– enthusiasm or theatrics on the part of the instructor helps in teaching.
– relate your material to the material learned before.

Seminar topics included: cultural issues in teaching, instructional strategies, communication, questioning strategies, higher-order thinking, transfer of learning and critical thinking. Activating a learner's prior knowledge of a topic, a frequently used instructional technique in the author's faculty development activities, heightens the meaningfulness of what is to be learned. When asked how they define critical thinking, one professor wrote:

Mechanical Engineering program has a broad spectrum consisting of engineering science at one end and design at the other end. Depending upon where you belong to in this program you may have different views. As far as I am concerned, critical thinking is brain storming, creating new ideas and designs, connecting the array of thought in an unusual way, finding new relationships between the input data of our thoughts. Perhaps, unusual way of thinking and connecting the elements of a thought together in the reverse order and trying to make some sense out of that is one way that one could think critically. 'Not accepting without satisfactory reasoning' is also a good banner for critical thinker in our program. This implies that any statement must be questioned and discussed. During the course of discussion of this kind critical thinking will be practiced. Maybe having question 'why' for all the statements is a good way of critical thinking.

Responding to a question about how to develop critical thinking in students, this professor wrote:

We as educators in M. E. program have a responsibility of creating this type of attitudes among our students. To generate this type of attitudes we must put out students in the spots that they will be questioned always. We can also promote this kind of attitude by conducting discussion sessions purposely designed for arguments and group discussions.

Another professor wrote in his diary:

Discussed the nature of critical thinking today and methods to foster this in the classroom. Need to be tentative, weigh parallel approaches, evaluate them and proceed with optimal strategy. In the classroom we should emphasize these key points in critical thinking.

When asked what characterizes effective instruction, a professor responded:

> Thorough knowledge of the subject and the background of the students are the two key elements of effective teaching. The procedure of presenting the subject is the artistic part of the teaching process. It may vary person to person, however.

Another professor wrote:

> One additional strategy in class is to assign problems which are closer to real life. Solutions should not be so straightforward. Tutoring sessions were demonstrated that demonstrated good/bad qualities in tutoring/teaching. I think every teacher/t.a. should be "forced" to see this material!

To help faculty use various types and levels of questions, examples from engineering were provided to maximize meaningfulness and utility by relating questioning to their personal needs and interests (Table 2). A session on transfer of learning focused on different types of transfer and areas for applying what was learned in new ways and situations. One exercise was mapping connections between course content to help students transfer knowledge and skills across topics within a course such as Computer Science in Fig. 3. Other areas of transfer addressed were across courses, professional applications and everyday life experience.

A particularly challenging activity, which was initially quite off-putting to some, required engineering faculty to conduct a lesson which was videotaped and then evaluate their own teaching using the Video Self-Assessment of Instruction (Hartman, 2001c, see the Appendix). One professor wrote:

> Also viewed our video tapes from Monday. We're not bad! [...] would like to see this videotaping extended to our t.a.'s and also would like our senior faculty to archive our first level courses. This will require some follow up.

Another commented that although I forced them "kicking and screaming" to have their teaching videotaped, it ended up being a very valuable experience.

At the end of the seminar, one professor wrote in his diary:

Table 2. Bloom's Taxonomy of Cognitive Objectives: Questioning in Engineering.

Cognitive Objectives: from Low to High Level	Engineering Question
Knowledge	What are the components of an electric circuit?
Comprehension	What is meant by "electric power engineering?"
Application	How can you use what you learned today to save money on your electric bill?
Analysis	What principles of electrical engineering are represented in the design of that power grid?
Synthesis	How could you maximize the efficiency of power use on our campus?
Evaluation	What are the strengths and weaknesses of the electric transformer that has been proposed for our campus?

DISCRETE MATH I - CSc 104

Interrelationships within Syllabus
by
Stephen Lucci

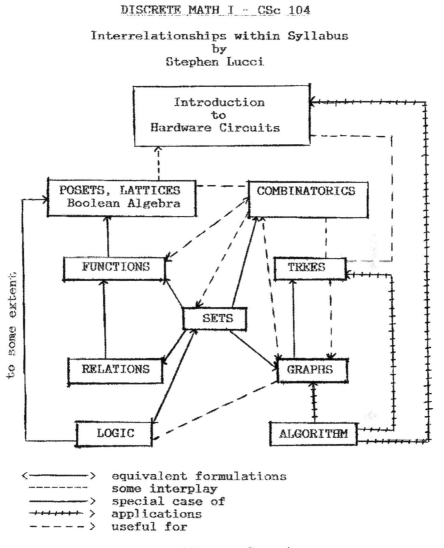

Fig. 3. Within-course Connections.

Next to last day! Almost finished! Not a sign of disrespect ... just feeling a bit tired. It has been an intensive month. I feel like we've accomplished a lot. Curious to see how many of our ideas will be implemented.

Another wrote:

One unexpected outcome of the seminar is that I've gotten to know several colleagues in Engineering that were merely faces before. Amazing how little interdepartmental communication transpires in our school. We could use more of this, albeit on a smaller scale. But good teaching methodology should be a college wide priority.

Applying the principle of self-evaluation to the author's own faculty development activities, upon learning from the engineering faculty that their students' academic difficulties were often due to calculus not being "second nature," the author began conducting faculty development with mathematics faculty teaching calculus to better prepare students for careers in engineering.

CONCLUSIONS

After many and varied experiences conducting holistic, learner-centered faculty development, it is clear that the approach made the efforts meaningful for faculty across the higher education curriculum teaching multicultural students at undergraduate and graduate levels. As substantiated by formal evaluations, diaries and anecdotal reports, faculty were motivated to reflect on their strengths and weaknesses as teachers, and to learn and try new instructional strategies because their prior knowledge, experiences, interests and attitudes were taken into account in planning and conducting workshops and seminars. Faculty's reflections heightened their metacognitive awareness of and critical thinking about themselves as professors and provided insights into how their students might experience learning in their classrooms. Faculty also experienced the campus as more welcoming and cohesive.

Recommendations and approaches in this chapter are consistent with Chickering and Gamson's (1987) seven principles of Good Practice in Higher Education: (1) encourage student–faculty contact, (2) develop reciprocity and cooperation among students, (3) encourage active learning, (4) give prompt feedback, (5) emphasize time-on-task, (6) communicate high expectations and (7) respect diverse talents and ways of learning. These principles can provide an umbrella for holistic, humanistic approaches to faculty development which impact undergraduate, graduate and post-graduate learners. Numerous instructional techniques consistent with this approach can be found in McKeachie's *Teaching Tips*, the classic treatise on teaching in higher education (McKeachie & Svinicki, 2006) and Bain's (2004) award-winning book, *What the Best College Teachers Do*, both of which emphasize learner-centered instruction.

Today, theories that embrace humanistic thought include Seligman's Positive Psychology and Pinker's Enlightenment. Positive psychology focuses on "... happiness, the effects of autonomy and self-regulation, how optimism and hope affect health, what constitutes wisdom, and how talent and creativity come to fruition" (Seligman & Csikszentmihalyi, 2000, p. 5). Pinker (2018) characterizes enlightenment as using science and reason to advance human welfare, and his research shows that in general, most people in the world are doing better than in the past, they are happier, and that people who live in liberal societies are the happiest. Using a holistic, humanistic approach to faculty development and teaching in general can help foster happiness in students and faculty.

By adopting these perspectives and approaches, higher education faculty can create humanized, stimulating, nurturing, safe and respectful classroom environments which promote student engagement, content mastery, cognitive skill development, intrinsic motivation and attitudes which foster thinking and self-directed learning and help students transfer what they learn to new contexts. Consequently, the holistic, learner-centered faculty development discussed in this chapter provides faculty, administrators and policymakers with knowledge, skills and attitudes that can be used to help students learn academic material and become enlightened global citizens with enhanced abilities for critical and creative thinking to meet current and future personal, professional and societal needs.

REFERENCES

Aronson, E., Blaney, N., Stephan, C., Sikes, J., & Snapp, M (1978). *The jigsaw classroom*. Beverly Hills, CA: Sage.

Bada, S. O. (2015). Constructivism learning theory: A paradigm for teaching and learning. OISR *Journal of Research and Method in Education*, 5(6), 66–70.

Bain, K. (2004). *What the best college teachers do*. Cambridge, MA: Harvard University Press.

Cassuto, L. (2013, November 4). Student-centered graduate teaching. *The Chronicle of Higher Education*. Retrieved from https://www.chronicle.com/article/Student-Centered-Graduate/142791

Chickering, A. W., & Gamson, Z. F. (1987). Seven principles for good practice in undergraduate education. *AAHE Bulletin. March*, 3–7.

Cornelius-White, J. H. D. (2006). A learner's guide to person-centered education. *The Person-Centered Journal*, 13(1–2). Retrieved from https://www.adpca.org/system/files/documents/journal/Cornelius-White%2C%20A%20Learner%27s%20Guide%20to%20Person-Centered%20Education_0.pdf

Cornelius-White, J. H. D., Hoey, A., Cornelius-White, C., Pitrik, R. M., & Figl, K. (2003). Person-centered education: A meta-analysis of care in progress. *Journal of Border Educational Research*, 3(1). Retrieved from https://journals.tdl.org/jber/index.php/jber/article/view/7278

Dewey, J. (1938). *Experience and education*. New York, NY: Macmillan.

Erikson, E. (1964). *Insight and responsibility*. New York, NY: W. W. Norton & Co.

Firdaus, F. A., & Mariyat, A. (2017). Humanistic approach in education according to Paulo Friere. *At-Ta'dib, Journal of Pesantren Education*, 12(2), 25–48. Retrieved from https://ejournal.unida.gontor.ac.id/index.php/tadib/index

Friere, P. (1968). *Pedagogy of the oppressed*. New York, NY: The Seabury Press.

Friere, P. (1981). *Education for critical consciousness*. New York, NY: The Continuum Publishing Co.

Gruber, H. E., & Richard, L. (1989). Active work and creative thought in university classrooms. In M. Schwebel, C. A. Maher, & N. Fagley (Eds.), *Promoting cognitive growth over the life span* (pp. 137–164). Hillsdale, NJ: L. E. Erlbaum.

Harris, B., & Harris, S. (1969). *Honore Daumier: Selected works*. New York, NY: Bounty Books.

Hartman, H. J. (1985). The holistic approach to improving thinking. In R. T. Hyman (Ed.), *Thinking processes in the classroom: Prospects and programs* (pp. 90–103). Blackwood, NJ: New Jersey Association for Supervision and Curriculum Development.

Hartman, H. J. (1989). Developing thinking holistically. *Scholar and Educator*, 12(2), 61–78.

Hartman, H. J. (2001a). *Metacognition in learning and instruction: Theory, research and practice*. Dordrecht: Springer.

Hartman, H. J. (2001b). Metacognition in science teaching and learning. In H. J. Hartman (Ed.), *Metacognition in learning and instruction: Theory, research and practice* (pp. 173–201). Dordrecht: Springer.

Hartman, H. J. (2001c). Teaching metacognitively. In H. J. Hartman (Ed.), *Metacognition in learning and instruction: Theory, research and practice* (pp. 149–172). Dordrecht: Springer.

Hartman, H. J. (2010). *A guide to reflective practice for new and experienced teachers*. New York, NY: McGraw-Hill.

Hartman, H. J., & Sternberg, R. J. (1993). A broad BACEIS for improving thinking. *Instructional Science*, 21, 401–425.

Jingna, D. U. (2012). Application of humanism theory in the teaching approach. *Higher Education of Social Science, 3*(1), 32–36. Retrieved from cscanada.net/index.php/hess/article/download/j.hess.1927024020120301.../2750

Johnson, R., & Johnson, D. (1992). *Cooperation and competition: Theory and research.* Edina, MN: Interaction Book Company.

Khatib, M., Sarem, S. N., & Hamidi, H. (2013). Humanistic education: Concerns, implications and applications. *Journal of Language Teaching and Research, 4*(1), 45–51. Retrieved from https://pdfs.semanticscholar.org/e989/d5a4f4fd764065de2358c4265ab72b2110bb.pdf

King. A. (1994). Guiding knowledge construction in the classroom: Effects of teaching children how to question and how to explain. *American Educational Research Journal, 31*(2), 338–368.

Knowles, M. (1970). *The modern practice of adult education: From pedagogy to andragogy.* Cambridge, MA: Cambridge Book Co.

Learner-Centered Work Group. (1997). *Learner-centered principles: A framework for school reform.* Washington, DC: American Psychological Association Press.

Lovell, R. B. (1980). *Adult learning.* London: Croom Helm.

Lyman, F. (1981). The responsive classroom discussion: The inclusion of all students. *Mainstreaming Digest.* College Park, MD: University of Maryland.

Maslow, A. (1956). Personality problems and personality growth. In C. Moustakas (Ed.), *The self: Explorations in personal growth* (pp. 36–47). New York, NY: Harper and Row.

Maslow, A. (1971). *Motivation and personality.* New York, NY: Harper & Row.

McKeachie, W., & Svinicki, M. (2006). *Teaching tips: Strategies, research, and theory for college and university teachers* (12th ed.). Boston, MA: Houghton Mifflin.

New York Times. (1996). Watch your hands! *New York Times,* August.

Piaget, J. (1971). *Science of education and psychology of the child.* New York, NY: Viking Press.

Piaget, J. (1973). *To understand is to invent.* New York, NY: Viking Press.

Pinker, S. (2018). *Enlightenment now: The case for reason, science, humanism and progress.* London: Penguin Publishing Group.

Rogers, C. R., Lyon, H. C., Jr, & Tausch, R. (2014). *On becoming an effective teacher.* London: Routledge.

Seligman, M., & Csikszentmihalyi, M. (2000). Positive psychology: An introduction. *American Psychologist, 55*(1), 5–14.

Sharan, Y., & Sharan, S. (1989/1990). Group Investigation expands cooperative learning. *Educational Leadership, 47*(4), 17–21.

Shih, Y-H. (2018). Rethinking Paulo Friere's dialogic pedagogy and its implications for teachers' teaching. *Journal of Education and Learning, 7*(4), 230–235.

Sigel, I. E. & McGillicuddy-De-Lisi, A.V. (1980). *Parental distancing, beliefs, and children's representational competence within the family context.* Princeton, NJ: Educational Testing Service.

University of Wyoming. (n.d.). Learning theories for educators, tenets of humanism. Retrieved from https://www.uwyo.edu/aded5050/5050unit9/education.asp

Weimer, M. (2013). *Learner-centered teaching: Five key changes to practice* (2nd ed.). San Francisco, CA: Jossey-Bass.

Whimbey, A., & Lochhead, J. (1982). *Problem solving and comprehension.* Philadelphia, PA: Franklin Institute Press.

Williams, M. K. (2017). Dewey in the 21st century. *Journal of Inquiry and Action in Education, 9*(1), 91–102. Retrieved from https://files.eric.ed.gov/fulltext/EJ1158258.pdf

Wlodkowski, R. (1986). *Enhancing adult motivation to learn.* San Francisco, CA: Jossey-Bass.

Wlodkowski, R., & Ginsberg, M. B. (1995). A framework for culturally responsive teaching. *Educational Leadership, 53*(1), 17–21.

APPENDIX. THINKING ABOUT COLLEGE
TEACHING (TACT)

Directions

This questionnaire asks you questions about your own thinking as a college teacher. Please answer them to the best of your own awareness about how often you think about these *issues*. There are no right or wrong answers. Circle one answer for each item.

1. Before I start teaching, I ask myself something like "What do the students need to know or understand?"

   never   hardly ever   sometimes   most of the time   always

2. When preparing to teach, I ask myself something like, "What steps should I take to ensure the students learn this?"

   never   hardly ever   sometimes   most of the time   always

3. When preparing to teach, I ask myself something like, "What should I do first, second, third ... ?"

   never   hardly ever   sometimes   most of the time   always

4. When preparing to teach, I ask myself something like, "What types of. problems/questions might arise and how should I handle them?"

   never   hardly ever   sometimes   most of the time   always

5. When preparing to teach, I ask myself something like, "Should I present the information verbally and/or diagrammatically?"

   never   hardly ever   sometimes   most of the time   always

6. When preparing to teach, I ask myself something like, "Can I teach this any other way?"

   never   hardly ever   sometimes   most of the time   always

7. When preparing to teach, I ask myself something like, "How long is it likely to take for students to learn this?"

   never   hardly ever   sometimes   most of the time   always

8. Before teaching, I ask myself something like, "What do the students already know about this topic?"

   never   hardly ever   sometimes   most of the time   always

9. While teaching, I ask myself something like, "Am I aware of any problems the students are having?"

   always   most of the time   sometimes   hardly ever   never

10. Before teaching, I ask myself something like, "Am I sure I'm comfortable enough with this material to teach it well?"

    always   most of the time   sometimes   hardly ever   never

11. While teaching, I ask myself something like, "Is what I'm doing leading the students where I want them to go?"

    always   most of the time   sometimes   hardly ever   never

12. While teaching, I ask myself something like, "Should I try a different approach?"
    always   most of the time   sometimes   hardly ever   never

13. While teaching, I ask myself something like, "Do the students understand what I just said?"
    always   most of the time   sometimes   hardly ever   never

14. Before teaching, I ask myself something like, "How will I check to make sure the students understand this?"
    never   hardly ever   sometimes   most of the time   always

15. Before teaching, I ask myself something like, "How have I successfully taught this before?"
    never   hardly ever   sometimes   most of the time   always

16. Before teaching, I ask myself something like, "Is there anything I should review in preparation for this class?"
    never   hardly ever   sometimes   most of the time   always

17. After teaching, I ask myself something like, "How did the class go overall?"
    always   most of the time   sometimes   hardly ever   never

18. After teaching, I ask myself something like, "What should I remember from this class that will improve my teaching of this topic next time?"
    always   most of the time   sometimes   hardly ever   never

19. After teaching, I ask myself something like, "What went well? what could have gone better?"
    always   most of the time   sometimes   hardly ever   never

20. After teaching, I ask myself something like, "Is there anything I could have done that might have made the class more effective?"
    always   most of the time   sometimes   hardly ever   never

21. After teaching, I ask myself something like, "Did I respond to the students appropriately?"
    never   hardly ever   sometimes   most of the time   always

22. After teaching, I ask myself something like, "Did I forget anything important?"
    never   hardly ever   sometimes   most of the time   always

23. After teaching, I ask myself something like, "Did I pick up on students' comprehension failures?"
    always   most of the time   sometimes   hardly ever   never

24. While teaching, I ask myself something like, "How is the pace? Should I slow down? Speed up?"
    always   most of the time   sometimes   hardly ever   never

Table A1. Video Self-Assessment of Instruction: Rate Degree of Weakness to Strength.

Classroom Behavior	1	2	3	4	5	Does Not Apply
Clearly state objectives						
Effectively organize material (structure/sequence)						
Appropriate scope						
Consider student background knowledge/skills						
Activate relevant background knowledge/skills						
Communicate short and long-term objectives						
Deliver instruction enthusiastically						
Use variety of instructional approaches						
Actively engage students with material						
Stimulate student motivation to learn						
Elaborate on abstract/difficult ideas						
Monitor students' comprehension						
Clarify areas of confusion						
Connect material within the course						
Connect material to other courses						
Apply material to professional context						
Apply material to everyday life						
Develop students' intellectual skills						
Monitor effectiveness of teaching strategies						
Change teaching strategies as needed						
Monitor students' nonverbal communication						
Monitor own nonverbal communication						

CHAPTER 7

ACTIVE LEARNING STRATEGIES FOR PROMOTING INTERCULTURAL COMPETENCE DEVELOPMENT IN STUDENTS

Leanne R. Havis

ABSTRACT

*Students entering higher education often lack a sense of cultural awareness and a basic understanding of what diversity, multiculturalism, and intercultural competence (ICC) have to do with their future goals. Ironically, student populations tend to be diverse in and of themselves. Yet the critical element that is often missing is their ability to interact across these differences, to confront (and engage with) their discomfort in the face of something new and unfamiliar. Getting students to overcome this discomfort so that meaningful learning and critical skill-building can take place is challenging for a number of reasons. Students are typically more motivated to expend effort in a course if they can recognize and appreciate the value and relevance that the material may have on other areas of their lives, most notably their professional pursuits. This appreciation can best be cemented though the use of active, rather than passive, learning strategies. This chapter introduces strategies for the intentional design of a classroom environment that will engage students and promote the development of ICC. Activities and assignments designated as promoting the accumulation of specific knowledge (**K**), the development of particular skills (**S**), or the exploration of certain attitudes (**A**) are shared.*

Developing and Supporting Multiculturalism and Leadership Development:
International Perspectives on Humanizing Higher Education
Innovations in Higher Education Teaching and Learning, Volume 30, 127–144
Copyright © 2020 by Emerald Publishing Limited
ISSN: 2055-3641/doi:10.1108/S2055-364120200000030011

Keywords: Intercultural competence; intercultural learning; intercultural communication; intercultural knowledge; active learning strategies; pedagogy; faculty development; self-reflection

In today's global environment, employers are looking for college and university graduates who are able to work competently and productively with individuals from diverse backgrounds (Eisenberg et al., 2013; Joy & Poonamallee, 2013). Institutions of higher education are expected to make intercultural learning and intercultural competence (ICC) a priority, given that their graduates will certainly come into contact with others from different cultures or backgrounds, or with persons who have different views or opinions than their own (Huang, 2017; Kedia, Harveston, & Bhagat, 2001; Liu & Dall'Alba, 2012; Sain, Kuznin, & Roje, 2017). Raising students' awareness about and sensitivity to intercultural differences is insufficient (Hickling-Hudson & McMeniman, 1996). What students need to be prepared for, ultimately, is a sense of world-mindedness that will allow them to live and work in different places with different people as "a socially responsible and interculturally knowledgeable citizen" (Schuerholz-Lehr, 2007, p. 181), which is where ICC becomes integral.

WHAT IS ICC?

Intercultural scholars have been unable to reach a consensus as to how intercultural competence (or competency) should be defined (Deardorff, 2006). For example, Bennett (1993) defines ICC as an individual's ability to accommodate cultural differences into his or her reality in such a way that the individual is able to move easily into and out of diverse cultures and to adjust naturally to the current situation. Likewise, Hammer (2009) further defines ICC as the capability to shift cultural perspective and appropriately adapt behavior to cultural differences and commonalities.

To avoid confusion, although the two terms are interchangeable, for the purposes of this chapter, *ICC* will be used to denote intercultural competency/competence, a concept understood as "the ability to communicate effectively and appropriately in intercultural situations based on one's intercultural knowledge, skills, and attitudes" (Deardorff, 2004, p. 194). *Knowledge* includes cultural self-awareness, a deep understanding of culture (including contexts, role, and the impact of culture and others' worldviews), culture-specific information, and sociolinguistic awareness (Deardorff, 2004, 2006). *Skills* refer to the ability to listen, observe, and interpret, as well as to analyze, evaluate, and relate (Deardorff, 2004, 2006); these are expected to lead to adaptability and flexibility, requiring cognitive flexibility and the capacity to pivot or adjust as needed in various environments. Finally, *attitudes* pertain to respect, openness (while withholding judgment), and curiosity (with a concomitant tolerance of ambiguity and uncertainty); that is, an individual who has developed these attitudes is able to lean into a feeling of discomfort borne out of intercultural interactions, rather than shying away from it (Deardorff, 2004, 2006). Deardorff's process model of ICC illustrates that the process orientation should begin with attitudes (individual-level) and progress to interaction-level outcomes; the degree of ICC attained, Deardorff explains, hinges on the degree of knowledge, skills, and attitudes achieved.

Deardorff (2011) further posits that ICC is an ongoing, dynamic process, one in which providing multiple opportunities for self-reflection is vital. Students need to take the time to ponder their own opinions, attitudes, and perspectives, and to think deeply and intentionally about both where these originated from and how they might impact their interactions with others who are different from them in some way. Deardorff (2004, 2006) clarifies that these opportunities for self-reflection are really where the greatest leaps in learning can take place so that individual-level attitudes can inform interaction-level outcomes. The aforementioned attitudes (i.e., respect, openness, and curiosity) serve as the foundation for the model (Deardorff, 2004, 2006), which naturally means that any endeavor to promote ICC in students must address attitudinal awareness and growth as much as the development of critical skills or the accumulation of new knowledge. Ideally, students' exposure to diverse cultures would be one way to further all three of these goals, yet this is rarely achieved in the higher education classroom.

CHALLENGES TO THE DEVELOPMENT OF ICC IN STUDENTS

Part of the problem is that students entering higher education often lack a sense of cultural awareness and a basic understanding of what diversity, multiculturalism, and ICC have to do with their future goals. Ironically, student populations tend to be diverse in and of themselves, with students coming from varied racial or ethnic backgrounds, socioeconomic levels, lived histories, languages, spiritual beliefs, and educational opportunities. Yet the critical element that is often missing is their ability to interact across these differences, to confront (and engage with) their discomfort in the face of something new and unfamiliar. For that reason, faculty members frequently witness self-segregation taking place in classrooms, where students separate themselves and choose to interact with others who are visibly like them (Crozier & Davies, 2008; Haynes, 2019; Villalpando, 2003). Villalpando (2003) references these same-race peer association patterns, noting that it is only when students of color are observed associating with one another that their same-race affiliations are bemoaned as a form of racial balkanization. Subsequent research into the phenomenon suggests that students' self-segregation is often symptomatic of more far-reaching systemic issues. Crozier and Davies (2008) describe South Asian youth in the United Kingdom who opt not to mix with their white peers, attend school trips, nor participate in extra-curricular activities because ethnocentrism and racist harassment relegate them to the margins, where they feel they have to stay out of concerns for their safety. Likewise, Haynes (2019) concludes that while African-American

women at midwestern universities in the United States do not have an aversion
to developing friendships with Caucasian women, both racial and gender tensions and the very real marginalization that they create motivate the former to
self-segregate.

Consequently, getting students to integrate (by overcoming more than merely
simple discomfort) so that meaningful learning and critical skill-building can take
place is imperative, especially given that research suggests racial and ethnic diversity enhances students' educational outcomes (Maruyama, Moreno, Gudeman, &
Marin, 2000). However, integration, intercultural communication, and a greater
emphasis on ICC are challenging to achieve for three reasons. Firstly, faculty
may not feel qualified to engage students in conversations about difference that
may become sensitive, confrontational, and potentially heated, without receiving
appropriate training or professional development in guiding facilitated discussions and conflict resolution. Secondly, faculty may be reluctant to devote pre-
cious class time to skill-building relating to ICC when there are only so many
weeks in a semester during which an extensive amount of curricular content must
be covered. Finally, students themselves may resist attempts to promote the development and application of critical skills. This phenomenon in particular provides
the basis for the current chapter.

Reinforcing the Relevance of ICC

Students are typically more motivated to expend effort in a course if they can recognize and appreciate the value and relevance that the material (and the assignment that they are expected to complete) may have on other areas of their lives,
most notably their professional pursuits (Eberly Center for Teaching Excellence
and Educational Innovation, 2014). This suggests that faculty members are likely
to enjoy greater success in promoting the development of skills relating to ICC
if students understand why developing and refining these skills is fundamental
for their post-graduation success. To some extent, this can be accomplished by
introducing guest speakers from diverse backgrounds into the classroom environment. In light of the fact that selecting teaching materials is often challenging for faculty members, providing cross-cultural exposure and interaction in the
form of professionals in the students' chosen field who can attest to the value
of intercultural communication and cultural awareness is tremendously valuable
(Calathes, 1994).

This traditional approach, while effective to an extent, is insufficient in and of
itself (Feng, 2016). Attempting to promote ICC development in students through
the introduction of a variety of guest speakers is inadequate. While professionals in the field from diverse backgrounds can certainly begin to raise students'
awareness to specific issues of note and heighten their desire to communicate
more effectively (or ask more questions) across racial, ethnic, and cultural groups,
the learning process involved is a passive one; and the preponderance of the literature about engaging teaching practices demonstrates that student learning can
best be cemented through the use of active, rather than passive, learning strategies
(Darling-Hammond, 2008; Perkins, 1993).

FACULTY CONSIDERATIONS IN IMPLEMENTING ACTIVE LEARNING APPROACHES

Active learning strategies are those that facilitate participation and encourage students to engage with the material more deeply (Buskist & Benassi, 2012). When it comes to ICC development, *how* the material is taught is as important as (if not more important than) the substance of *what* is taught. Yet studies suggest that even when faculty members are willing to introduce an element of multiculturalism and ICC into their work, they often struggle with understanding how to identify and implement strategies to incorporate those attitudes into their teaching (Johnson & Inoue, 2003; Liu & Dall'Alba, 2012). For that reason, a significant number report that they only seldom or very seldom incorporate multicultural instructional materials in their teaching (Johnson & Inoue, 2003). Moreover, in a survey of more than 500 faculty from Carnegie Research-1 institutions, only one-third responded that they had adjusted their pedagogical approach as a result of increased diversity in their classes (Maruyama et al., 2000).

The rationale behind this reticence to implement a new pedagogical approach that would seek to promote students' ICC development is often fairly straightforward: faculty may simply be at a loss as to where and how to start. Despite being content experts in their own respective areas, few faculty members are trained on active learning strategies during their graduate or doctoral studies. Fewer still are exposed to methods or techniques specifically designed to foster ICC in their students. The task can seem quite daunting. Faculty members tend to teach the way they were taught, and when they do implement new pedagogical approaches, they tend to do so slowly, tentatively, and cautiously, using more of a trial-and-error approach than any truly systematic process (Halpern & Hakel, 2003). Svinicki (2017) observes that being an effective teacher is quite complicated, not least because faculty members are at the mercy of conflicting demands (i.e., building ICC skills vs covering content in the curriculum). Moreover, she suggests that faculty members who teach the same course repeatedly for years are likely to lose motivation over time (Svinicki, 2017). In short, it is simply easier to teach the same course the same way each time, despite the fact that doing so may fail to stimulate both the students and the teacher. Consequently, becoming self-aware with respect to one's own teaching practices is a necessary first step.

Attending to the Classroom Environment

One initial consideration for creating a classroom environment conducive to accomplishing the desired outcomes is how to make the physical and psychological space welcoming and inviting. What neuroscience teaches about learning and stress suggests that students enjoy the educational process and retain information best when they feel safe and secure (Kohn, 2004). This may be achieved through small measures taken by an instructor, such as thinking about the layout of the classroom itself; arranging the desks and chairs in a configuration that is conducive to fruitful, open discussions (such as in a circle or U-shape, where students can observe each other's – and the instructor's – expressions and mannerisms during dialogue) may yield tremendous results.

Class climate. Crose (2011) posits that one way to create a non-threatening classroom environment is to establish an inviting, welcoming tone from the first day. Faculty members should be prepared to devote a significant portion of the first class session to allow students to get to know one another. Icebreakers are informal interactions that allow students to begin to identify, for example, common ground with their peers (i.e., likes and dislikes), what classmates like to be called, or how names are to be pronounced. These interactions are crucial in laying the foundation for forming bonds and relationships outside (as well as inside) of the classroom (De Vita, 2000). Examples of icebreakers are provided below.

Sharing of personal information. Another preliminary consideration involves a determination by the instructor regarding how much of his or her own personal background to share; students may feel more comfortable making themselves vulnerable in conversation if they can see a similar inclination on the part of their faculty member. Faculty members may share details about their experiences with microaggressions, with cross-cultural encounters, or with stereotyping, but only to the extent that they are comfortable doing so. The idea here is to model the practice of reflecting on and exploring personal biases and histories, so if an instructor feels anxious or apprehensive in sharing a particular story out of a fear of losing credibility or crossing boundaries, that concern is to be respected; if students see their instructor becoming uncomfortable, refusing to make eye contact, or shutting down a conversation, the exercise may actually become counterproductive. What they will learn, rather than how to practice the necessary skills associated with ICC, is that such actions result in negative sorts of outcomes and should be avoided, and that is certainly not the intention.

Minimal lecture time. De Vita (2000) further asserts that faculty members should aim to minimize the time spent lecturing and incorporate more active learning approaches instead. Considerable research suggests that students' attention begins to wane after 10–15 minutes of a lecture (Goss Lucas & Bernstein, 2005, p. 63; Stuart & Rutherford, 1978; Wankat, 2002, p. 68), and retention of material drops considerably after ten minutes (Hartley & Davies, 1978). Integrating active learning strategies can help, given that most people learn better from actively engaging with material than they do from being passive (Wilson & Fowler, 2005). Active learning strategies require students to *do* something: analyze, create, reflect, and so on. This type of pedagogical approach is ideal for promoting the development of ICC in students, especially since the emphasis is on fostering self-reflection and practicing particular skill sets.

EXAMPLES OF ACTIVE LEARNING STRATEGIES TO PROMOTE ICC DEVELOPMENT

The next section of this chapter introduces specific examples of tried-and-tested activities, exercises, and assignments that engage students, foster integration by breaking down barriers to intercultural communication, and promote the development of ICC. According to Deardorff (2011), the foundation for ICC must be established at the attitudinal level; students can only be expected to work at developing the necessary skills and competencies to achieve the desired outcomes if they have (or can be encouraged to foster) an initial appreciation for cultural diversity and a tolerance for ambiguity. In other words, they must feel comfortable with leaning into their discomfort so as to learn some valuable truths about themselves and the ways in which they interact with those who are different from them. Accordingly, what follows are examples of in-class activities and out-of-class assignments that encourage students to consider issues of difference critically and to reflect on these in a way that is both personally meaningful and culturally sensitive.

Students' Cultural Self-awareness

It is important to note that students often lack either the awareness or the vocabulary (or both) for discussing and analyzing their own cultures (Yueh, 2015), and for that reason it may be easier for them to focus on other cultures; that is, the more unusual elements may draw their attention immediately, whereas asking them to reflect on their own social norms or world views may be a fruitless exercise. For that reason, several of the activities and assignments described in the next section include an analysis of students' native culture as well as one which is alien or foreign to them.

Origins and Designation of Activities and Exercises

The activities and assignments listed below were developed across a variety of disciplines and course levels, in a number of different countries (and, in the case of the European University Viadrina at Frankfurt's PeerNet program, devised by students themselves). They are discussed as originally presented in the literature, with a brief discussion of the goals and aims of the assignment, and additional modifications or suggestions for alternative approaches are provided where appropriate. Each activity and assignment is also designated as one that promotes the accumulation of specific knowledge (K), the development of particular skills (S), or the exploration of certain attitudes (A); faculty members seeking to address one outcome rather than another are encouraged to select activities or assignments that are closely aligned with their pedagogical goals.

In-class Activities and Exercises

Icebreaker: Speed Dating (Hiller, 2010) K, S.
This exercise is based on the "speed dating" concept, wherein everybody involved talks to everybody else, collecting as much information as possible under time constraints. For example, students would be given one minute with each classmate to collect information about their background, intercultural experience, and any expectations about the course.

What would be useful to add to this process is a whole-group discussion and post-activity de-briefing. Once students have interacted one-on-one with each of the other students in the class, the group could meet back together and share not only the content of what they learned about one another but also their observations about the process. This would provide an appropriate forum for students to begin to pinpoint the source of any discomfort and brainstorm possible courses of action for ameliorating it.

A possible modification for the exercise would be to provide students with a list of prompts or questions, with the aim being that they can identify as many similarities and differences as possible based on a variety of factors (i.e., likes and dislikes, background, family life, previous education, course expectations, etc.). Then they would be able to begin to explore why there are particular people with whom they may have a lot in common, as opposed to why they may have had very different life experiences to date than some of their classmates. This would promote the acquisition of culture-specific information and cultural self-awareness while enhancing students' abilities to listen, analyze, and relate.

Icebreaker/Coping with the Language Barrier: Suomi (Hiller, 2010) S, A.
This is an exercise aimed at reducing the anxiety surrounding language barriers while demonstrating how content can be understood (and shared) despite not knowing or understanding a particular language. All students receive a worksheet with a few basic words in the target language (one unfamiliar to them), including three pattern sentences and a phonetic pronunciation guide. For example, Hiller (2010) uses the phrases, "My zodiac sign is Leo," "my favorite color is red," and "I speak Finnish." All participants stand in a circle, with one student in the center. That student builds a sentence based on the words on the worksheet, simultaneously sharing information about him- or herself. All participants who share those characteristics (i.e., all students whose favorite color is also red) join the person in the middle. Then the circle re-forms and the next student takes a turn.

The sample provided by Hiller (2010) utilizes Finnish, which is typically underutilized in a German classroom; however, the instructor should feel free to adapt the activity to any language not spoken by students in the class. While there may be particular challenges involved in selecting a language that does not use a Roman or Latin alphabet (i.e., Mandarin, Hebrew, Russian, etc.), exposure to a written form of communication that looks different from what students may be accustomed to (i.e., because the alphabet uses characters instead of letters, or is read from right to left or from top to bottom) is another significant step in promoting stronger intercultural acceptance and communication. Besides, a phonetic guide is provided, so students can also begin to get a sense of how other cultures communicate and the sounds that their written words produce.

Another possible modification to the activity involves listing more than three sentence patterns on the worksheet and transforming it into more of an icebreaker where students can get to know one another. The instructor can add a variety of prompts, such as "I am an only child," "I am a resident student on campus," "I play sports," "I am artistic," and so on. If at any point students want to add to the sentence choices in ways that are not provided on the worksheet, they may be allowed to use the translate feature on their smart phones or other electronic devices. This too would provide an additional aspect to de-brief when the activity is over; the instructor can ask students to reflect on when they felt they needed to consult their phone for translations or phonetic pronunciations, and can similarly identify some of the drawbacks or disadvantages incurred by relying on electronic sources and apps to communicate with others.

Like the previous activity, students are expected to listen, analyze, and relate, but they must do so in an unfamiliar environment in which they will inevitably experience ambiguity and linguistic uncertainty. This would encourage the development of curiosity and discovery, and, one would hope, empathy for others who may be struggling in intercultural interactions where language barriers impede communication.

Self-Reflection: Values in Proverbs (Hiller, 2010) K, S, A.

This is an activity designed to promote students' self-reflection and their articulation of particular cultural (and personal) beliefs. Students are afforded an opportunity to reflect on statements, proverbs, and clichés that mean something to them (i.e., that have "emotional resonance") and to begin to unpack where and why their belief systems originated the way that they did. All students begin by taking five to ten minutes to identify proverbs and sayings that they believe are typical for their culture, such as "the early bird catches the worm" or "treat others the way that you would want to be treated." The most important thing here is that students choose sayings that are meaningful to them, either because their parents or grandparents frequently repeated them, or because they are often heard in the media, or for some other reason that they can verbalize. They then present the sayings they chose and explain what these mean to them and why they chose them. Other students should feel free to ask questions during this time.

The group is then asked to dive deeper and think about the values expressed in the proverbs or sayings; in other words, what does a saying convey about the beliefs, assumptions, and motivations of the group of people that uses it? Collectively, a list of up to thirty proverbs or sayings is compiled by the students as a group and then, individually, students are asked to rank them by order of personal significance. Then the second phase of the activity commences: the auction. Students are each awarded 10,000 Valutas (auction currency) that can be used in any amount to buy specific values. Values are announced and auctioned off, one by one. The highest bid wins the value. A hammer may be used to create a realistic auction-like atmosphere. The auction ends when all values have been sold. The de-briefing component at the end of the auction prompts students to think about how they felt when they had to rank the values, when they did not have enough money to bid on a value that was important to them, and when values that meant nothing to them sold at a high price.

The reason that this particular exercise is so critical is because it requires students to take an introspective, critical look at their own value systems. A frequent lament about the current generation is that students may be apathetic, or that they espouse beliefs and opinions without truly understanding some of the deeper assumptions and justifications behind them. This is a necessary first step in sparking students' self-reflection so that they can begin to understand

(and then defend) their belief systems, but in non-confrontational, safe contexts where specific political and social debates will not be discussed.

There are a couple of modifications that may be utilized with this activity. The first involves making the initial step (of identifying sayings and proverbs that are personally meaningful to them) an out-of-class assignment rather than an in-class one. There are two advantages to this; the first is that students can take more than 5 or 10 minutes as they brainstorm and jot down their thoughts, and the second is that they will effectively be starting to think about these issues prior to coming to class. This may establish a greater sense of receptivity to the in-class portion of the assignment. The second modification relates to the second step, wherein students share their choices (and the reasons behind them) with the group as a whole. In larger classes (i.e., those with more than twenty students), this can be both time-consuming and unnerving for students with anxieties about public speaking. Instead, the sharing can take place in small-group discussions, where three or four students exchange what they came up with. This can easily be accomplished in under ten minutes and in a more informal, casual setting.

This exercise manages to address all three ICC goals. Students will formulate a sense of cultural self-awareness as they reflect on their own beliefs while simultaneously learning about their classmates' worldviews. They will hone their ability to interpret, analyze, and evaluate, as well as to relate to one another. They will also demonstrate respect in valuing other cultures while withholding judgment as they manifest an openness to intercultural learning.

Role-playing: Hosts (Hiller, 2010) K, A.
Hiller (2010) contends that role-playing is a particularly effective method for promoting ICC development since knowledge and intentions can only go so far; it is truly only in an actual situation where someone's behavioral choices become tested. She describes a creative acting approach involving a dyadic role-play, where two "differently poled groups" (Hiller, 2010, p. 155) have to interact while sensitizing students to characteristic differences in other nationalities. The activity was originally designed for German and Polish students at Viadrina to think about how people from other nations may behave while visiting their homes, and to break down existing stereotypes in the context of their roles as welcoming hosts.

All students form homogenous teams of three to four players per team from one country (if possible). Each group identifies characteristics of the other nation and writes them down with the overall goal of answering one question: how do you think the other nation would receive a family at their house (assuming the two families know each other from a mutual vacation that took place years earlier)? Each group presents its findings to the audience, ideally acting it out in a short, creative, theatrical performance. Hiller (2010) notes that this activity promotes tolerance, empathy, and acceptance of others while raising awareness of cultural differences. The de-briefing component is especially important for this activity so that stereotypes and prejudices can be broken down.

There are several modifications that may make this activity applicable to a variety of classes and student populations. In institutions and/or programs where it would be impossible to assemble homogenous national teams, the hosts and guests may differ along other lines: religion, gender, race, even national region. The instructor must make it very clear at the outset of the activity that the aim is to create a welcoming environment, and that accusations and discriminatory or prejudicial statements will not be considered appropriate. If any student or team does engage in this type of discriminatory or prejudicial language or conduct, extra time must be set aside during the de-briefing component to address this and turn it into a productive learning experience.

An alternative approach would involve deliberately making the teams as diverse as possible, so that team members would have to engage in perspective-taking on a number of levels both during the brainstorming stage and during the theatrical performance. In other words, they would have to try to act like the very people they are seeking to understand. A successful approach in the past has involved showing a brief two-minute clip from the 1993 film, *The Joy Luck Club,* before beginning the activity. The clip can be easily accessed on YouTube and shows one character (Waverly) bringing her fiancé, Rich, to dinner at her Chinese parents' home. Rich fails to observe the appropriate Chinese table manners, is unable to use chopsticks, and insults his host's cooking; yet his offensive, boorish, and even cruel actions are solely the result of his cultural ignorance. This is an effective way to introduce students to the idea that awareness of and sensitivity to intercultural differences may have a significant impact on how welcome guests may be made to feel or how hospitable hosts may be perceived to be.

Although some of what students are expected to do in this activity involves a need to interpret and relate, the emphasis is on gaining culture-specific information and a deeper understanding and awareness of culture while demonstrating that they value other cultures and withhold judgment in situations that are ambiguous and/or uncertain.

Activities and Assignments with Out-of-Class Components

The "Outsider/Insider" Assignment (Garcia, 2014) K, S, A.

This assignment utilizes an outsider/insider framework to promote students' conceptualization of cultural difference and simultaneously teach skills for managing cross-cultural encounters. The assignment requires students to write two short papers, one in which the student describes a situation in which he or she was an outsider, and another in which he or she observed a newcomer to a group where the student was an insider. Very clear prompts and directives are provided. For the Outsider paper, students are asked to consider, for example, the experience of living in or visiting a foreign country, being a new kid in a school where everyone else already knew each other, or getting to know someone from a different racial or ethnic group after a lifetime spent in a relatively homogenous environment. Their reflection should include answers to such questions as what it was like being an outsider, what others knew that the student did not know, how others reacted to the student, whether the student was able to gain entry into the group and become accepted ultimately, and, if so, how the student's perspective changed as an insider.

For the Insider paper, students are asked to shift their perspective to consider a situation when they were the insiders and someone else (an outsider) was joining the group; for example, hosting a visitor from another country, having new neighbors, classmates, or co-workers move in who are immigrants, or meeting a new kid who just moved to their school or joined a team or club to which they belong. From this perspective, students are asked to consider how it felt to have the newcomer join the situation, how they (and others) treated the newcomer, how the newcomer reacted, whether they were able to get to know the person (or whether they remained an outsider), what challenges arose in integrating this newcomer to the new group or environment, and then, in conclusion, what were the hardest and best aspects of the process. Garcia (2014) describes that students' greatest struggle with this assignment is often taking the role of the other, and that individual conversations (as well as additional class time) may be required in order to make the distinction between the outsider and the insider clear.

In order to facilitate in-class discussion, Garcia (2014) suggests culling the best paragraphs from each essay and arranging them by theme. Then students take turns reading excerpts (not necessarily their own) aloud to the class. What makes this added dimension so innovative is that students may be forced to read a first-person account from the point of view of someone else (who may be of a different race, age, gender, ethnicity, etc.). Students who do not occupy minority status may become exposed to their classmates' perceptions of being treated and perceived as such, which makes the experience more intense; at the same time, students may feel less vulnerable on a personal level, since they are not expected to share publicly (or admit to) anything about which they might feel uncomfortable.

A possible modification to this exercise would be to convert it from an out-of-class, wholly written assignment to an interview-based in-class activity with a written reflective component. Students could pair up and ask one another the questions for each of the two scenarios, making note of the responses provided. Then the written paper that they submit would include the information provided by their peer, but more importantly, it would also reveal how they made sense of the information that was shared. For example, in describing how a classmate felt when she moved and had to face a scary first day at a new school, the student writing the paper could reflect about his own actions in making new students feel welcome; likewise, he could compare his own experience feeling like an outsider and share areas of commonality or possible coping strategies. This self-reflection would add another layer of cross-cultural understanding to the activity.

The assignment promotes a deeper understanding and knowledge of culture (including contexts, role, and the worldviews of others), as well as the development of students' abilities to observe, interpret, and relate. Simultaneously, they are being encouraged to show respect by valuing diversity and withholding judgment while learning about the experiences of peers from other cultures.

The Human Differences Paper (Muzumdar, Holiday-Goodman, Black, &
Powers, 2010) K, S.
This assignment is intended as an experiential counterpart to heighten students'
awareness of difference vis-á-vis participation in an intentional experience in
diversity, supplementing course content, particularly as it relates to pharmaceutical students or those in nursing and allied health professions. The paper centers
around a "human difference activity." Students are expected to identify a group
or person different from themselves on the basis of race, ethnicity, religion, or
ability (among other characteristics) and experience that difference through, for
example, a visit to a homeless shelter, a personal interview conducted with persons from diverse cultural backgrounds, or attendance at a program, function,
or organizational meeting of an unfamiliar group. The first part of the paper
is the students' pre-visit "Intention Form." Students submit a brief outline of
a group or individual that they intend to visit, primary questions that they have
about that group or individual, and the process by which they intend to gather
the information. The second part of the paper is submitted once the experiential
activity has concluded. Students provide background information on the selected
group or person, identify the major issues faced by the group or person, describe
the "human difference activity" undertaken, demonstrate answers to questions
gleaned from the experiential activity, and reflect on what pharmacists, for example, would need to know about the group or person in order to provide more
effective care.

Faculty may use the pre-visit "Intention Form" as an opportunity to provide
feedback to students on their choice of subject and/or on the questions they
would like to answer. This could also lead to an interesting class discussion on
the importance of cross-cultural communication, openness, and curiosity. The
instructor can compile a list of all of the subjects or groups in which students
have expressed an interest and publicize this in class, so that students with similar
subjects or topics could be inspired to work together on the project. Although
they would each be submitting separate papers, comparing and contrasting their
reflections on the singular experience could be very telling. Alternatively, the
instructor could organize the questions students submit by theme and utilize that
framework as the basis for a conversation in class. This kind of approach could
prompt students to think about the process in which they propose to engage and
to anticipate (and brainstorm for possible ways to overcome) any discomfort or
strangeness that they might encounter. Since the instructor would be presenting
the ideas anonymously and as common ground across the entire class, no one student would feel awkward or singled out; instead, this could prove to be an excellent forum for exchanging ideas about breaking through certain barriers while
handling sensitive subjects respectfully.

A de-briefing session would be helpful as a final component to the assignment.
Students can share highlights of their experience in class, focusing on how it was
similar to and/or different from their expectations. Ideally, this could circle back
to an open conversation about stereotypes, where students could reflect, knowing
what they now know, on why they believed an experience with the group or person in question would be what they had envisioned it to be in their minds. Faculty

should also bear in mind that although the exercise and paper ask students to consider what they have learned in the context of pharmaceutical studies, these can be applied to virtually any discipline. The key is to deepen students' understanding and knowledge of other cultures and to foster their ability to observe, analyze, and relate through the experiential and reflective process in a way that applies to their own respective fields of study, given that greater perceived relevance on the part of the student is strongly correlated with greater transfer of learning and retention (Anderson, Reder, & Simon, 1996; Campione, Shapiro, & Brown, 1995; Sternberg & Frensch, 1993).

Interview-based Reflections (Havis, 2019) K, S.
These assignments are designed to promote intercultural learning and ICC development by requiring students to interview an individual from a different background than their own (with the point of difference varying across assignments) and reflect on that experience both in writing and orally. One assignment asks students to interview someone from a different religious or spiritual tradition and to glean as much information as possible (respectfully and sensitively) about their beliefs, habits, customs, taboos, and rituals. Another emphasizes cultural differences in non-verbal communication, particularly in relation to such aspects as gestures, facial expressions and expressiveness, eye contact, and physical or conversational distance. A third interview focuses on microaggressions and subjects' feelings, reactions, and responses following microaggressive incidents. Students are told that the specific questions they should ask are up to them, and no specific directions are provided other than a general reminder to be respectful to the interview subject and a prompt to pay particular attention to details that might be important to know for someone in their discipline or intended professional field.

For each assignment, students are instructed to reflect on what they asked, what they learned, and what they still might be curious about in a short paper (approximately one to two pages). They are also invited to share what they learned from their interviews in class and to make connections between their experiences and those of their peers. The in-class sharing component should be encouraged but not mandated. For students who are more introverted, or who are reluctant to "say the wrong thing" or "appear stupid," the written component of the assignment affords sufficient opportunity to reflect on their discomfort and to articulate what (if anything) they would do differently, given the chance. Forcing them to speak up in a more public way could potentially increase feelings of anxiety and vulnerability. However, if faculty members observe that several students in the class are reluctant to share, then a valuable teaching opportunity would present itself in the form of a discussion about objectivity; students could take away from the experience the notion that there is more than one "correct" approach to take and that doing or seeing something differently than a classmate does not necessarily equate to one person being "right" and the other being "wrong."

These interview-based assignments are intended to aid in the acquisition of culture-specific information and a deeper understanding of the role and context of culture while enhancing students' abilities to listen, interpret, and relate. In the event that in-class sharing becomes uncomfortable and produces feelings of anxiety for students, an ideal opportunity for exploring attitudes of ambiguity and uncertainty (and brainstorming ways to address these) would present itself.

CONCLUSION

Examples of activities, exercises, and assignments that faculty may opt to integrate into their classes abound, both online and in various books and journal articles. Yet, to revisit the point made earlier in the chapter, faculty may be reluctant to make use of these, either because so much content needs to be covered in the curriculum that they feel they simply cannot devote the time to knowledge acquisition or skill-building that is not directly relevant to the learning outcomes associated with the course (what Svinicki, 2017, described as conflicting demands), or because they themselves feel unequal to the task; they may be concerned that a discussion would devolve into a political debate or a shouting match, that they would not know how to referee arguments over a potentially sensitive subject without inserting themselves into the dialogue, or simply that they feel uncomfortable talking about particular topics. Faculty who fall into the former group may find it relatively simple to use assignments with out-of-class components so that a minimal amount of class time is sacrificed (although, ideally, some in-class de-briefing would take place to facilitate students' self-reflection process). Faculty who fall under the general heading of "apprehensive," on the other hand, will find that a simple solution is not so readily available.

Faculty development may be one possible answer, and it may take a "variety of forms" (Lancaster, Stein, MacLean, Van Amburgh, & Persky, 2014, p. 1), from individual-level conversations to the establishment of committees or centers. There is no right or wrong way for faculty to seek out resources or advice from their peers on best evidence-based practices for promoting ICC development in students. Faculty development committees can create repositories of pedagogical strategies on course management systems that faculty members across an institution would be able to access; they might also invite speakers to campus to provide formal training. Alternatively, like-minded faculty can form teaching and learning communities, possibly as circles or squares (Haave, 2014), to meet on a regular basis, share materials electronically, and experiment with various strategies that they learn from one another. Such a collegial approach in particular would assuage feelings of anxiety and nervousness because human nature is such that people are often comforted when they hear that others like them are struggling in similar ways.

Yet formal models of faculty development are not the sole way to increase faculty knowledge and behaviors when it comes to ICC development, nor is it necessarily the best way to stimulate faculty motivation and enthusiasm (by lessening their apprehension and unease about tackling "difficult" conversations or subjects in their classes). The best way for faculty members to become more comfortable with these types of activities and exercises may be to model the very same learning processes that they want their students to undertake; that is, to lean into the ambiguity and uncertainty, acknowledge them, embrace them, and persist until they dissipate. The more faculty members participate in conversations that make them uncomfortable, and learn to recognize and articulate (and subsequently address) what it is about the situation that makes them feel so ill at ease, the more qualified they will be to scaffold this self-reflective, curious approach for their students and to model what it looks like when these fears are overcome and when new attitudes and skills emerge. It is not so much that practice makes perfect in this particular instance, but it certainly does make for deeper, more profound learning all around.

REFERENCES

Anderson, J. R., Reder, L. M., & Simon, H. A. (1996). Situated learning and education. *Educational Researcher*, 25(4), 5–11.

Bennett, M. J. (1993). Towards ethnorelativism: A developmental model of intercultural sensitivity. In R. M. Paige (Ed.), *Education for the intercultural experience* (pp. 21–71). Yarmouth, ME: Intercultural Press.

Buskist, W., & Benassi, V. A. (2012). *Effective college and university teaching: Strategies and tactics for the new professoriate*. Los Angeles, CA: Sage.

Calathes, W. (1994). The case of a multicultural approach to teaching criminal justice. *Journal of Criminal Justice Education*, 5(1), 1–14.

Campione, J. C., Shapiro, A. M., & Brown, A. L. (1995). Forms of transfer in a community of learners: Flexible learning and understanding. In A. McKeough, J. Lupart, & A. Marini (Eds.), *Teaching for transfer: Fostering generalization in learning* (pp. 35–68). Mahwah, NJ: Lawrence Erlbaum Associates.

Crose, B. (2011). Internationalization of the higher education classroom: Strategies to facilitate intercultural learning and academic success. *International Journal of Teaching and Learning in Higher Education*, 23(3), 388–395.

Crozier, G., & Davies, J. (2008). "The trouble is they don't mix": Self-segregation or enforced exclusion? *Race, Ethnicity, and Education*, 11(3), 285–301.

Darling-Hammond, L. (Ed). (2008). *Powerful learning: What we know about teaching for understanding*. San Francisco, CA: Jossey-Bass.

Deardorff, D. K. (2004). *The identification and assessment of intercultural competence as a student outcome of international education at institutions of higher education in the United States*. Unpublished doctoral dissertation. North Carolina State University, Raleigh.

Deardorff, D. K. (2006). The identification and assessment of intercultural competence as a student outcome of internalization at institutions of higher education in the United States. *Journal of Studies in International Education*, 10(3), 241–266.

Deardorff, D. K. (2011). Assessing intercultural competence. *New Directions For Institutional Research*, 149, 65–79.

De Vita, G. (2000). Inclusive approaches to effective communication and active participation in the multicultural classroom: An international business management context. *Active Learning in Higher Education*, 1(2), 168–180.

Eberly Center for Teaching Excellence and Educational Innovation. (2014). Students lack interest or motivation. Retrieved from www.cmu.edu/teaching/solveproblem/strat-lackmotivation/lackmotivation-01.html

Eisenberg, J., Lee, H. J., Brück, F., Brenner, B., Claes, M. T., Mironski, J., & Bell, R. (2013). Can business schools make students culturally competent? Effects of cross-cultural management courses on cultural intelligence. *Academy of Management Learning & Education*, 12(4), 603–621.

Feng, J. B. (2016). Improving intercultural competence in the classroom: A reflective development model. *Journal of Teaching in International Business*, 27, 4–22.

Garcia, A. C. (2014). The "outsider/insider" assignment: A pedagogical innovation for teaching cross-cultural understanding. *International Journal of Teaching and Learning in Higher Education*, 26(3), 453–462.

Goss Lucas, S., & Bernstein, D. A. (2005). *Teaching psychology: A step by step guide*. Mahwah, NJ: Lawrence Erlbaum Associates, Inc.

Haave, N. (2014). Teaching squares: A teaching development tool. *The Teaching Professor, 28*(10), 1.

Halpern, D. F., & Hakel, M. D. (2003). Applying the science of learning to the university and beyond: Teaching for long-term retention and transfer. *Change, 35*(4), 36–41.

Hammer, M. R. (2009). The intercultural development inventory: An approach for assessing and building intercultural competence. In M. A. Moodian (Ed.), *Contemporary leadership and intercultural competence: Exploring the cross-cultural dynamics within organizations* (pp. 203–217). Thousand Oaks, CA: Sage.

Hartley, J., & Davies, I. K. (1978). Note taking: A critical review. *Programmed Learning and Educational Technology, 15*, 207–224.

Havis, L. (2019). Promoting intercultural competence among criminal justice students using interview-based signature assignments. *Transformative Dialogues: Teaching & Learning Journal, 12*(1), Article 4.

Haynes, C. S. (2019). There's no place like home? African American women in the residence halls of a predominantly white Midwestern University. *Gender and Education, 31*(4), 525–542.

Hickling-Hudson, A., & McMeniman, M. (1996). Pluralism and Australian teacher education. In M. Craft (Ed.), *Teaching education in plural societies: An international review* (pp. 16–26). London: Falmer.

Hiller, G. G. (2010). Innovative methods for promoting and assessing intercultural competence in higher education. *Proceedings of Intercultural Competence Conference, 1*, 144–168. Retrieved from http://cercll.arizona.edu/ICConference2/malgesini.pdf

Huang, L. (2017). Co-curricular activity-based intercultural competence development: Students' outcome of internationalisation at universities. *Innovations in Education and Teaching International, 54*(3), 184–193.

Johnson, K., & Inoue, Y. (2003). Diversity and multicultural pedagogy: An analysis of attitudes and practices within an American Pacific Island university. *Journal of Research in International Education, 2*, 251–276.

Joy, S., & Poonamallee, L. (2013). Cross-cultural teaching in globalized management classrooms: Time to move from functionalist to postcolonial approaches? *Academy of Management Learning & Education, 12*(3), 396–413.

Kedia, B. L., Harveston, P. D., & Bhagat, R. S. (2001). Orienting curricula and teaching to produce international managers for global competition. *Journal of Teaching in International Business, 13*(1), 1–22.

Kohn, A. (2004). Feel-bad education. *Education Week, 24*(3), 44–45.

Lancaster, J. W., Stein, S. M., MacLean, L. G., Van Amburgh, J., & Persky, A. M. (2014). Faculty development program models to advance teaching and learning within health science programs. *American Journal of Pharmaceutical Education, 78*(5), Article 99.

Liu, S., & Dall'Alba, G. (2012). Learning intercultural communication through group work oriented to the world beyond the classroom. *Assessment & Evaluation in Higher Education, 37*(1), 19–32.

Maruyama, G., Moreno, J., Gudeman, R. H., & Marin, P. (2000). *Does diversity make a difference? Three research studies on diversity in college classrooms*. Washington, DC: American Council on Education.

Muzumdar, J. M., Holiday-Goodman, M., Black, C., & Powers, M. (2010). Instructional design and assessment: Cultural competence knowledge and confidence after classroom activities. *American Journal of Pharmaceutical Education, 74*(8), Article 150.

Perkins, D. (1993). Teaching for understanding. *American Educator: The Professional Journal of the American Federation of Teachers, 17*(3), 28–35.

Sain, Z. F., Kuznin, M., & Roje, R. C. (2017). Teaching intercultural competence in undergraduate business and management studies – A case study. *Croatian Journal of Education, 19*(1), 55–71.

Schuerholz-Lehr, S. (2007). Teaching for global literacy in higher education: How prepared are the educators? *Journal of Studies in International Education, 11*(2), 180–204.

Sternberg, R. J., & Frensch, P. A. (1993). Mechanisms of transfer. In D. K. Detterman & R. J. Sternberg (Eds.), *Transfer on trial: Intelligence, cognition, and instruction* (pp. 25–38). Norwood, NJ: Ablex.

Stuart, J., & Rutherford, R. J. (1978). Medical student concentration during lectures. *Lancet, 2*(8088), 514–516.

Svinicki, M. D. (2017). From Keller's MVP model to faculty development practice. *New Directions for Teaching & Learning, 2017*(152), 79–89.

Villalpando, O. (2003). Self-segregation or self-preservation? A critical race theory and Latina/o critical theory analysis of a study of Chicana/o college students. *Qualitative Studies in Education, 16*(5), 619–646.

Wankat, P. C. (2002). *The effective, efficient professor: Teaching, scholarship, and service.* Boston, MA: Allyn & Bacon.

Wilson, K., & Fowler, J. (2005). Assessing the impact of learning environments on students' approaches to learning: Comparing conventional and action learning designs. *Assessment & Evaluation in Higher Education, 30*(1), 87–101.

Yueh, H. S. (2015). Playing the role of an outsider within: Teaching intercultural communication through an ethnographic project. *Communication Teacher, 29*(1), 13–20.

CHAPTER 8

APPLYING FREIRE AND UBUNTU TO HUMANIZING HIGHER EDUCATION LEADERSHIP

Victor Pitsoe and Moeketsi Letseka

ABSTRACT

This chapter explores the relationship between higher education leadership and humanizing pedagogy. It is premised on the assumption that higher education leadership, as a social construct, is both a philosophical problem and policy imperative. Yet, the fourth industrial revolution and artificial intelligence (AI) imperatives have far-reaching implications for the "dominant" higher education leadership theory and practice. With this in mind, this chapter advocates for a broader and culturally inclusive understanding of higher education leadership perspectives. Among others, this thesis is that in a developing country context such as South Africa, for example, the dominant approach of higher education leadership should be guided by the Ubuntu *principles and humanizing pedagogy. The author argue that the humanizing pedagogy and* Ubuntu *principles, in a culturally diverse setting of the fourth industrial revolution era and AI, have the prospects of changing the current unacceptable levels of performance and bring change in a larger scale in higher education institutions.*

Keywords: Humanizing pedagogy; dehumanizing pedagogy; dehumanize; Ubuntu; higher education leadership; fourth industrial revolution; open distance and e-learning; dominant culture

Developing and Supporting Multiculturalism and Leadership Development:
International Perspectives on Humanizing Higher Education
Innovations in Higher Education Teaching and Learning, Volume 30, 145–158
Copyright © 2020 by Emerald Publishing Limited
All rights of reproduction in any form reserved
ISSN: 2055-3641/doi:10.1108/S2055-364120200000030012

1. INTRODUCTION AND BACKGROUND

Globally, higher education leadership is undergoing a process of rapid change. Higher education leadership encompasses primarily the academic disciplines of leadership and organizational theory. Yet, there is a growing body of literature that recognizes the symbiotic relationship between higher education leadership and industrial revolutions. There is a paucity of literature on higher education leadership in culturally diverse settings. With this in mind, the work of Paulo Freire might be useful to the debates on higher education leadership. This is because higher education leadership is a territorial area. As a discourse, it does not exist independently of psychological experiences and social/cultural contexts. This chapter notes that dominant higher education leadership strategies, procedures and behaviors seem to be trapped in the functionalist framework and perpetuate dehumanizing pedagogy. Such strategies, procedures and behaviors ignore the nature of leadership as a form of personal expression and social stewardship. Moreover, they deny ambiguity.

The purpose of this chapter is to generate debate on the evolving field of artificial intelligence (AI) in higher education leadership. We shall argue that humanizing pedagogy and the philosophy of *Ubuntu* have the potential to change the current unacceptable levels of performance and bring change on a larger scale in higher education institutions, especially in Open Distance and e-Learning (ODeL) institutions. As Tutu (2008) aptly puts it, *Ubuntu* is a belief that a person is a person through other persons, that my humanity is caught up, bound up, inextricably, with yours. When I dehumanize you, I inexorably dehumanize myself. It is worthwhile noting that effective and efficient higher education leadership practices are marked by responsiveness to the students' needs, as well as clearly articulated learning destinations of the diverse students. Nevertheless, the dominant higher education leadership practice has three fundamental blind spots – it continues, (1) to be trapped in dehumanizing pedagogy, (2) it lacks the attributes of cultural hybridization and (3) it eschews the principles of humane approaches. Our thesis in this chapter is that basing higher education leadership practices on one set of values, namely the dehumanizing pedagogy, in culturally diverse settings can potentially lead to what Italian Marxist Antonio Gramsci (1971) calls "cultural hegemony."

Central to this chapter is the assumption that no set of pedagogical principles can claim to be the final word or arbiter on higher education leadership. The complex and porous nature of culturally diverse learning environments of the era of the fourth industrial revolution calls for higher education institutions to move away from one-size-fits-all paradigms and instead to focus on humane approaches to reaching and learning such as a humanizing pedagogy. Our view is that Freire and *Ubuntu* can address the specific humanizing needs in higher education leadership created by AI and the Fourth Industrial Revolution. That is, higher education leadership should to be adaptive to diverse cultures. Drawing mainly on the works of Paulo Freire and the philosophy of *Ubuntu* this chapter: (1) conceptualizes the notion of higher education leadership through the fourth industrial revolution lens; (2) presents higher education leadership as a tool for the social construction of docile bodies; (3) explores the thoughts on human-izing pedagogy; (4) argues a case for the philosophy of *Ubuntu* as a humanizing pedagogy; and finally (5) proposes a rethinking of higher education leadership through *Ubuntu* framework and humanizing pedagogy.

2. THE CONCEPT OF HIGHER EDUCATION LEADERSHIP THROUGH THE FOURTH INDUSTRIAL REVOLUTION LENS

The literature on "higher education leadership" is abundant but diverse. There is no fixed definition and the literature changing at a fast rate. Higher education leadership as a rubric for the bureaucratic organizing of higher education insti-tutions is rooted in a particular identity and involves a multitude of definitions, interpretations, aims and strategies. For Spicer (2019):

> good leadership is essentially about being an adept and versatile performer, responding to the needs and wants of your followers and giving them, more than anything, a sense of security, whether that means encouraging chats about their career development or focused targets for them to work towards. (*https://www.chronicle.com/campusViewpointArticle/What-Makes-a-Good-Leader-/669/*)

It is worthwhile mentioning that the *being-ness* of "higher education leadership" is influenced and shaped by industrial revolutions and different situations/con-text. Our starting point is that from an industrial revolutions perspective, changes in society and higher education leadership have a symbiotic relationship and are interconnected. As Xing and Marwala (2017) observe:

> The connection between education and society is often implied to be one-way, where educa-tion is expected to fit in with economic and political trends, rather than opposing them and representing something different. (p. 11)

Leadership in higher education is tough. Yet, a radical fourth industrial revolution in the higher education space calls for a range of leadership skills. Notwithstanding the fact that different situations require different leadership styles, the question: *What makes a good leader in the higher education fourth industrial revolution era?* becomes critical. Just like the past industrial revolutions, "which called for the remake of education to prepare a labor force for new forms of work and citizenship," the fourth industrial revolution calls for "new forms of education to prepare a locally and globally-oriented workforce and citizenry" (Maila & Pitsoe, 2014, p. 99). As Xing and Marwala (2017) put it, "The factory floor is moving towards self-regulating production that can be adapted to indi-vidual customer demands and has self-learning capability" (p. 10).

Notwithstanding that the fourth industrial revolution technologies and AI are tools for human survival, our take is that higher education practitioners should embrace technology rather than resist it. While we acknowledge the fact that AI perpetuates hegemonic practices, creates docile bodies and dehumanizes higher education our position is that AI is a more symbiotic both/and opportunity that affords growth for higher education practitioners, and the organizations they work for, through thoughtful technology advancements. For us, AI empowers humans and machines to do what each does best. Most importantly, AI is a strategic endeavor, it helps organizations to create better human–machine product experiences; boost performance through more sophisticated and precise insights; and accelerate development, automate the mundane and tap human potential. Xing and Marwala (2017) remind us, "This period requires certain skills that are not exactly the same as the skills that were required in the third industrial revolution where information technology was the key driver" (p. 13). They argue that "in the era of the 4th industrial revolution, higher education needs to deepen its technology system reforms by breaking down all barriers to innovation" (p. 13). Against this backdrop therefore, the key questions for us are: (1) To what extent is higher education leadership transformed consistent with the basic requirements of the fourth industrial revolution? (2) How can value be extracted from the use of AI to guide higher education leadership?

Drawing on the work of Klaus Schwab (2017), *The Fourth Industrial Revolution*, Yang and Chen (2018) state that:

> The fourth industrial revolution is not merely an extension or prolongation of its predecessor, but is a distinct phase distinguished by the extraordinary velocity, scope, and system impacts of its technological advancements. (p. 40)

Schwab (2017) describes *The Fourth Industrial Revolution* as a fusion of technologies such as, among others, gene sequencing, nanotechnology, cloud computing, AI and how these technologies interact across the physical, digital and biological domains that make this revolution fundamentally different from previous revolutions. Schwab (2017) picks out advances such as self-driving cars, auto-piloting of commercial planes, unmanned commercial and military drones, global positioning systems (GPS), virtual assistants, translation software, "intelligent" robots, the Internet of Things, as well as applications such as Apple's Siri, as some of the distinguishing features of *The Fourth Industrial Revolution*.

It is Schwab's (2017) contention that "it is almost inevitable that *The Fourth Industrial Revolution* will have a major impact on labour markets and workplaces around the world" (p. 43). It will "demand and place more emphasis on the ability of workers to adapt continuously and learn new skills and approaches within a variety of contexts" (p. 47). He warns that:

> labour markets … are becoming biased towards a limited range of technical skill sets, and that globally connected digital platforms and marketplaces are granting outsized rewards to a small number of 'stars'. (p. 87)

The Economist magazine (2014) projects that "the combination of big data and smart machines will take over some occupations wholesale." In others, it will allow firms to do more with fewer workers. Text mining programs will displace professional jobs in legal services. Biopsies will be analyzed more efficiently by image processing software than lab technicians. Accountants might follow travel agents and tellers into the unemployment line as tax software improves.

For Schwab (2017):

> the winners will be those who are able to participate fully in innovation-driven ecosystems by providing new ideas, business models, products and services, rather than those who can offer only low-skilled labour or ordinary capital.

In their book titled *Work in the Digital Age: Challenges of the Fourth Industrial Revolution*, Neufeind, O'Reilly, and Ranft (2018) note that the enormous growth in the rate of IT computing power, storage capacity, connectedness and software applications is transforming employment, disrupting businesses and challenging labor regulations. They caution that it should be the goal of our politics to ensure industrial and societal transformations provide opportunities for social mobility and citizens' personal and professional development. If we are not proactive in our education and human resource development plans, Neufeind et al. (2018) caution, the unintended consequences of *the fourth industrial revolution* will be rising levels of wealth inequality, low social mobility, and increasing regional disparities within and between countries.

The dominant higher education leadership was designed to meet the needs of past industrial revolutions. Higher education leadership in the advent of the fourth industrial revolution has different demands. These include AI, robotics, the internet of things, biotechnology, 3D-printing, nanotechnology and autonomous vehicles. Xing and Marwala (2017) observe that:

> the need for higher education to respond is urgent as the power of the fourth industrial revolution technologies for either positive social impacts or devastating environmental damage is upon us. (p. 17)

Thus, the dynamics of higher education are driving the demand for a new set of skills and capabilities for the fourth industrial revolution era's leadership. Xing and Marwala (2017) note that "Higher education in the fourth industrial revolution is a complex, dialectical and exciting opportunity which can potentially transform society for the better." It should be mentioned that the fourth industrial revolution has far-reaching and deep ramifications for the dominant higher education leadership. For instance, for higher education institutions to stay relevant in the fourth industrial revolution era they require a drastic reconsideration and modification of the leadership framework. The new frameworks and contexts of higher education leadership need to be responsive to the increasing and complex rate of change in the fourth industrial revolution space. Like the fourth industrial revolution curriculum, the fourth industrial revolution higher education leadership needs to be responsive:

> to the political and social tensions that will accompany the accelerating pace of technological change, and to respond to the paradox of technologies that simultaneously increase democratization and centralize wealth and political influence. (Penprase, 2018, p. 221)

Summing up, we have highlighted the fact that the fourth industrial revolution technologies and AI create different opportunities and challenges for higher education systems. Hence, the fourth industrial revolution technologies and AI call for a dramatic shift away from the dominant conventional education leadership. It is important to note that, the precise impacts of such fourth industrial revolution technologies on higher education leadership are still unknown, but will bring deep and rapid change. As Penprase (2018) puts it, the fourth industrial revolution (1) "challenges some of our fundamental assumptions of what it means to be human and the conditions of our relationship with the natural world" and (2) will "shape the future of education, gender and work" and how the fourth industrial revolution will require" "accelerating workforce reskilling" (p. 221). We now turn to the view that higher education can be attributed to the construction of what French philosopher Michel Foucault calls "docile bodies." As Foucault (1995) puts it:

> Discipline produces subjected and practised bodies, 'docile' bodies. Discipline increases the forces of the body (in economic terms of utility) and diminishes these same forces (in political terms of obedience). In short, it dissociates power from the body; on the one hand, it turns it into an 'aptitude', a 'capacity', which it seeks to increase; on the other hand, it reverses the course of the energy, the power that might result from it, and turns it into a relation of strict subjection. (p. 138)

3. HIGHER EDUCATION LEADERSHIP AS A TOOL FOR THE SOCIAL CONSTRUCTION OF DOCILE BODIES

It is reasonable to suppose that the canonical work of Michel Foucault, *Discipline and Punish, Madness and Civilization, The Birth of the Clinic,* is fundamental to analyzing and understanding the social construction of higher education leadership and the problem of power in the fourth industrial revolution era. Regardless of whether Foucault wrote about the prison system, his work offers a useful conceptual lens through which to view educational leadership as a *regulatory* mechanism in the shaping of the *subject* (student). Viewed within a Foucauldian framework, higher education leadership serves to *normalize* and *regulate* conduct and/or behavior that are regarded as acceptable and desirable. Among others, higher education leadership sees the body as an object, a target of power, to be manipulated, shaped, trained, and made to obey and learn skills and rules of conduct. Hence, educational leadership seeks to mold a "docile [body] that may be subjected, used, transformed, and improved" (Foucault, 1995, p. 136).

It should be mentioned that as a power relations construct, higher education leadership is a philosophical issue. It has the potential to turn individuals into "docile bodies" and into objects and targets of power. It might be argued that through higher education leadership, cultures, institutions and individuals are reproduced. Most importantly:

> power is exercised on the bodies and souls of individuals, and it has the paradoxical effect of increasing an individual's power, at the same time it is making the individual more docile. (Coverston, 2001, p. 45)

Foucault (1982) believed that:

> this form of power applies itself to immediate everyday life which categorizes the individual, marks him by his own individuality, attaches him to his own identity, [and] imposes a law of truth on him which he must recognize and which others have to recognize in him. (p. 212)

As a major source of social discipline and conformity, power is what makes higher education leadership what it is. From the Foucauldian perspective, higher education leadership is the product of power. It is established in "culturally standardized discourses formed by constellations of talk patterns, ideas, logics, and assumptions that constitute objects and subjects" (Fairhurst, 2007, p. 7). Foucault (1982) observes that "the exercise of power is not simply a relationship between partners, individual or collective; it is a way in which certain actions modify others" (p. 789). For him "power exists only when it is put into action, even if, of course, it is integrated into a disparate field of possibilities brought to bear upon permanent structures" (p. 789). In his book, *Power, A Radical View*, Steven Lukes' (2005, p. 41) central project is to answer the questions "What is an exercise of power" and "What is it to exercise power?" He argues that effective exercise of power occurs when "*A* gets *B* to do what he [*B*] would not otherwise do" (Lukes, 2005, p. 43). But Lukes (2005, p. 12) is quick to point out that "power is a capacity not the exercise of that capacity (it may never be, and never need to be, exercised)." It is his contention that "power as domination, is only one species of power." One "can be powerful by satisfying and advancing others' interests." Thus the definition of power and any use of it "are inextricably tied to a given set of (probably unacknowledged) value-assumptions which predetermine the range of its empirical application" (Lukes, 2005, p. 30).

Power is ubiquitous at every level of the social body, and the exercise of power is strategic and war-like. It is Foucault's view that "power is not something that is acquired, seized, or shared, something that one holds on to or allows to slip away; and power is employed through a net-like organization." Foucault (1982) insists that:

> a power relationship can only be articulated on the basis of two elements which are each indispensable if it is really to be a power relationship: that 'the other' (the one over whom power is exercised) be thoroughly recognized and maintained to the very end as a person who acts; and that, faced with a relationship of power, a whole field of responses, reactions, results, and possible inventions may open up. (p. 228)

Foucault argues that:

> power is implicit within everyday social practices which are pervasively distributed at every level in all domains of social life, and are constantly engaged in; moreover, it 'is tolerable only on condition that it masks a substantial part of itself. Its success is proportional to its ability to hide its own mechanisms. (p. 86)

In brief, power is exercised through higher education leadership. It might therefore be concluded that the notions of power and docile bodies are regarded as the main drivers of effective higher education leadership. As Foucault (1995) writes, a docile body is "one that may be subjected, used, transformed, and improved. And that this docile body can only be achieved through strict regiment of disciplinary acts" (p. 156). It is highlighted that "The body, required to be docile in its minutest operations, opposes and shows the conditions of functioning proper to an organism" (p. 156). It can therefore be inferred that the main bio-political functions of higher education leadership is the creation of *docile bodies*. Foucault suggests that "bodies are the site upon which power is contested." For this reason, the bodies are a *sine qua non* the site upon which higher education leadership is conducted.

4. HUMANIZING PEDAGOGY

Most scholars (Bartolome, 1994; Freire, 1970; Price & Osborne, 2000) regard humanizing pedagogy as a process of *becoming* for students and teachers. Freire (1970/1993) asserts that "Concern for humanization leads at once to the recognition of dehumanization, not only as an ontological possibility, but also as a historical reality" (p. 43). Notwithstanding that Freire (1970) has often been criticized for the "universalist" nature of his theory of oppression and liberation, the notion of humanizing pedagogy is integral to educational leadership. Freire urges us to recognize that humanizing pedagogy is about transforming oppressive relations of power which lead to the oppression of the ordinary people. Most importantly, humanizing pedagogy "transforms oppressed people and saves them from being objects of education to subjects of their own autonomy and emancipation" (Aliakbari & Faraji, 2011, p. 77).

In *Pedagogy of the Oppressed*, Freire (1970) writes that "humanizing pedagogy is a teaching method that ceases to be an instrument by which teachers can manipulate students, but rather expresses the consciousness of the students themselves" (p. 51). It holds that:

> teachers who are able to promote a humanizing pedagogy are more apt to develop mutual humanization in a dialogic approach with their students in which everyone ultimately develops a critical consciousness. (p. 56)

With this in mind, Huerta (2011) posits that:

> teachers who embrace a humanizing pedagogy recognize the socio-historical and political context of their own lives and their students' lives, including the influence of societal power, racial and ethnic identities, and cultural values. (p. 39)

She argues that "these teachers believe that marginalized students (due to race, economic class, culture, or experience) differ in how they learn, but not in their ability to learn" (p. 39). For Huerta:

> (1) teachers who practice a humanizing pedagogy incorporate students' language and culture into the academic context to support learning and to help students identify with, and maintain pride in, their home cultures; and (2) teachers who practice a humanizing pedagogy explicitly teach the school's codes and customs, and/or mainstream knowledge, to enable students to fully participate in the dominant culture. (p. 39)

Our position in this chapter is that higher education leadership should be a "people-centered activity and must not be reduced to a form of hegemony by tech-enthusiasts" (Makhanya, 2019, p. 9). Within this context, the question: to what extent can higher education systems humanize leadership? becomes critical. As Freire (1970) observes:

> dehumanization, which marks not only those whose humanity has been stolen, but also (though in a different way) those who have stolen it, is a distortion of the vocation of becoming more fully human. (p. 44)

For him:

> dehumanization, although a concrete historical fact, is not a given destiny but the result of an unjust order that engenders violence in the oppressors, which in turn dehumanizes the oppressed. (p. 44)

It is worthwhile mentioning that dehumanization, as a psychological process and the denial of full humanness to others, still exists in the twenty-first century because it suits the interests of those in the management training industry. For this reason, Petriglieri and Petriglieri (2015) write that "dehumanizing leadership into models and methods makes it easier to trademark and sell" (p. 636).

To conclude, seen from Freirean perspective, dehumanizing higher education leadership, as social and power relations construct carries the attributes of the oppressor – the oppressed internalize the image of the oppressor and adopts his guidelines through dehumanizing leadership theory and practice. As Petriglieri and Petriglieri (2015, p. 632) aptly put it, "this dehumanization consists of reducing leadership to a disembodied set of skills and romanticizing it as a virtue that is disembedded from any group, institution, or society." For them, "the reduction of leadership to a set of skills is evident in models of leadership development based on the assumption that the essence of leadership is influence." The concept of a humanizing pedagogy is vital to HEL and for this reason, there is need to balance educational leadership instrumental and humanistic aims to transform the status quo. One plausible way is to reconsider humanizing leadership that requires recognizing, tolerating, and respecting, if not celebrating, ambiguity and tension. In the next section, we tease out the potential role of the philosophy of Ubuntu in humanizing pedagogy in higher education.

5. *UBUNTU* AS A HUMANIZING PEDAGOGY

Barely "a day goes by without some reference to the potential impact of artificial intelligence in our lives" (Dennis, 2018a, 2018b). Unsurprisingly, AI profoundly impacts the nature of services in higher education and opens new possibilities and challenges for the sector. Popenici and Kerr (2017) observe that "the future of higher education is intrinsically linked with developments on new technologies and computing capacities of the new intelligent machines" (p. 1). They further argue that:

> In this field, advances in artificial intelligence open to new possibilities and challenges for teaching and learning in higher education, have a potential to fundamentally change governance and the internal architecture of institutions of higher education. (p. 1)

It is Popenici and Kerr's (2017) view that:

> As significant advances in machine learning and artificial intelligence open new possibilities and challenges for higher education, it is important to observe that education is eminently a human-centric endeavor, not a technology centric solution. (p. 3)

They argue that:

> Despite rapid advancements in AI, the idea that we can solely rely on technology is a dangerous path, and it is important to maintain focus on the idea that humans should identify problems, critique, identify risks, and ask important questions that can start from issues such as privacy, power structures, and control to the requirement of nurturing creativity and leaving an open door to serendipity and unexpected paths in teaching and learning. (p. 3)

While AI is currently progressing at a fast pace, the question, "what philosophical positions shape artificial intelligence?" becomes critical. It is necessary to mention that in the Southern African context the philosophy of *Ubuntu* provides pertinent lenses for reflecting on the fourth industrial revolution and AI. Our take in this chapter is that higher education leadership in the fourth industrial revolution and AI space is devoid of the humanizing component. There is no doubt that the advances in fourth industrial revolution higher education leadership and AI have a potential of benefiting from the philosophy of *Ubuntu*. Makhanya (2019) argues that "Blind artificial intelligence enthusiasm may inadvertently lead to a dehumanization of the higher education experience" (p. 9). He reminds us that:

> We are a species that is interactive and care for each other, a species that understands that 'I am because of you; and you are because of me'. This is what we call the *Ubuntu* philosophy of life. (p. 10)

The concept of *Ubuntu* is a fundamental framework for enacting a humanizing pedagogy. Much has been written about the concept *Ubuntu* (Bodunrin, 1981; Broodryk, 2002; Letseka, 2000; Masolo, 1994; Oruka, 1990; Ramose, 2002; Sindane, 1994). As an African view that grounds societies *Ubuntu* embraces communal ways of living. It represents the epistemological paradigm that informs the cultural practices (Letseka, 2013) and is based on the etiquette of humanity, which includes caring for each other's well-being and reciprocating kindness (Letseka, 2012). Letseka (2000) argues that "*Ubuntu* has normative implications in that it encapsulates moral norms and values such as altruism, kindness, generosity, compassion, benevolence, courtesy, and respect and concern for others" (p. 180).

The concept of *Ubuntu* has a symbiotic relationship with *humaneness*. Philosophically, the two imply the essence of being human. It emphasizes human obligations toward others and their relationships. Notably, both concepts carry the attributes of beneficence, benevolence, compassionateness, good-heartedness, humanity, kindheartedness, softheartedness, tenderheartedness, virtue and warm-heartedness. It is worthwhile mentioning that "*Ubuntu* embellishes cultural beliefs and values and is the essence of being human"; and it "comes in many guises in many cultures" (Jolley, 2011, p. 2). Jolley (2011) underscores that *Ubuntu* ignores "cultural barriers and goes beyond cultural beliefs and values, and is within the heart" (p. 18). In his work *Education for Critical Consciousness,* Freire (2005) observes that:

> to be *human* is to engage in relationships with *others* and with the world. It is to experience that world as an objective reality, independent of oneself, capable of being known. (p. 3)

He argues that "animals, submerged within reality, cannot relate to it; they are creatures of mere contacts" (p. 3).

In this regard, developing critical consciousness is an inescapable concern for the humanization of the world. For higher education leadership, to embrace *Ubuntu* or humaneness in the advent of the fourth industrial revolution is to promote humanism.

6. RETHINKING HIGHER EDUCATION LEADERSHIP THROUGH THE PHILOSOPHY OF *UBUNTU* AND HUMANIZING PEDAGOGY

South Africa is experiencing a bourgeoning need to decolonize and Africanize higher education leadership in line with the political and cultural imperatives of transformation and demographic representivity. Concomitantly, higher education leadership's job requirements and skills profiles are changing. There is a need for skills and expertise that are responsive to the above-mentioned national mandate. Such skills and expertise would be marked by a preponderance of creative, empathetic and interpersonal inclinations. Adding to this demand is the fact that the advent of the fourth industrial revolution itself not only demands the reinvention of higher education leadership *praxis*. However, it also has the potential to disrupt the sector through large-scale automation, adoption of emergent technologies, big data and AI. Ravarini and Strada (2018) note that the:

> Fourth Industrial Revolution, which includes developments in previously disjointed fields such as artificial intelligence and machine-learning, robotics, nanotechnology, 3-D printing, and genetics and biotechnology, will cause widespread disruption not only to business models but also to labor markets over the next five years, with enormous change predicted in the skill sets needed to thrive in the new landscape. (p. 98)

Our stance in this chapter is that for higher education leadership in South Africa to be culturally relevant to the demands of the fourth industrial revolution, it should be guided by the principles of humanizing pedagogy, *Ubuntu*, *humanness* and *human kindness*. As Blessinger, Sengupta, and Reshef (2019) point out, "Higher education should be a place of caring, support and the meaningful pursuit of academic and professional goals." Wiredu (2002, p. 313) notes that according to *Ubuntu*, "people should be treated humanely and be recognized as persons associated with dignity and equal respect." Thus, embracing *Ubuntu* as a humanizing pedagogy has the potential to redirect the focus of higher education leadership in the fourth industrial revolution space. Taking up *Ubuntu* as a humanizing pedagogy entails innovating within higher education leadership and labor-related policymaking, requiring a skills evolution of its own.

Ubuntu is an all-inclusive worldview (values shared across cultures) that encapsulates caring, respect, tolerance, honesty, hospitality, compassion and empathy (Blackwood, 2018). As such, *Ubuntu* is pertinent to rethinking and humanizing higher education leadership consistent with the demands of the fourth industrial revolution. Freire's work on humanizing pedagogy is crucial to higher education leadership. The state of dehumanization in dominant higher education leadership practices calls for counter hegemonic practices to dehumanization. In order to come to grips with Freire's philosophy, a great deal hinges on understanding his views on the "banking concept" of education. Freire is explicit that there is a need to move away from a dehumanizing to humanizing education.

Humanizing pedagogy is rooted in critical pedagogy. As such, humanizing pedagogy is consistent with the "right" teaching strategies. It values students' (and teachers') background knowledge, culture and lived experiences. Among others, humanizing pedagogy is compatible with the emergent framework – it negates the "banking" concept of education. As Freire (1970) writes:

> the banking concept of education as an instrument of oppression – its presuppositions – "a critique"; the problem-posing concept of education as an instrument for liberation – its presuppositions; the "banking" concept and the teacher-student contradiction; the problem-posing concept and the supersedence of the teacher-student contradiction; education: a mutual process, world-mediated; people as uncompleted beings, conscious of their incompletion, and their attempt to be more fully human. (p. 71)

From a historical point of view, humanizing pedagogy was first enunciated by Freire In his book, *Pedagogy of the Oppressed*. Freire (1970, p. 56) presents humanizing pedagogy as a philosophical approach that fosters critical dialogue and liberatory practices. He calls for counter hegemonic education practices to dehumanizing pedagogies. On the whole, with the growing influence of AI and the fourth industrial revolution, there is a need for a revolutionary shift in higher education leadership in terms of theory and practice. Among others, higher education leadership should be driven in such a way that it meets the needs of culturally diverse students. One plausible solution is to rethink higher education leadership practices through the lenses of the philosophy of *Ubuntu* and humanizing pedagogy. The philosophy of *Ubuntu* and humanizing pedagogy has the potential to guide and inform higher education leadership in the ODeL institutions.

7. CONCLUSION

In this chapter, we explored the link between higher education leadership, AI, the fourth industrial revolution, the philosophy of *Ubuntu* and humanizing pedagogy. We argued that the imperatives of the fourth industrial revolution and AI have far-reaching implications for the "dominant" higher education leadership theory and practice. The reason for this is that the fourth industrial revolution and AI are disruptive phenomena. We argued a case for a broader and culturally inclusive understanding of higher education leadership, noting that in a developing and culturally diverse setting such as South Africa, the dominant approaches to higher education leadership should be guided by humanizing pedagogy and the philosophy of *Ubuntu*. The latter is an African worldview that encapsulates the moral virtues of caring, respect, tolerance, honesty, hospitality, compassion and empathy.

REFERENCES

Aliakbari, M., & Faraji, E. (2011). Basic principles of critical pedagogy. In *2nd international conference on humanities, historical and social sciences. IPEDR* (vol. 17). Singapore: IACSIT Press.

Bartolome, L. (1994). Beyond the methods fetish: Toward a humanizing pedagogy. *Harvard Educational Review, 64*(2), 173–194.

Blackwood, A. (2018). A review of you can't teach us if you don't know us and care about us: Becoming an Ubuntu, responsive and responsible urban teacher. *Multicultural Perspectives, 20*(4), 257–260. doi:10.1080/15210960.2018.1467768

Blessinger, P., Sengupta, E., & Reshef, S. (2019). Humanising higher education via inclusive leadership. *University World News: The Global Window on Higher Education.* Retrieved from https://www.universityworldnews.com/post.php?story=20190218081816874

Bodunrin, P. O. (1981). The question of African philosophy. *Philosophy, 56*(216), 161–179.

Broodryk, J. (2002). *Ubuntu: Life lessons from Africa.* Pretoria: Ubuntu School of Philosophy.

Coverston, C. R. (2001). *A Foucauldian analysis of power in nursing education.* Published doctoral thesis, The University of Utah.

Dennis, M. (2018a). Artificial intelligence and recruitment, admission, progression, and retention. *Enrollment Management Report, 22*(9), 1–3.·

Dennis, M. (2018b). How will artificial intelligence change admissions? *University World News.* Retrieved from https://www.universityworldnews.com/post.php?story=20181024090311655

Fairhurst, G. T. (2007). *Discursive leadership: In conversation with leadership psychology.* Thousand Oaks, CA: Sage.

Foucault, M. (1982). The subject and power. In H. L. Dreyfus, & P. Rabinow,(Eds.), *Beyond structuralism and hermeneutics* (pp. 208 -226). Chicago, IL: University of Chicago.

Foucault, M. (1995). *Discipline and punish The birth of the prison.* [Trans. A. Sheridan, 1977.]. New York, NY: Vintage

Freire, P. (1970/1993). *Pedagogy of the oppressed.* London: Continuum.

Freire, P. (2005). *Education for critical consciousness.* New York, NY: Continuum.

Gramsci, A. (1971). *Selections from the prison notebooks* (Q. Hoare & G. N. Smith, Eds. & Trans.). New York, NY: International Publishers.

Huerta, T. M. (2011). Humanizing pedagogy: Beliefs and practices on the teaching of Latino children. *Bilingual Research Journal, 34*(1), 38–57. doi:10.1080/15235882.2011.568826

Jolley, D. R. (2011). *U b u n t u: A person is a person through other persons.* Published M.Ed. dissertation, Southern Utah University.

Letseka, M. (2000). African philosophy and educational discourse. In P. Higgs, N. C. G. Vakalisa, T. V. Mda, & N. T. Assie-Lumumba (Eds.), *African voices in education* (pp. 179–193). Landsdowne: Juta.

Letseka, M. (2012). In defence of Ubuntu. *Studies in Philosophy and Education, 31*(1), 47–60.

Letseka, M. (2013). Educating for Ubuntu/Botho: Lessons from Basotho indigenous education. *Open Journal of Philosophy, 3*(2), 337–344.

Lukes, S. (2005). *Power: A radical view* (2nd ed.). London: Palgrave Macmillan.

Maila, M. W., & Pitsoe, V. J. (2014). Teaching practice as communities of inquiry. *Journal of Social Sciences, 41*(1), 99–106. doi:10.1080/09718923.2014.11893345

Makhanya, M. (2019). *UNESCO mobile learning week 2019.* Paris: UNESCO.

Masolo, D. A. (1994). *African philosophy in search of identity.* Bloomington, IN: Indiana University Press.

Neufeind, M., O'Reilly, J., & Ranft, F. (2018). *Work in the digital age: Challenges of the fourth industrial revolution.* London: Rowman & Littlefield International.

Oruka, H. O. (1990). *Sage philosophy: Indigenous thinkers and modern debate on African Philosophy.* Leiden: E. J. Bill.

Penprase, B. E. (2018). The fourth industrial revolution and higher education. In N. W. Gleason (Ed.), *Higher education in the era of the fourth industrial revolution* (pp. 207–229). Singapore: Springer.

Petriglieri, G., & Petriglieri, J. L. (2015). Can business schools humanize leadership? *Academy of Management Learning & Education, 14*(4). Retrieved from https://journals.aom.org/doi/pdf/10.5465/amle.2014.0201

Popenici, S. A., & Kerr, S. (2017). Exploring the impact of artificial intelligence on teaching and learning in higher education. *Research and Practice in Technology Enhanced Learning, 12*(22), 1–13. doi:10.1186/s41039-017-0062-8

Price, J. N., & Osborne, M. D. (2000). Challenges of forging a humanizing pedagogy in teacher education. *Curriculum and Teaching, 15*(1), 27–51.

Ramose, M. B. (2002). The philosophy of Ubuntu and Ubuntu as a philosophy. In P. H. Coetzee & A. P. J. Roux (Eds.), *Philosophy from Africa* (pp. 230–238). Cape Town: Oxford University Press.

Ravarini, A., & Strada, G. (2018). From smart work to digital do-it-yourself: A research framework for digital-enabled jobs. In R. Lamboglia, A., Cardoni, R. P. Dameri, & D. Mancini (Eds.), *Network, smart and open: Three keywords for information systems innovation* (pp. 97–108). Cham: Springer.

Schwab, K. (2017). *The fourth industrial revolution*. New York, NY: Crown Publishing Group.

Sindane, J. (1994). *Ubuntu and nation building*. Pretoria: Ubuntu School of Philosophy.

Spicer, A. (2019). What makes a good leader? *The Chronicle of Higher Education*. Retrieved from https://www.chronicle.com/campusViewpointArticle/What-Makes-a-Good-Leader-/669/

The Economist. (2014). The future of jobs: The onrushing wave. January 18.

Tutu, D. (2008). *"One Hour"* on CBC Interview.

Wiredu, K. (2002). The moral foundations of an African culture. In P. H. Coetzee & A. P. J. Roux (Eds.), *Philosophy from Africa* (pp. 287–296). Cape Town: Oxford University Press Southern Africa.

Xing, B., & Marwala, T. (2017). Implications of the fourth industrial age for higher education. *The Thinker*, *73*, 1–10.

Yang, P., & Chen, Y. (2018). Educational mobility and transnationalization. In G.N. Webster (Ed.), *Higher education in the era of the fourth industrial revolution* (pp. 39–63). Singapore: Palgrave Macmillan.

CHAPTER 9

ACADEMIC FREEDOM AT THE BUSINESS SCHOOL: TEAPOT'S TEMPEST OR MODERNITY'S KNIFE EDGE?

Timothy J. Fogarty

ABSTRACT

The development and progressive refinement of the concept of academic freedom has generally occurred without material participation by the American business school. Whereas the business school looms large as a component of higher education in the twenty-first century, most believe that it is indifferent or perhaps hostile to the concept of academic freedom. For the most part, business school faculty fail to share the liberal political leanings of their colleagues from across the university, and therefore are less likely to find themselves to need academic freedom protection from those who would like to squelch opinions that run contrary to government and establishment elites. This chapter recognizes the fundamental alignment of what is taught in the business school and what business faculty research. However, that does not gainsay prospects for academic freedom protection when such is not the case. The chapter explores public interest dimensions of being a faculty member in a business school and how these might be manifested. Examples of controversial work are offered for each of the major business disciplines.

Keywords: Academic freedom; business schools; university rankings; research; teaching; capitalism; publicity; commodification; public interest; business scandals

Developing and Supporting Multiculturalism and Leadership Development:
International Perspectives on Humanizing Higher Education
Innovations in Higher Education Teaching and Learning, Volume 30, 159–174
Copyright © 2020 by Emerald Publishing Limited
All rights of reproduction in any form reserved
ISSN: 2055-3641/doi:10.1108/S2055-364120200000030013

Academic freedom has been a long and lustrous norm in US higher education (Russell, 2002) that has, in many ways, allowed the higher education to flourish. Very few people would support interference with the full operation of the marketplace of ideas that is supposed to describe the collegiate community. However, the doctrine as it is understood and practiced at the business school of the twenty-first century, puts the university's administration in a curious place. A faculty person with controversial opinions has to be understood as a threat to the large consequence of business school rankings in the media (Wedlin, 2006). With business schools at the fulcrum of university alumni development (Wunnava & Okunade, 2013), another point of tangency exists for administrators who might prefer to abandon doctrines such as academic freedom, in favor of, as they say, running the operation "like a business" (Holbrook, 2018).

That which we know or assume about academic freedom in higher education was created and matured when the university was a much different place than it is today (Fuchs, 1963). This chapter highlights only one important change – the emergence of the business school as a central unit for faculty, administrators and students (Kaplan, 2014). The general thesis of this chapter is that academic freedom takes on different meanings within the business school. Whereas the political is not wholly subsumed by the economic, the latter provides the dominant perspective to understand academic freedom in this domain.

In order to organize this topic, several issues are addressed after a brief consideration of the general nature of academic freedom. The rise of the business school is contemplated along lines of potential relevance. This leads to the development of the symbiotic relationships among business, governments and business schools. The fault lines for academic freedom at the business school are next discussed, both at the macro and micro levels. The latter incorporates predictable perspectives available to business disciplines and their faculty. This chapter concludes with some of the projected futures for academic freedom at the business school.

ACADEMIC FREEDOM

Society is always marked by division. That people see important questions and their correct answers differently would be the source of healthy dialogue if it were not for the ability of some to use power to impose their solutions. Whereas dictators use physical coercion to get their way, subtler forms of control are exerted by elites in democratic societies (Bourdieu, 2013; Foucault, 2012). Speaking truth to power can therefore be perilous even for those who have expertise on certain subjects. Academic freedom provides those employed by colleges and universities from feeling harsh repercussions for the positions they have taken. Academics regularly retain their positions and privileges as university employees. Thus, tenure needs to be understood in the context of faculty efforts in enforcing academic freedom.

Political controversy is the usual strata wherein academic freedom is tested. When the country moves in a particular direction, a non-trivial group of people are likely to protest (Hughes, 1949). The vagaries of constitutional interpretation are considerable, leading many to the justifiable expression of contrary ideas

(Alexy, 2010). That which is political seems to have expanded in recent times (schools, guns, religion), as we find ourselves in a nonstop culture war leading many toward the expression of ideas that make the current winner somewhat uncomfortable (Hartman, 2019). With institutions of higher education normally seen as uncharacteristic bastions of liberalism (Zipp & Fenwick, 2006), the sides are not difficult to imagine. Academics, with the strength of their educations and a bully pulpit of sorts built into their positions, have strong incentives to voice their opinions. This puts the professoriate in the crosshairs of those able to command resources and accustomed of getting their way.

We might like to think that academic freedom is an absolute. In fact, it represents a negotiated position where principles are compromised in exchange for limited guarantees (Slaughter, 1980). There usually are some time line resolutions, where the academics of today obtain some desired outcome, but only in exchange for a less promising future visited upon the academics of tomorrow (Loveless, 2011).

We also like to imagine the drama of academic freedom: show-downs precipitated by bold faculty expression followed by heavy-handed threats of sanctions. In fact, academic freedom is more likely to erode (Neem, 2019) than be canceled by fiat. Important degrees of disappearance are likely to happen without much notice or protest. For present purposes, this accretion is made possible by changes to the university itself. These changes may be those that compromise the shared interests of college administration and faculty, and those that compromise the essential community of faculty.

THE RISE OF THE BUSINESS SCHOOL

A time traveler from one or two hundred years ago would recognize a good deal if able to see today's universities. Many of the disciplines being taught would be familiar even in the presence of updated content and new teaching technology. However, the business school would be an alien life form. One hundred years ago, only embryonic forms of the disciplines now with large faculties and student majors would have been present. Any critical mass of people wishing to study things like accountancy or marketing would have been either in fly-by-night trade schools or employed within divisions of employing corporations. Other disciplines like finance and logistics were yet to be invented. Now, "the business school grow(s) bigger and ever wealthier while humanities departments shrink and suffer and starve ..." (Conn, 2018). The reasons that this has happened are well beyond the scope of this chapter. The fact that it has means everything to this piece. If business is the future of higher education, the future of academic freedom also resides here.

Suffice it to say that universities needed at some point to give people what they wanted. The expansion of that which was suitable college content and the gradual erosion of roadblocks that did not have pragmatic purposes, facilitated scale and scope of the higher education sector. The growth of the business school denoted the point where colleges themselves became a business, and higher education became an industry (Teixeira, Jongbloed, Dill, & Amaral, 2006). The many forces such as which either made this possible (globalization, technology, anti-intellectualism) or served as a collateral consequence thereof would alter the university going forward. As the university became that which it had not been, a new version of academic freedom would take root.

The growth of the business school, and its propagation of that which many in academe thought had no legitimate place at the university, brought with it a new type of research that generally was weaker than existed in more traditional disciplines (Pfeffer & Fong, 2002). Committed to spread ideas that are useful and to celebrate whatever practices generated the largest fortunes, business schools have serious content problems. They are prone to ideas not well grounded in theory, substituting anecdotal cases for solid empiricism. Professors, lacking any real theory or laboratories, were also hamstrung in comparison with the sciences, both natural and social. Business school research also tended to be devoid of a commitment to any public good, championing instead private wealth creation. Periodic reforms were necessary to tether the business schools to the norms of the university, despite fundamental flaws in their origins.

Business school faculty also were a different breed than those that taught at the rest of the university (Huczynski, 1994). Many came from business, with some maintaining their practice involvement. For many years, teaching was thought by many to be a part-time occupation. As doctoral level education become more the norm, the professoriate became more of a main pursuit, but only to the extent that practice was relegated to the margins. Selling consulting services on the side became normalized. Even those without side bets in business maintain a business worldview. This is exemplified by what Gendron (2015) calls a "paying off" mentality whereby scholarship is not important for itself but instead as that which generates short-term benefits and rewards for its producer. This prevailing attitude is consistent with much earlier findings that business school faculty tended toward complacency and self-satisfaction (Porter & McKibbin, 1988). These attitudes were even more surprising in the context of an educational product that paled in comparisons with the lessons of the "real world."

The research of the business school, even at its best, represents applications of theories developed elsewhere (Starkey & Tiratsoo, 2007). In longest measure, economics has served as the mothership to which most business schools connect. Across the United States, the positioning of economics departments vis-à-vis business schools illustrate the ambivalence of the relationship. Some universities have opted for a middle ground wherein the pre-existing economics faculty remains outside the business school and a shadow business economic group takes up residence as a business discipline. Those inside tend to self-impose a constrained view of economics, often furthering what has been called agency theory (Jensen & Meckling, 1976), which could be understood as the business school's re-invention of the discipline. The business school also has been selectively penetrated by psychology. Of great interest to the business school is how people make decisions. Psychology has been embraced and selectively reformulated as organizational behavior. In other sectors, mathematics has been introduced to solve classic business problems such as the time value of money, double entry bookkeeping and inventory reorder points. These became the stock in trade for departments of accountancy, finance and operations.

Both teaching and research in the business school is saturated with the logic of private sector markets. Much of the thinking that occurs in its classrooms and journals perpetuated the idea that markets produce outcomes that are usually correct, and therefore work best when left alone. The efficient market hypothesis (Malkiel & Fama, 1970) works as a benchmark against which measurement is made. Grades given to students and publications achieved by faculty are understood by virtue of market metaphors (Beatty, 2004). Members of the business school community express surprise when they encounter someone that does not subscribe. Although the idea of markets and their supremacy does not amount to a particularly strong culture, the business school has had some success in exporting a certain and particular way of thinking to university-level administration (see Daniel & Wellmon, 2018).

THE BUSINESS SCHOOL, CORPORATIONS AND THE STATE

More than a century has passed since Thorstein Veblen (1917) warned of the corrupting influence of business upon the university. Writing well in advance of the business school's emergence, his fear of fundamental incompatibility now seems both apocalyptic and quaint. The business school represents both the corporate constituency's broadest wish fulfillment for a platform from which its interests can be furthered, and a theoretical quarantine of such influence that works in favor of the rest of the university. That readers have accepted the appropriateness of this interpretation makes us wonder why Veblen was so frightened. That he saw the progressive encroachment of business people as such a pure evil serves to remind us how much the university has changed.

Perhaps more of a surprise is the role of the state in this alignment. Rather than protecting the university as an important institution of the public welfare, the state has in many ways facilitated the blurring of the lines that had separated higher education from commerce. The university, led by its business school, has now become an agent of change rather than a bulwark of stability that only reluctantly reflects its times (Boyce, 2002). A good deal of the state's role in this is invisible, in that an important element is the passive refusal to use the legal system to make what business wants either illegal or more expensive to pursue. In other countries, the state has been more active in its efforts to rationalize state funding by designating productivity measures and essentially creating a market for professorial work (Dominelli & Hoogvelt, 1996).

The corporate community works as a force of rationalization and standardization. The tools they bring to accomplish these objectives are hardly anathema to the business school. For most, instruction in their use represents the highest note of achievement for students. Ironically, the simplification of such calculations and their purposeful de-contextualization makes the business school a stronger and less nuanced believer in them than business. Little tension exists in the goals that are sought by these tools, and in their collateral consequences. Perhaps because the business school engages in little of the creative or imaginative research that Veblen advocated, whatever conflict exists is not structural.

The specific mechanisms which are used by business to co-opt the business school are many, making their importance collectively much greater than any individual one. Most prominent is the ritualized necessity of advisory bodies used by the school and by some of its departments. Business school accreditation rules make advisory bodies nearly synonymous with the proper management of the school and its sub-units (Mello, 2019). Corporate presence is also exerted now that internships and practicums have been regularized as official learning experiences. Business people are a regular feature on campus as guest speakers, competition judges and honorees for an always expanding set of awards concocted by the schools. In such an environment, the line between the business school and the corporate community is difficult to find. Progressively, the ability to criticize these businesses becomes more difficult by virtue of their routinized proximity.

We should not characterize the business school as dupes in their current relationships with business. It may be more appropriate to consider this to be a situation of mutual exploitation. Business gets access to the "best and brightest" students the business school has to offer. Their efforts neutralize a potential problematic adversary in their efforts to secure favorable treatment from the state. Business also basks in the reflection of a high-prestige apparently disinterested ally whose reputation helps purify business motives. Businesses get a non-negligible amount of discretionary cash that can be useful to do things not necessarily sanctioned by legislative approval or university budgetary constraints. They also can use these associations to become more legitimate to students and their parents who prioritize real-world connections to worthwhile employment. Preserving these advantages argues toward usually not focusing on the bad behaviors of the other party and being "functionally stupid" about the overall ethics of non-independence (Mintz, Dang, & Savage, 2013).

The consequences of being a bedfellow of business would not be as large if business were a relatively unchanging phenomenon. Once you become a partner, you are mostly obligated to what your partner becomes. Fueled by more advanced technologies, and by a more permissive state, capitalism has become more concentrated, thereby creating a larger divide between winners and losers. Even in the name of heightened efficiency, the distributional consequences are becoming more difficult to accept. Similar consequences will be vested upon students with many finding it difficult to sustain themselves in the middle class while disproportionate wealth accrues to a few that are very well positioned (Knorringa & Guarin, 2015). Capitalism has also become more global, inflicting transition costs upon many US communities (Wallerstein, 2000). Again, business schools are asked to either swallow hard on the sidelines, or help by becoming apologists for moving economic activity abroad and for maneuvers to avoid regulation. A little closer to home, colleges have felt the pain of the new rules of competition as corporations support the many ways of privatizing the public sector (Newfield, 2008). Such thinking has led to the decline of public funding for higher education (Djelic 2012; John & Parsons, 2005). One might conclude that colleges have been hoisted by their own petard.

That which the business school has become reflects the lessons learned at the knee of business. These lessons have made the college experience less *sui generis* learning and maturing experiences for students, and more a rehearsal for their post-graduation work lives. The bureaucratic logic of the business school is that this entity needs to be run at the profit. Programs are judged by their ability to attract students, not by their intellectual appropriateness or necessity. Faculty are evaluated by their ability to create student satisfaction and by the citations that their publications can garner. Nobody wants to make difficult judgements on the merits when these bad measures will suffice. Low-cost temporary instructors will be leveraged wherever possible. The bad currency called online courses will never be closely scrutinized. The business school represents the first step down a slippery slope in part because its economizing maneuvers are not offset by valued added research as one might find in medical or engineering schools.

Difficulties do exist between business schools and businesses. Not everything that business wants has been willingly provided. Although great strides have been made in re-defining education as vocational education, there has been resistance. Whereas business has blurred the functional areas, the academic continues to believe in disciplinary lines. Required courses persist, providing exposures that no job would need. Curriculums change slowly and cannot quickly reflect the vocational flavor of the month. Businesses would probably prefer that all faculty spend more time on their school's educational mission and less on producing the research that they see little value in. Faculty that stay research active do it for a variety of reasons that do not further the interests of the corporate constituency. Some of this work may actually put businesses in a less than favorable light. Finally, business interests are heterogeneous along several dimensions. Since business schools cannot always please all the companies, some are therefore marginalized.

MODALITIES OF ACADEMIC FREEDOM IN THE BUSINESS SCHOOL

Academics have the power, through research and related advocacy, to attract the attention of others. Not all of this visibility is positive. By far and away, faculty at the business school write about business matters and therefore occasionally raise ire within that constituency.

The most likely type of academic freedom triggered by the business school faculty could be called public interest work. Although perhaps with lower frequency than non-business school faculty, academics tend to have passion for social causes. These would include environmental problems, charitable causes and labor advocacy. Chances are good that they would see corporate opposition to the success of these causes. Corporate prioritization of maximizing profits often involves not taking responsibility for "externalities" when this is made possible by law (Shum & Yam, 2011). Corporations can also be taken to task for their general failure to support the public sector, usually by engaging in extraordinary measures to minimize their payment of income taxes (Crocker & Slemrod, 2005) and evading their responsibility for much beyond the maximization of shareholder value (McSweeney, 2008).

At the heart of public interest work done by business school faculty is the desirability of some state of nature or society that does not exist. In that most corporate actors follow the letter of the law, this work tends to be more of a critique of government than of business. Corporations tend to be the beneficiary of what is characterized as bad public policy. Whereas some companies (usually larger ones) derive more benefit than others, they are not specifically targeted for criticism in this line of work. One would be correct in the observation that public interest work is the most political version of academic freedom seen at the business school. While public interest work is readily publishable, it tends not to appear in the mainstream journals of choice for business schools. The broad concern with the contours of the good society makes this work visible in lower tier specialty publications, where one finds some treatment of distributional consequences, collateral damage and sustainability. This happens with sufficient regularity that it creates the appearance to business that not all of the business school is aligned with their interests. However, this corpus is not sufficient to suggest a counter-hegemony, except perhaps in a long-run perspective (Boyce, 2002; Lehman, 2013; Parker, 2011).

The second modality of academic freedom-relevant work at the business school is less common than the first, but more potent. Faculty members occasionally go on crusades against particular industries or specific companies in an industry. Whereas there might be a particular public interest offense that triggered the work, the idea that a target exists comes to the forefront. Here the scope of the inquiry may broaden, or the researcher may uncover how one problem is related to another inside a company. For these purposes, questionable accounting leads to a more microscopic look at the transactions that aggregate into the externally reported accounts. This may reveal purposeful distortion and ulterior motives, having nothing to do with the accounting choices. For these purposes, academics tend to collaborate with insiders because proprietary information is usually required. On occasion, work of this sort garners the attention of regulators who possess power to compel more disclosure and ultimately to impose sanctions.

Academics doing investigations of particular companies tend not to be motivated by the publications that this work could produce. In fact, as case studies, the career-enhancing publication potential for work of this sort is very limited in the United States. This work would more likely appear in mass market outlets, in part because of its high drama, high stakes characteristics. Therefore, it requires passion for the topic above and beyond typical academic career pursuits. In fact, the controversy caused by such work is likely to be injurious to most careers.

The last modality of academic freedom occurs with the lowest frequency but in a way is the most extreme. Unlike the other ideal types that tend toward high levels of specificity regarding a societal problem or an industry perpetration, a small minority of scholars in the business school take issue with the capitalistic mode of production. Hearing this, external parties are more surprised that there are *any* socialists in the business school, than they are surprised that there are few (Ladd & Lipset, 1975).

As mentioned previously, some business schools have subsumed the entirety of the economics discipline at their universities. Since Marxian economics is a legitimate branch of that discipline, a scholar who has made a career positing the superiority of alternative methods of productive organization may have been reluctantly introduced into the business school in the middle of their career. Such an individual tends not to be excessively problematic to the corporate community because of their tendency toward abstract theoretical writing. That these situations are few in number prevents their perspective from being too visible, even within the limited scope of their academic units. In other words, whereas there are Marxist professors, there are no Marxist economic departments in business schools. Very few of the very few will follow Marx's suggestions about praxis, therefore keeping the academic freedom issue one that is merely "on paper" (Green, Hibbins, Houghton, & Ruutz, 2013).

The bulk of the appearances for Marxist thought is soft-peddled by some academics who do not explicitly identify themselves or their analyses as Marxist. Ironically, their usual target is the current state of higher education in the United States (Bowles & Gintis, 1976). This usually produces high-level critiques regarding student labor exploitation and the managerial attempts to direct faculty research outcomes (Saravanamuthu & Tinker, 2002).

RESIDENT DISCIPLINARY LOGIC

Although this chapter concerns the business school, one should recognize that such an administrative unit actually comprises several distinct disciplines, usually formed as academic departments with some degree of autonomy. At this level, more specificity about potential academic freedom issues can be identified.

Accounting fashions itself as the language of business, a statement that understates the ambiguity in these communications and disclosures. Accounting standards allow a degree of choice in methods, which taken together, may allow high levels of aggressiveness and unrealistic future assumptions (Richardson, Sloan, Soliman, & Tuna, 2006). Auditing for publicly traded companies is similarly riddled with estimates and dependent upon the trust that can be placed in the client (Espejo, 2001). Aspersions can be cast on how well this has been done, as well as upon the intervening financial incentives of the parties to construct a reality that is in actuality a fiction (Gendron & Bédard, 2001).

Finance concerns itself mostly with the operation of money markets. Utilizing assumptions about the efficiency with which information affects security pricing, the field has become highly esoteric and mathematical. The few academics that take forensic approaches to this data are able to isolate suspect trading patterns and the bypassing of controls. Insider trading and backdating are only two of many abuses that industry insiders would prefer that academics not explore.

How products and services are sold is the domain of marketing departments. The cultivation of demand among potential buyers is well-recognized as an art form that is subject to many abuses. The *caveat emptor* bedrock has been replaced in many sectors with a panoply of consumer protection regulations that invite clever "work arounds." Academics who reveal the specifics of sales practices often identify a rather callous corporate indifference to people's health and financial security embedded in messaging. Although examples from the marketing efforts of alcohol and tobacco sellers immediately come to mind, they represent situations that differ from many others only in degree, not in kind.

A specialty of some management departments (sometimes called organizational behavior) is the treatment of human beings within organizations. Work in this area rarely is pointed at a specific company and rarely identifies problems that are not shared by most companies. This work tends to be positive, at least to the extent that suggestions are routinely offered to make dysfunctional conditions better. In that this field delves more into the psychological than the economic, it presents only a limited zone of controversy addressable by corporations.

The hot business field of our current time goes by several different names, the most general being management science, but more recently business analytics. The hallmark of the area is the applied use of mathematics and statistics. Although there has been some recognition of the collateral consequences of algorithms left on their own (O'Neil, 2016), the vast majority of faculty will become willing collaborators (Wixom et al., 2014). Artificial intelligence and other "big data" applications have such enormous profit-enhancing potential to weather occasional ethical pinpricks. One cannot expect those that work in the area to need academic freedom protection, although we might need protection from them.

SPECIAL COMPLICATIONS FOR ACADEMIC FREEDOM AT THE BUSINESS SCHOOL

Earlier in this chapter, the complications for academic freedom that resulted from the very idea of the business school and its sudden ascendancy within the modern university were discussed. In this section, descriptions of other salient conditions that bear upon the prospects for academic freedom are offered. Many of these pertain to the position likely to be taken by the school after a faculty member has done or said that which is contrary to the already conflicted positioning of the business school in the modern economy.

Any discussion of the modern business school soon moves toward the many attempts by the mass media to rank its quality. Perhaps because of the dearth of anything offered by the business school for its students other than extrinsic value-for-money, rankings have been the marching tune for business schools to an unprecedented degree for several decades. The real resource consequences of changes in ratings requires business school leaders to pay attention to them even if they are based on questionable measures and aggregations. *Ceteris paribus*, the fish bowl world that this has created makes business schools much more protective of their reputations and especially leery about bad publicity. Faculty members doing research that requires academic freedom protection might make this defensiveness problematic, and might even incline the business school to align itself with popular opinion and against its own faculty. Rankings heighten the importance of appearances at the cost of merit and substance (DeAngelo, DeAngelo & Zimmerman, 2005).

In keeping with the commodification of the business school produced by arbitrary rankings, accreditation agencies induce even more isomorphic influence. Although other units of the university (and universities as a whole) are subject to accreditation, the appropriateness of this external judgment has gained considerable power over the business school. Accreditors, preaching a mission-driven education process, have brought very distinct ideas about how business schools ought to be managed. They demand mission statements, formal strategic plans, SWOT charts and external advisory boards, whether or not they add value, mostly because they such practices are found in modern business. Together with a distinct preference for formal management and documentation have transferred power from the faculty to the Dean's Office. Accreditation has been successful at inculcating the belief that faculty are white-collar employees who should be rationally managed and whose work product accrues to the school's credit. Academic freedom thrives more where faculty reasonably see themselves as independent contractors. Whereas accreditation is silent on academic freedom, its general thrust is inconsistent with the independence of spirit and intellectual choice that serve as the foundations of this doctrine. Even though accreditation is binary and not nearly as fanciful as popular press rankings, the power it actually exerts may be not more substantive than the stigma of its loss in the eyes of mostly uninformed constituents.

Elite control exists in many sectors of the academy, and the business school is no exception. The domination of critical gatekeeping functions such as editorial boards, trade associations and data control has been well documented for several of the business disciplines. This is exacerbated in the business school because of the abundant financial support of business elites who desire to elevate their own brand capital through an association with education's elite (Fogarty, 1995). That business schools arose in an era more marked by the rhetoric of a meritocracy and egalitarianism makes elite control less easy to accept. As schools not at the top of the hierarchy look to elites for direction, they typically do not find support for any oppositional views adopted by individual faculty (Williams, Jenkins, & Ingraham, 2006).

Publishing in the top business journals, compared to the broader space for content, presents the unique challenges of a stronger conservative default positioning of editors and reviewers. With very few exceptions, that which is innovative or especially critical is not particularly welcomed (Fogarty & Ravenscroft, 2000). This manifests itself in many ways. Strong editors willing to override reviewers are not often seen. Bad measures tend to possess a life of their own once they enter the literature at high places. Replications are not welcomed in part for fear that their results would offend (Koole & Lakens, 2012). People with findings that strongly question business practices often have to seek publication outlets outside the United States. Qualitative methods are frowned upon since the obvious agenda is to render work that has the appearance of true science (Bennis & O'Toole, 2005). Perhaps business faculty doing research are too easily dissuaded from doing path-breaking research and have been collaborators in their own subrogation. Socialized into accepting the preferences of superiors from their preacademic careers, they are less likely to pursue the work that will need academic freedom protection. As put by Gendron (2015), research in this area is excessively "tightly coupled" with that which has already been successful, and too little the result of "raw curiosity" (Hopwood, 2007).

Business faculty are also called upon to serve as expert witnesses in commercial litigation. This might range from opinions about the reasonableness of certain practices to interpretations of how accounting standards should be implemented. The many parties that seek normative expertise to oppose corporate envelop pushing should be able to come to the business faculty for assistance. We would like to hope that success in this regard is not impeded by the support a business has shown for a business school from hiring its students to providing faculty with honorific titles.

THE FUTURE OF ACADEMIC FREEDOM AT THE BUSINESS SCHOOL

Daniel and Wellmon (2018) suggest that today's university may be the last truly public institution. It continues to further many aspirations, both public and private, both collective and individual. We suspect that academic freedom will remain a cornerstone of this edifice. This is a maintained belief, despite the real risk faced by the sector is the "fake news" constructed by damaging myths about it (see Newfield, 2008).

This chapter has portrayed the business school as an outlier at the modern university. This resulted from its unique emergence with the scene, and its special positioning regarding both educational and scholarly missions. The consequence of this distinction is fairly unique academic freedom needs and contingencies.

Perhaps the most important thing about academic freedom at the business school is the simple truth that it will less likely to be put to a stern test. This will be the case for the unvarnished reason that academic freedom tends to have a predictable political alignment that is less likely to occur at the business school. Generally speaking, faculty members need the protection of this sacred doctrine because they have voiced an opinion or published an article that others find excessively liberal (in the vernacular, left of center). Conservative voices let their displeasure be known. Pressure is put on the faculty person for daring to take such a position. Belatedly, more reasonable people note that the opinion should be protected by our collective understanding of academic freedom. The same drama should also take place at the business school, with those taking offense likely to be businesses or other well-financed interests. The only difference might be that business faculty are less likely to have liberal attitudes and tend to see things as would the corporate establishment. This is not a necessity, but a likely empirical truth (Rothman, Lichter, & Nevitte, 2005).

The aggressive nature of the pursuit of profits and other efforts designed to bolster share prices still makes a good target. Even if fewer business faculty are willing to make a stand, either against abuses of the rules of the game or in furtherance of a public interest neglected in the process, this effort still stands as the most predictable alignment of the parties to any dispute that might engage academic freedom. A business school faculty person is more likely than a faculty person from the liberal arts or social sciences to take a position somewhat to the political right of constituents (Gross, Medvetz, & Russell, 2011). Such a position might draw the righteous indignation of university officials, but it represents a much less problematic scenario.

For the bulk of the business faculty, academic freedom is a doctrine of relevance to other types of professors (Woodhouse, 2009). This silent majority do not see their intellectual life as political. They are very much aligned with the business school's important constituents in that they believe that markets provide efficient results and should be only lightly regulated. They believe that stock markets are level playing fields that allocate capital in accordance with risk-adjusted returns. They favor low taxes and ample rewards for wealth and innovation. They are skeptical about redistribution programs. Their research tends to be on very neutral matters that for the most part ignores long run complications and remote collateral consequences. They mostly are content to be narrow specialists.

Most versions of the future grant a much larger presence to technology (McCarthy & Wright, 2004). This very well could be an important battleground for academic freedom (Simmons, 2001). One could easily imagine academic work warning of the dangers of over-reliance and over-delegation to new automatic means of operations such as promised by artificial intelligence. Business school faculty should be positioned to know more about these technologies, and be more aware of the dangers that they might pose. One could also easily project that businesses would have much to gain as unabashed advocates of full-scale implementation. Unfortunately, business school faculty are more likely to take up the role of cheerleader more than that the mantle of Jeremiah.

All bets might be off as the tools of modern business are increasingly turned on higher education to disrupt the delivery of higher education services. We shall have to see where the sympathies of the business faculty lie in such personal circumstances. As it currently stands, the business school faculty tends to believe that business is the supportive friend that would never harm us. However, outsider observers tend to believe that higher education itself is not sustainable (Scott, 2018). Business school faculty well-paid relative to others in the academy seem to be willing to roll with these punches, having a major stake in the status quo. Even those who have taken a serious look at the threatening forces of change (e.g., Pincus, Stout, Sorensen, Stocks, & Lawson, 2017) have chosen to believe their glass is solidly half-full.

This chapter may not have given sufficient credence to opposing viewpoints. We do not say that academic freedom has no meaning at the business school, or that there is no room for it to be made more meaningful in the future. On the spectrum of business school faculty exists many types, some of which are now poised to benefit from a classic form of academic freedom. What we seek to establish is the existence of the structures that mitigate to the contrary.

In summary, some may look at the situation of academic freedom in the business school as a tempest in a teapot. Business school faculty, as people who either were formerly business people or are heavily predisposed toward business, are less likely to take the courageous positions that would be enshrined in the academic freedom's hall of fame. On the other hand, the business school might be the vanguard of modernity wherein a faculty member's privilege to be the proverbial "loose cannon" might be more severely constrained than would be projected by a linear extension of the tradition of academic freedom.

REFERENCES

Alexy, R. (2010). *A theory of constitutional rights.* New York, NY: Oxford University Press.
Beatty, J. E. (2004). Grades as money and the role of the market metaphor in management education. *Academy of Management Learning & Education, 3*(2), 187–196.
Bennis, W. G., & O'Toole, J. (2005). How business schools lost their way. *Harvard Business Review, 83*(5), 96–104.
Bourdieu, P. (2013). *Distinction: A social critique of the judgement of taste.* London: Routledge.
Bowles, S., & Gintis, H. (1976). *Schooling in capitalist America.* New York, NY: Basic Books.
Boyce, G. (2002). Now and then: Revolutions in higher learning. *Critical Perspectives on Accounting, 13*(5–6), 575–601.
Conn. S. (2018). Business schools have no business in the university. *Chronicle of Higher Education,* February 20, pp. R1–R5.
Crocker, K. J., & Slemrod, J. (2005). Corporate tax evasion with agency costs. *Journal of Public Economics, 89*(9–10), 1593–1610.
Daniel, A., & Wellmon, C. (2018). The university run amok. Higher education's insatiable appetite for doing more will be its undoing. *Chronicle of Higher Education,* July 29, B1–B3.
DeAngelo, H., DeAngelo, L., & Zimmerman, J. L. (2005). What's really wrong with US business schools? Working Paper. University of Rochester. Retrieved from Social Science Research Electronic Paper, http://ssrn.com/abstracts=766404.
Djelic, M. L. (2012). Scholars in the audit society: Understanding our contemporary iron cage. In L. Engwall (ed.) *Scholars in Action: Past, Present, Future* (Vol. 2, pp. 97–121). Upsaliensis: Acta University.
Dominelli, L., & Hoogvelt, A. (1996). Globalisation, the privatisation of welfare, and the changing role of professional academics in Britain. *Critical Perspectives on Accounting, 7*(1), 191–212.
Espejo, R. (2001). Auditing as a trust creation process. *Systemic Practice and Action Research, 14*(2), 215–236.
Fogarty, T. (1995). Sponsored academic positions by large public accounting firms: An analysis of quid pro quo. *Advances in Public Interest Accounting, 6,* 133–162.
Fogarty, T., & Ravenscroft, S. (2000). Making accounting knowledge: Peering at power. *Critical Perspectives on Accounting, 11*(4), 409–431.
Foucault, M. (2012). *Discipline and punish: The birth of the prison.* New York, NY: Vintage.
Fuchs, R. F. (1963). Academic freedom. Its basic philosophy, function, and history. *Law and Contemporary Problems, 28*(3), 431–446.
Gendron, Y. (2015). Accounting academia and the threat of the paying-off mentality. *Critical Perspectives on Accounting, 26,* 168–176.
Gendron, Y., & Bédard, J. (2001). Academic auditing research: An exploratory investigation into its usefulness. *Critical Perspectives on Accounting, 12*(3), 339–368.
Green, W., Hibbins, R., Houghton, L., & Ruutz, A. (2013). Reviving praxis: Stories of continual professional learning and practice architectures in a faculty-based teaching community of practice. *Oxford Review of Education, 39*(2), 247–266.
Gross, N., Medvetz, T., & Russell, R. (2011). The contemporary American conservative movement. *Annual Review of Sociology, 37,* 325–354.
Hartman, A. (2019). *A war for the soul of America: A history of the culture wars.* Chicago, IL: University of Chicago Press.
Holbrook, M. B. (2018). A subjective personal introspective essay on the evolution of business schools, the fate of marketing education, and aspirations toward a great society. *Australasian Marketing Journal, 26*(2), 70–78.

Hopwood, A. G. (2007). Whither accounting research?. *The Accounting Review, 82*(5), 1365–1374.

Huczynski, A. A. (1994). Business school faculty as gatekeepers of management ideas. *Journal of Management Development, 13*(4), 23–40.

Hughes, E. C. (1949). *Social change and status protest: An essay on the marginal man* (Vol. 129). London: Ardent Media.

Jensen, M. C., & Meckling, W. H. (1976). Theory of the firm: Managerial behavior, agency costs and ownership structure. *Journal of Financial Economics, 3*(4), 305–360.

John, E. P. S., & Parsons, M. D. (Eds.). (2005). *Public funding of higher education: Changing contexts and new rationales.* London: JHU Press.

Kaplan, A. (2014). European management and European business schools: Insights from the history of business schools. *European Management Journal, 32*(4), 529–534.

Knorringa, P., & Guarin, A. (2015). Inequality, sustainability and middle classes in a polycentric world. *The European Journal of Development Research, 27*(2), 202–204.

Koole, S. L., & Lakens, D. (2012). Rewarding replications: A sure and simple way to improve psychological science. *Perspectives on Psychological Science, 7*(6), 608–614.

Ladd, E. C., Jr, & Lipset, S. M. (1975). *The divided academy: Professors and politics.* New York, NY: McGraw-Hill

Lehman, C. R. (2013). Knowing the unknowable and contested terrains in accounting. *Critical Perspectives on Accounting, 24*(2), 136–144.

Loveless, T. (Ed.). (2011). *Conflicting missions?: Teachers unions and educational reform.* Washington, DC: Brookings Institution Press.

Malkiel, B. G., & Fama, E. F. (1970). Efficient capital markets: A review of theory and empirical work. *The Journal of Finance, 25*(2), 383–417.

McCarthy, J., & Wright, P. (2004). Technology as experience. *Interactions, 11*(5), 42–43.

McSweeney, B. (2008). Maximizing shareholder-value. *Critical Perspectives on International Business, 4*(1), 55–74.

Mello, J. A. (2019). Creating and developing effective business and professional school advisory boards. *Journal of Higher Education Theory and Practice, 19*(2), 88–97.

Mintz, S. M., Dang, L., & Savage, A. (2013). Ethics of relationships between accounting academics and external sponsors. *Issues in Accounting Education, 28*(3), 555–580.

Neem, J. (2019). The subtle erosion of academic freedom. *Chronicle of Higher Education,* April 16, pp. R7–R8.

Newfield, C. (2008). Public universities at risk: 7 damaging myths. *Chronicle of Higher Education, 55*(10), A1–2.

O'Neil, C. (2016). *Weapons of math destruction: How big data increases inequality and threatens democracy.* New York, NY: Broadway Books.

Parker, L. (2011). University corporatisation: Driving redefinition. *Critical Perspectives on Accounting, 22*(4), 434–450.

Pfeffer, J., & Fong, C. T. (2002). The end of business schools? Less success than meets the eye. *Academy of Management Learning & Education, 1*(1), 78–95.

Pincus, K. V., Stout, D. E., Sorensen, J. E., Stocks, K. D., & Lawson, R. A. (2017). Forces for change in higher education and implications for the accounting academy. *Journal of Accounting Education, 40,* 1–18.

Porter, L. W., & McKibbin, L. E. (1988). *Management education and development: Drift or thrust into the 21st century?.* Hightstown, NJ: McGraw-Hill Book Company, College Division.

Richardson, S. A., Sloan, R. G., Soliman, M. T., & Tuna, I. (2006). The implications of accounting distortions and growth for accruals and profitability. *The Accounting Review, 81*(3), 713–743.

Rothman, S., Lichter, S. R., & Nevitte, N. (2005). Politics and professional advancement among college faculty. *The Forum, 3*(1). doi: https://doi.org/10.2202/1540-8884.1067.

Russell, C. (2002). *Academic freedom.* London: Routledge.

Saravanamuthu, K., & Tinker, T. (2002). The university in the new corporate world. *Critical Perspectives on Accounting, 13*(5–6), 545–554.

Scott, P. (2018). *The crisis of the university.* London: Routledge.

Shum, P. K., & Yam, S. L. (2011). Ethics and law: Guiding the invisible hand to correct corporate social responsibility externalities. *Journal of Business Ethics, 98*(4), 549–571.

Simmons, J. (2001). Educational technology and academic freedom. *Techné: Research in Philosophy and Technology, 5*(3), 158–166.

Slaughter, S. (1980). The danger zone: Academic freedom and civil liberties. *The ANNALS of the American Academy of Political and Social Science, 448*(1), 46–61.

Starkey, K., & Tiratsoo, N. (2007). *The business school and the bottom line.* New York, NY: Cambridge University Press.

Teixeira, P., Jongbloed, B. B., Dill, D. D., & Amaral, A. (Eds.). (2006). *Markets in higher education: Rhetoric or reality?* (Vol. 6). Dordrecht: Springer Science & Business Media.

Veblen, T. (1917). *The higher learning in America.* New York, NY: Hill and Wang.

Wallerstein, I. (2000). Globalization or the age of transition? A long-term view of the trajectory of the world-system. *International Sociology, 15*(2), 249–265.

Wedlin, L. (2006). *Ranking business schools: Forming fields, identities and boundaries in international management education.* Cheltenham: Edward Elgar Publishing.

Williams, P. F., Jenkins, J. G., & Ingraham, L. (2006). The winnowing away of behavioral accounting research in the US: The process for anointing academic elites. *Accounting, Organizations and Society, 31*(8), 783–818.

Wixom, B., Ariyachandra, T., Douglas, D., Goul, M., Gupta, B., Iyer, L., & Turetken, O. (2014). The current state of business intelligence in academia: The arrival of big data. *Communications of the Association for Information Systems, 34*(1), 1.

Woodhouse, H. (2009). *Selling out: Academic freedom and the corporate market.* Quebec: McGill-Queen's Press.

Wunnava, P. V., & Okunade, A. A. (2013). Do business executives give more to their alma mater? Longitudinal evidence from a large university. *American Journal of Economics and Sociology, 72*(3), 761–778.

Zipp, J., & Fenwick, R. (2006). Is the academy a liberal hegemony? The political orientations and educational values of professors. *International Journal of Public Opinion Quarterly, 70*(3), 304–326.

CHAPTER 10

HUMANIZING HIGHER EDUCATION THROUGH ETHICAL LEADERSHIP TO SUPPORT THE PUBLIC SERVICE

Vimbi Petrus Mahlangu

ABSTRACT

The chapter focuses on humanizing higher education by infusing ethical leadership in the curriculum to improve the public service. Its design is qualitative in nature and literature reviews and document analysis were employed in compiling the chapter. It followed an interpretive paradigm and used Kolb's Experiential Learning Theory as a lens in understanding humanizing education in higher education. Nowadays ethical leadership is of paramount importance in higher education and in the public service. Ethical leadership should be based on the moral person and on the moral manager. The moral person component focuses on desirable personal qualities of leaders such as being perceived as honest, fair and trustworthy. The moral manager focuses on the leader and uses transactional efforts such as rewards and punishments to reinforce desired behaviors. Soft skills are very important in higher education and should be transferred through coursework. Students need to be supported in all aspects of education including the academic, emotional and social demands in higher education.

Keywords: ethical leadership; higher education; respect; fairness; public service; experiential learning; access; democracy; social and political relations; humanizing education

Developing and Supporting Multiculturalism and Leadership Development:
International Perspectives on Humanizing Higher Education
Innovations in Higher Education Teaching and Learning, Volume 30, 175–190
Copyright © 2020 by Emerald Publishing Limited
ISSN: 2055-3641/doi:10.1108/S2055-364120200000030014

This chapter provides an exciting opportunity to advance our knowledge of humanizing higher education by infusing ethical leadership in the curriculum to improve the public service. The main reason for choosing this topic is personal interest. Kolb's Experiential Learning Theory was used as a lens in understanding ethical leadership in the public service. Blessinger and Bliss (2016) are of the view that education is recognized as a fundamental human right. Hence, the establishment of open universities is part of a wider effort to democratize education. They argue that the way higher education is designed there is a possibility that students can have access, ownership, participation and experience the opportunity to exercise this basic human right. In this chapter, I am adopting the idea of Geduld and Sathorar (2016) that humanizing education should be understood to constitute a set of social and political relations that connects the apparently self-contained act of teaching with culture, structure and the mechanisms of social control. Therefore, humanizing education must be a philosophy of education informed by positionalities, ideologies, Ubuntu and standpoints of instructors and students.

Humanizing education must consider the relationships between the purpose of higher education, the context of education, the content of what is being taught and the methods of how it is taught. In addition, it must include aspects such as who is being taught, for whom, who is teaching, the relationship to each other and the relationship that higher education must structure and power. Power relations also mark the scope and content of higher education curricula. Students' approaches to learning or getting by in their university education will differ. These differences have an impact on how they apply themselves in the workplace environment, and eventually society, based on their ability to engage in the discourse of the field or discipline they have chosen (Khene, 2014).

Humanizing education must aim to heal the effects of traumatic events that produce guilt, anxiety, resentment and injustice that persist and distort individual and national well-being. A range of conflicting differences, power relations, embedded interests, fears and anxieties that intersect with educational processes in a variety of ways are assumed within humanizing education. For example, interests, power relations and concomitant elements are resident within, between and among students, instructors and other role players and stakeholders in higher education (Keet, Zinn, & Porteus, 2009).

Instructors must understand the essence of humanizing education and have greater educational awareness, so that students can lead healthy and fulfilling lives in the workplace. Students are nations' most important assets and hope (Shih, 2018). Students need instructors' care and love, and instructors must respect students' rights and fundamental freedoms, freedom of expression and opinion to create a humanizing climate of learning. Therefore, the humanization of education is necessary. Instructors and students both have important roles in classrooms. Therefore, Morris (2019) is of the view that is to effectively solve problems situated in the workplace that are posed during the learning process, considering the details of the conditions of the context seems imperative because problems are inherently context specific.

RESEARCH QUESTION

The question, which the chapter intends to investigate, is the following: To what extent do we understand humanizing higher education by infusing ethical leadership in the curriculum to improve the public service? The next section reviews the "Literature."

LITERATURE REVIEW

Experiential Learning Theory

Kolb's theory is called Experiential Learning Theory, which has two parts or levels: the Experiential Learning Cycle, which has four stages, and the other is the Learning Styles, which has four types. According to Healey and Jenkins (2000) there are different stages of effective learning. They explain these stages of effective learning in terms of four stages, namely: (1) Having a concrete experience (Where the student is actively experiencing an activity); (2) observation of and reflection on that experience (where the student is consciously reflecting on that experience); (3) the formation of abstract concepts (analysis) and generalizations (conclusions) (where the learner is being presented with/or trying to conceptualize a theory or model of what is (to be) observed) which are then and (4) used to test hypothesis in future situations, resulting in new experiences (where the learner is trying to plan how to test a model or theory or plan for a forthcoming experience). Similarly, Moseley, Summerford, Paschke, Parks, and Utley (2019) are of the view that using Kolb's Experiential Learning Style Theory, higher education institutions can introduce students to a humanizing education concept (Active Experimentation stage) and participate in active experiences with the concept (Concrete Experiences stage) within higher education. Some examples of abstract humanizing education concept interactions include role playing, or problem solving. Next, students should be able to discuss, analyze and reflect on the active experience, relate it to past experiences and do observations, and reflections with their peers (Reflective Observation stage). Lastly, students need to discuss and apply the humanizing education concept learned to their work situation (Abstract Conceptualization stage). The learning process can begin at any stage; however, the students should complete the cycle for maximum learning.

In support of Moseley et al. (2019), Morris (2019, p. 1) is of the view that "experiential learning theory places life experience as a central and necessary part of the learning process, where knowledge is created through the transformation of experience." Similarly, Healey and Jenkins (2000, p. 186) are of the view that this theory provides a rationale for a variety of learning methods, including independent learning, learning by doing, work-based learning and problem-based learning. Its advantages are that it provides ready pointers to application; directs higher education to ensure that a range of teaching methods is used in a course; provides a theoretical rationale for what instructors already do and then offers suggestions on how to improve on that practice (ensuring effective links between theory and application).

Again, it makes explicit the importance of encouraging students to reflect and providing them with feedback to reinforce their learning. In addition, it supports instructors in developing a diverse, aware lecture rooms. Generally, it makes instructors aware of the way in which different learning styles must be combined for effective learning; and it can be readily applied to all areas of the discipline and can be used by individuals and course teams. On the other hand, Moseley et al. (2019), describe experiential learning as a philosophy of education based on a theory of sociocultural experiences and interactions to guide students through reflection to "increase knowledge, develop skills, clarify values and develop people's capacity to contribute to their workplace." To them, the ways of knowing must be connected to the social, cultural and physical situations students experience in learning.

Moral Competence, Respect of Others and Notions of Managing Diversity

Higher education has a major contribution to make to the moral and ethical standards in humanizing education for students to fit in the workplace. Scholars have found that moral development does not occur automatically but depends on the instructors instilling them in students. Bronikowska and Korcz (2019) found that in education policies in most countries, institutions equip students with moral competences for the workplace. However, at the same time, educational programs are expected include some aspects of moral education geared to raising the knowledge of moral conceptions, which are easy to be tested in students, and to be common with workplace behavior. In humanizing education, ethics can be used to promote the responsibility and autonomy of the students by applying themselves to the fundamental moral principles needed in the workplace. Moral development can be influenced by the experiences of students in various settings and contexts. According to Alhadabi et al. (2019), moral intelligence is a major quality that determines students' behavior in the workplace environment and social context. It is the capacity to understand right from wrong, to have strong ethical convictions and to act on them to behave in a right and honorable way. Generally, moral values determine students' cognitive and behavioral attitudes toward life dilemmas. The degree of adopting humanizing educational values underlines students' concerns about the issues of justice, equality, abstaining from harm and caring for others in the workplace.

The opportunity to voice one's own opinion in interactions and discourses is an important precondition for psychological well-being and participation and therefore for social justice in humanizing education. For example, respectful relations empower students and respect experiences promote their awareness of their equal entitlement concerning equal say in their well-being. In this part, respect can be explained as the recognition of individuals' equal rights and equal worth and this recognition of people's equal rights need to be grounded in the idea of equal dignity. The core idea is that students may feel respected when they have the feeling that they and their opinions are considered equally and are taken seriously in the workplace. The importance of equality-based respect for individuals' autonomy and life satisfaction is an important form of social recognition such as need-based care or achievement-based social esteem. Equality-based respect strengthens personal autonomy and the awareness of having equal rights (i.e., self-respect) and can foster students' ability to express their ideas and opinions and to stand by their rights (Renger, Mommert, Renger, Miché, & Simon, 2019).

In this chapter, respect of others can be associated with social trust of which it can be understood as an expectation that students will behave with good will, that they intend to honor their commitments, and that they will avoid harming others. The notion that connects humanizing education is moral trust, which is trust based not on personal experience, but on the assumption of shared fundamental values. This leads to trusting other people, however different they are, caring for them and treating them equally will make their experiences meaningful to them (Łopaciuk-Gonczaryk, 2019).

According to Amirkhanyan, Holt, Mcrea, and Meier (2019), diversity is a multifaceted concept that includes building cultural awareness and promoting pragmatic management policy within organizations. So, in managing diversity in higher education, especially in preparing the students for workplace, higher education institutions must be able to manage and address diversity issues. Therefore, diversity management practices can enhance operations and service delivery and to create higher education environments in which the input and participation of diverse staff and students can be used to achieve its goals. Diversity management practices targeting racially heterogeneous institutions and students can be beneficial to internal institutional climate and can benefit the students as clients (Amirkhanyan et al., 2019). Similarly, Dhiman, Modi, and Kumar (2019) are of the view that managing diversity means changing the culture of standard operating procedures that require data, experimentation and the discovery of the procedures that work best for each higher education. It is further argued that managing diversity can be regarded as a process of management based on certain values that recognize the differences between people and it can be identified as a strength but at the same time is directed toward the achievement of institutional outcomes. In managing diversity, higher education institutions must be responsive to students needs in terms of race, gender, class, native, language, religion, personal preferences and work styles.

Fairness and Justice through the Transformation of Society

Karam et al. (2019) argue that an understanding of the relationships between leader behaviors and justice perceptions is important. Employee–leader relationships must be characterized by social exchange relationships and distinguishable from other forms of exchanges by having expectations of longer-term, interdependent interactions that generate trust, reciprocal behaviors and high-quality relationships. For example, examining only leader-focused justice perceptions, particularly in relation to an explicit "event" (e.g., a single episode such as a performance appraisal), fails to consider the broader task, relational and change interactions between the leader and the employee and these interactions may impact justice. For Samara and Paul (2019), the two concepts justice and fairness seem to be overlapping and perhaps should be understood as alternative terms for the same basic concepts. Yet, justice and fairness start from the notion that all employees have a similar frame of reference for judging actions. Therefore, failing to consider the role of preconceived expectations, emotions and relations affecting employees' ethical perceptions and fairness judgments will be a mistake. While justice simply refers to adherence to rules of conduct, fairness refers to subjective perceptions of whether rules of conduct are ethical and fair. Similarly, Rasooli, Zandi, and DeLuca (2019) highlight that fairness is a moral issue with its theoretical roots tracing back to moral philosophy that is comprised of meta ethics, normative ethics and descriptive ethics. Meta ethics deals with several ontological and epistemological questions such as what fair or unfair means and whether fairness and unfairness exist. Normative ethics prescribes and evaluates ethical or unethical acts based on standards or frameworks. Fairness in normative ethics refer to the extent to which a given action, outcome, or circumstance is in alignment with a certain ethical paradigm (Rasooli et al., 2019).

Descriptive ethics describes what individuals consider as ethical or unethical conduct without conforming to an evaluation of their ethical values. Kim, Choi, and Lee (2019) are of the view that recognition justice requires that individuals be objectively represented in humanizing education within institutional and cultural process without their identity being degraded, discriminated or disrespected. Recognition justice is when the ideal of justice is ranked higher than the ideal of self-realization and justice is the highest of all moral values (Juul, 2010). It is the fundamental concept in the tenets of justice because the lack of recognition serves as not only an impediment to humanizing education but also the foundation for unjust distribution. When not recognized as an equal member of an organization or society with due respect, one's membership and participation may decline in institutional or political decision-making procedures. Under this circumstance, an organization may eventually end up with maladministration of resources. Even when redistributive policies or affirmative remedies are employed to resolve problems of maladministration (e.g., financial indemnification for student fees and loans), they may merely make shift solutions unless there are substantive efforts to redress the problems of recognition injustice that contribute to maladministration at the same time. The next section presents humanizing education.

Humanizing Education

Hwang (2001) is of the view promoting human rights education is confronting the traditional values in any society. Culturally speaking, human rights, a concept spurred from individualism in the West, can contrast with traditional values. Promoting human rights education such as in Confucian societies, for example, Taiwan, can have a considerable impact on the different levels of interpersonal relations in different sectors such as in workplace, society, politics and education. Therefore, humanizing education in higher education must impart values and ethical leadership to students in preparing them for the workplace. The concept of morality is categorized into the ethics of autonomy, the ethics of community and the ethics of divinity. Within this classification system, the morality of individualism in Western culture belongs to the ethics of autonomy, which stresses personal rights as an individual. However, the morality of Confucianism stresses interpersonal duties in social situations and belongs to the ethics of community. There is a huge gap in how the East and West define "morality." The moralities developed from individualism are rights-based conceptions of natural law.

All moral standards involve personal rights, duties and social goals, but each of them implies a different priority (Hwang, 2001). On the other hand, Robson and Martin (2019) are of the view that the ethic of justice requires ethical leaders to consider whether a formal policy or law provides a resolution to an issue in humanizing education. The ethic of critique encourages leaders to move beyond the implementation of policies and, instead, consider issues of power and oppression inherent in policy. The ethic of care supports leaders in showing concern for others, including, for example, students, instructors and communities. Ethic of profession is the moral responsibility of higher education to engage in processes that will assist students to pursue the moral purposes of their professions in preparing them for their work places (Furman, 2003). This can be achieved by addressing the challenges that students may encounter in their respective programs in higher education settings. An ethic of profession needs to be informed by engagement with the ethics of justice, critique and care, but also reflections on life histories and practice.

Neal, Justice, and Baron (2019, p. 98) believe that as students grow within education social systems (e.g., family, church, and work); both ethics and values are formed. Education social systems refer to systems of communications between home, society, work, etc., and education institutions in which communication determine what further communications is needed (Hendry & Seidl, 2003).

Some would argue that ethics are taught first by external forces, which define right and wrong. This same process needs to happen in higher education. Instructors and students need to share the main roles in education (Shih, 2018). Instructors usually have experience with a variety of different students, so it is important for them to know how to handle certain situations that are specific to students, especially when these involve behavioral problems that affect the workplace. However, instructors must deal with behavioral problems of students in ways that are humane in nature. Hence, humanizing education should use Ubuntu principle when instructors try to influence, navigate and coexist within the sociopolitical context and practices of organizations where leaders, students, administration and community members are involved. The Ubuntu principle refers to an African philosophy of life which originates from within African idioms, which means "A person is a person through other persons," or, "I am because we are; we are because I am." Ubuntu attitude is the one who is noted to be hospitable, friendly, generous, compassionate and caring for his fellow human being (Arthur, Issifu, & Marfo, 2015).

Humanizing education must fit each student and must address each student's specific needs and individual potentialities. Navarretea, Vásqueza, Montero, and Cantero (2019) suggest that humanizing education should be based on a didactic principle that is based on dialogue, which will allow horizontal pedagogic relations between instructor and student. In this pedagogic relationship, humanizing didactics needs to be understood as accompanying students in such a way as to provoke them into critical attitudes, especially with respect to topical social work issues and their own behavior. To this end, the choice of humanizing didactic methodologies should be focused on reformulating the contents of human rights education by means of representations (symbolism), until they can be given real existence in human rights education. Thus, humanizing education ought to educate by developing capacities and forming values, through contents and methods. To them (Navarretea et al., 2019), human rights values such as respect for dignity, respect for life, etc., need to be part of the human rights teaching and learning contents in education. The humanizing education must be educational in that it ought to appeal to the contents and methods of each culture. In this chapter, humanizing education should be considered open, multidisciplinary, intercultural in nature. The next section presents experiences of human rights education.

Experiences of Human Rights Education

Humanizing education must be a political activity and through employing the principle of mutual vulnerability higher education institutions can be able to acknowledge that certain pedagogical alignments and calibrations further an agenda of critical social justice and empowerment and understand how other alignments militate against such possibilities (Keet et al., 2009). Concern for humanizing education can lead to the recognition of dehumanization in the workplace, not only as an ontological possibility, but also as a historical reality. In this case, humanizing education can be used as a strategic component in societal healing if racism prevails in the workplace.

Renner, Brown, Stiens, and Burton (2010) think that in terms of social justice, humanizing education must begin from a premise that the world is deeply flawed. Higher education institutions must believe that the condition of the poor students is not only unacceptable, but it is the result of structural separation that is man-made. Relative to this notion, humanizing education must be there to ensure that higher education is satisfying all students, because the world can be utterly devastating to them all, the privileged and the oppressed. Thus, higher education institutions are all implicated in the creation or maintenance of structural differentiation so a posture of penitence and indignation in higher education is critical. This sort of approach implies not a working for, but a working with – a humble, more contextual, more connected approach. This approach can be linked to the concept of "structural transformation," which must aim to alleviate unmet needs, but also to develop critical consciousness concerning social realities, and to organize and act against destructive higher education conditions that obstruct humanizing education.

Gill and Niens (2014) posit that education can provide a framework for teaching and learning about reconciliation that will have a long-term impact as it may help to avoid transgenerational transmission of conflict in the workplace. They further emphasize that the transformative power of reconciliation building in higher education lies in its potential to redress processes of dehumanization, which are root causes of institutional violence, which also result in the denial of some students' moral values and human rights. According to them, humanizing education is vital in the development and maintenance of a culture of tolerance diversity and inclusion; and in the establishment and promotion of democratic citizenship and critical engagement with politics and society in the workplace.

The Characteristics of Humanizing Education

Osorio (2018) opine that humanizing education must be valuing the students' background knowledge, culture and life experiences, and creating learning contexts where power is shared among students and instructors. To her, instructors who infuse a humanizing education into their teaching are the ones who must actively pursue a path toward mutual humanization. So, a mutual humanization education needs to be understood as a process that welcomes shared ownership between the instructor and students in problem posing education where students become coinvestigators rather than simply the receivers of information. Consequently, instructors, instead of seeing students as empty vessels that needed to be filled, they must highlight students' linguistic and cultural resources in their programs. Therefore, instructors must see themselves as learners together with students as they grapple with issues of power and privileges related to the topics in the curriculum. Huerta (2011) maintains that instructors who embrace a humanizing education are aware of the socio-historical and political context of their own lives and those of their students, including the influence of societal power, racial and ethnic identities and cultural values. They believe that marginalized students (due to race, economic class, culture or experience) are different in how they learn, but not in their ability to learn. For example, when students' home and community language and culture correspond closely to that of the higher education institution, academic performance can be enhanced. Yet academic performance can be compromised for students whose home culture and/or language differ from that of the institution.

Instructors who practice a humanizing education need to incorporate students' language and culture into the academic context to support learning and to help students identify with, and maintain pride in, their home cultures. Those who care about their students' emotional, social and academic well-being ought to practice humanizing education. Humanizing instructors must listen to students and communicate regularly with them (in their native language) about their progress in a more holistic manner. Such humanizing instructors must exhibit kindness, patience and respect toward others, and take time to instill these values in students. In addition, instructors who practice a humanizing education explicitly teach the institutions' codes and customs, and mainstream knowledge, to enable students to participate in the dominant culture. These instructors have a responsibility to assist students in appropriating knowledge bases and discourse styles deemed desirable by the workplace. As Geduld and Sathorar (2016) write, higher education programs need to be designed in such a manner that students can acquire, integrate and apply a range of knowledge types, such as disciplinary knowledge, pedagogical knowledge, practical knowledge, fundamental knowledge and situational knowledge. In higher education, programs should be designed to enable students to acquire and apply these knowledges in an integrated, fused manner in the workplace.

According to Roux and Becker (2016), humanization and dehumanization remain historical and ontological possibilities for incomplete human beings, and they assume humanization as the premise of education. To them, the telos of education is critical and can be used as reflective understanding of the world and one's place in higher education. In their argument, they think that Freire suggests that education, as a practice of freedom toward humanization, should focus on dialogue as praxis. This does not necessitate an integration, accommodation, or assimilation of all within the structures in higher education and social practices that cause exclusion and discrimination, but a transformation of the very structures and practices that cause exclusion of students. According to them, the idea of Freire is that education is the entanglement of philosophy, politics and practice, which demands that higher education institutions are to engage themselves with the students in transforming oppressive social conditions. In this sense, then, all education is political and functions as "public education," that is, as a form that constantly involves pedagogical encounters with others. This broadened conception of education includes public sites of education, offering opportunities for higher education to mobilize alternative forms of counterhegemonic learning (Zembylas, 2018). The next section presents supporting and participation in humanizing education.

Supporting and Participation in Humanizing Education

Khene (2014), in espousing Freire's idea, is of the view that practicing and developing a humanizing education requires that instructors learn to see and treat students as human beings, because naturally we should treat each other as human beings. However, some instructors can become so disconnected in the process of higher education and begin to see students as objects that will help them reach tenure, get publications through, or maintain their "guru" stature. Instructors are expected to engage with students appropriately so that they may realize their full potential in higher education. Similarly, Gill and Niens (2014) maintain that humanization education needs to be characterized by fostering respect for human dignity, reconciliation and relation building, celebrating shared humanity as a common identity and reconstructing a vision for a humane society where there is the possibility of a culture of peace in the workplace. Therefore, higher education institutions need to shift in their approaches to accommodate dialogic education as a key element for students' participation and to transform the workplace. On the other hand, Salazar (2013) is of the view that successful students of color experience academic success at the expense of their cultural and psychological well-being. In addition, these students may demonstrate a race-less persona. In other words, for them to navigate the educational system, they need to sacrifice an essential part of their humanity by acting White to fit into the white stream. Therefore, students of color may experience subtractive schooling through the denial of their heritage and assimilation into White culture.

Roux and Becker (2016) support Freire's idea that if higher education wants to teach and learn for freedom and humanization, it needs to acknowledge situated selves. To them, situated selves are positioned within intersections of past, present and future place and space in higher education. For example, racism is based on unequal relations of power and is intertwined with other forms of discrimination such as class, gender, ethnicity, religion and language and utilizes these to justify and reproduce itself. That is why people in different power positions interconnect differently in changing relational contexts. Higher education institutions have the legal authority to decide which students to admit, but they need to do so based on a published and transparent set of criteria that will guide them in making such decisions on which students are admitted. In addition, higher education institutions ought to set out the minimum requirements that students are expected meet for them to be considered for admission (Higher Education South Africa, 2011).

Sometimes higher education institutions' admission processes may be filled with uncertainty for both students and the institutions. For example, if students are guaranteed admission before their senior year, they tend to take risks by reducing their performance effort, and then the cost of this behavior is not fully borne by students, as many higher education institutions may provide costly remedial services to students who show up on campuses underprepared (Leeds, McFarlin, & Daugherty, 2017). Furthermore, many students may experience problems because of the "invisibility" of their disabilities because of a breakdown in communication within the higher education institutions. Students may have the assumption that higher education institutions, knowing of their disabilities, would not offer them access if it could not provide the necessary support (Borland & James, 1999). At times, higher education institutions face challenges in realigning their undergraduate mission and environment in support of different number of students who need support. For example, vulnerable disadvantaged undergraduate students who happen to have undetected disabilities.

There are specific factors in different contexts that make students' admission different, such as whether discrimination occurs because of gender, social class, race or ethnicity. In turn, these factors are affecting higher institutions' strategies in responding to admissions and access challenges in higher education. Similarly, there may not be enough resources in all countries to fund the kind of students' admission systems that would accommodate humanizing education, nevertheless, lack of resources at higher education institutions should not constrain the reasoning around humanizing admission and access criteria to education (McCowan, 2016). In some instances, after going through entry tests students are faced with problems of selecting their preferred subjects among different types of courses due to lack of knowledge of intake merits and they may not be treated well. Therefore, humanizing education is needed and to be applied by administrators and instructors as well. In such cases, problems arise when students are waiting for admissions in specific higher education institutions, whereas, others have finished their admission processes and have selected eligible students, but some students cannot take admission in any higher education institutions because there is no prediction system for admission in them (Usman et al., 2017). The next section presents humanizing education access.

Humanizing Education Access

In terms of breaking down and pushing through the spatial walls of whiteness on campuses, research has found that white students often voice resistance to participation in diverse learning communities. It has been found that at histori- cally white colleges and universities, walls of whiteness spatially separate white and non-white students. In addition, race has functioned as a central axis of social organization in white supremacist societies. Thus, affirmative action poli- cies can produce a "welcoming" effect for students of color. It stands to reason that humanizing pedagogies are needed for students to access higher education. Affirmative action has been an important policy for challenging past and pre- sent discrimination in admission for black students to historically white colleges and universities (Brunsma, Brown, & Placier, 2012). Brown, Boser, Sargrad, and Marchitello (2016) assert that different forms of tests for admission have existed for centuries. In addition, admission to higher education, testing methods that discriminated correctly for every student's admission may not exist. The demand for higher education and the competition for seats in them had left admissions officers with the overwhelming task of choosing the most meritorious from an excess of highly qualified candidates. That is the reason why higher education institutions admit students with demonstrated high levels of academic talent in their academic programs (Giancola & Kahlenberg, 2016).

In addition, humanizing education can be used as a useful tool to ensure the heterogeneity of the student population or as an unfair advantage given to stu- dents who might otherwise be deemed inadmissible based on their academic per- formance. On the other hand, test scores (without the use of a student's race or ethnicity as a factor) might reduce the racial and ethnic diversity of the admit- ted student population at higher education institutions (Clarke & Shore, 2001). Similarly, Frawley, Larkin, and Smith (2017) support the notion that engagement that supports admission and access in higher education ought to be character- ized by humanizing education through teaching and learning, curriculum design, policies, research, external relations, social and cultural engagement, partner- ships with school and higher education providers, workplace and organization and participation of students. Ubuntu can be used to help students to participate in higher education (Frawley et al., 2017).

Students need to be enabled to participate in knowledge communities and engage with other students, as well as in human rights education. Humanizing education should be viewed as enabling participation in "knowing," enabling stu- dents to acquire membership in wider discourse in higher education, to poten- tially become knowledgeable about human rights (Khene, 2014). Similarly, Fields (2015, pp. 24–25) in support of Khene (2014) is of the view that pre-orientation programs can enhance an undergraduate students' sense of belonging and can provide a solid foundation for the start of their academic career. However, pre- orientation programs are sometimes fee-based and many low-income and first- year students may not have the funds to register for these programs. They may not appreciate their value due to the expense and may not recognize their potential importance due to lack of previous, related experiences.

In support of Fields (2015), Iannelli, Smyth, and Klein (2016) contend that standardized systems of admission to higher education may produce a more egalitarian educational outcome. Decisions about admissions must be based on the availability of university places and not on students' language ability for university study (Coley, 1999). This means that most Australian higher education institutions make decisions to admit or reject on academic grounds without considering humanizing education. Hence, a minority of them make an initial assessment of acceptability but take the final decision to admit students with a disability only after they have checked their policies and an "assessment" is made of their abilities and the institutions' facilities. Students are selected based on their language abilities rather than on humanizing education. Other higher education institutions will only admit students if they are convinced of the students' ability to cope with their disabilities irrespective of their level of academic achievement (Borland & James, 1999).

DISCUSSION

Humanizing education is meant to bring about valuing human rights in the workplace. Moral intelligence is a major quality that determines students' behavior in the workplace Affirmative action is an important policy that can be used to redress the past imbalances that discriminated people in the workplace. Equality-based respect strengthens personal autonomy and the awareness of having equal rights of employees in the workplace. The next section presents the Implications for policy and practice. Humanizing education can be used as a useful tool to ensure the heterogeneity of the student population or as an unfair advantage given to students who might otherwise be deemed inadmissible because of their academic or test performance. There is a need for education to be race-sensitive and governments' policymakers need to invest more financial resources in programs that seek to increase humanizing education. The responsibility of humanizing education should be tied to all institutions of education in their policies. Financial resources should be provided to those education institutions that support and encourage human rights education. Ethical leaders interested in discouraging deviance in the workplace, it is important for them to exhibit ethical behavior in terms of treating employees in a fair and ethical manner. However, leaders should also note that ethical leadership might not always guarantee that employees will approve behaviors intended to benefit the organization as well as refrain from behaviors that are harmful in the workplace. It is recommended that caring relationships should be encouraged in higher education and in the workplace so that employees can experience feelings of inclusion. Higher education institutions need to have programs that will enable students to care for the needs of others, such as outreach programs or community projects. Also, ethical leaders should be able to turn their followers' mind-set of self-interest into the organizational goals and to involve all stakeholders in the running of the organization so that they can experience humanizing education.

CONCLUSION

Students need to be prepared in advance and to be supported by humanizing education to help them to cope and to reduce anxiety associated with workplace environments. Students need to know that working together and soft skills are important in the workplace. They need to be made aware that humanizing education is a requirement to perform well in the workplace.

REFERENCES

Alhadabi, A., Aldhafri, S., Alkharusi, H., Al-Harthy, I., Alrajhi, M., & AlBarashdi, H. (2019). Modelling parenting styles, moral intelligence, academic self-efficacy and learning motivation among adolescents in grades 7–11. *Asia Pacific Journal of Education, 39*(1), 133–153. doi:10.1080/02188791.2019.1575795

Amirkhanyan, A. A., Holt, S. B., Mcrea, A. M., & Meier, K. J. (2019). Managing racial diversity: Matching internal strategies with environmental needs. *Public Administration Review, 79*(1), 69–81. doi:10.1111/puar.12977

Arthur, D. D., Issifu, A. K., & Marfo, S. (2015). An analysis of the influence of Ubuntu principle on the South Africa peace building process. *Journal of Global Peace and Conflict, 3*(2), 63–77.

Blessinger, P., & Bliss, T. J. (Eds.). (2016). *Open education international perspectives in higher education.* Cambridge: Open Book Publishers.

Borland, J., & James, S. (1999). The learning experience of students with disabilities in higher education. A case study of a UK university. *Disability & Society, 14*(1), 85–101.

Bronikowska, M., & Korcz, A. (2019). The level of moral competences of pre-service PE teachers – A reason to worry? *Biomedical Human Kinetics, 11*, 19–27. doi:10.2478/bhk-2019-0003

Brown, C., Boser, U., Sargrad, S., & Marchitello, M. (2016). *Implementing the every student succeeds act toward a coherent, aligned assessment system. Implementing the every student succeeds act.* Washington, DC: Center for American Progress. Retrieved from www.americanprogress.org

Brunsma, D. L., Brown, E. S., & Placier, P. (2012). Teaching race at historically white colleges and universities: Identifying and dismantling the walls of whiteness. *Critical Sociology, 39*(5), 717–738.

Clarke, M., & Shore, A. (2001). *The roles of testing and diversity in college admissions: National board on educational testing and public policy.* Newton, MA: Lynch School of Education, Boston College.

Coley, M. (1999). The English language entry requirements of Australian universities for students of non-English speaking background. *Higher Education Research & Development, 18*(1), 7–17. http://dx.doi.org/10.1080/0729436990180102

Dhiman, S. K., Modi, S., & Kumar, V. (2019). Celebrating diversity through spirituality in the work place: Transforming organizations holistically. *The Journal of Values-Based Leadership, 12*(1), 1–18.

Fields, H. R., Jr. (2015). *Increasing undergraduate socioeconomic diversity at Washington University in St. Louis: Building capacity in the existing university infrastructure final report.* St. Louis, MO: Washington University.

Frawley, J., Larkin, S., & Smith, J. A. (2017). *Indigenous pathways, transitions and participation in higher education: From policy to practice.* Singapore: Springer Nature Singapore Pty Ltd.

Furman, G. C. (2003). Moral leadership and the ethic of community. *Values and Ethics in Educational Administration, 2*(1), 1–8.

Geduld, D., & Sathorar, H. (2016). Humanising education: An alternative approach to curriculum design that enhances rigour in a B.Ed. programme. *Perspectives in Education, 34*(1), 40–52.

Giancola, J., & Kahlenberg, R. D. (2016). *True merit: Ensuring our brightest students have access to our best colleges and universities.* Lansdowne, VA: Jack Kent Cooke Foundation.

Gill, S., & Niens, U. (2014). Education as humanisation: A theoretical review on the role of dialogic education in peacebuilding education, *Compare: A Journal of Comparative and International Education, 44*(1), 10–31. doi:10.1080/03057925.2013.859879

Healey, M., & Jenkins, A. (2000). Kolb's experiential learning theory and its application in geography in higher education. *Journal of Geography, 99*(5), 185–195. doi:10.1080/00221340008978967

Hendry, J., & Seidl, D. (2003). The structure and significance of strategic episodes: Social systems theory and the routine practices of strategic change. *Journal of Management Studies, 40*(1), 176–196.

Higher Education South Africa. (2011). Message from Prof Duma Malaza, Chief Executive Officer (CEO), Higher Education South Africa (HESA). *Insight.* Issue 03 – September, 1–24.

Huerta, T. M. (2011). Humanizing education: Beliefs and practices on the teaching of Latino children. *Bilingual Research Journal, 34*(1), 38–57. doi:10.1080/15235882.2011.568826

Hwang, K.-K. (2001). Introducing human rights education in the Confucian society of Taiwan: Its implications for ethical leadership in education. *International Journal of Leadership in Education, 4*(4), 321–332. doi:10.1080/13603120110077981

Iannelli, C., Smyth, E., & Klein, M. (2016) Curriculum differentiation and social inequality in higher education entry in Scotland and Ireland. *British Educational Research Journal, 42*(4), 561–581.

Juul, S. (2010). Solidarity and social cohesion in late modernity: A question of recognition, justice and judgement in situation. *European Journal of Social Theory, 13*(2), 253–269.

Karam, E. P., Hu, J., Davison, R. B., Juravich, M., Nahrgang, J. D., Humphrey, S. E., & DeRue, D. S. (2019). Illuminating the 'Face' of justice: A meta-analytic examination of leadership and organizational justice. *Journal of Management Studies, 56*(1), 134–168.

Keet, A., Zinn, D., & Porteus, K. (2009). Mutual vulnerability: A key principle in a humanising education in post-conflict societies. *Perspectives in Education, 27*(2), 109–119.

Khene, C. P. (2014). Supporting a humanizing education in the supervision relationship and process: A reflection in a developing country. *International Journal of Doctoral Studies, 9*, 73–83. Retrieved from http://ijds.org/Volume9/IJDSv9p073-083Khene0545.pdf

Kim, J. D.-Y., Choi, E., & Lee, E. (2019). Social justice, fairness and exclusion in the South Korean electricity sector. *Energy Research & Social Science, 51*, 55–66.

Leeds, D. M., McFarlin, I., Jr, & Daugherty, L. (2017). Does student effort respond to incentives? Evidence from a guaranteed college admissions program. *Research in Higher Education, 58*, 231–243.

Łopaciuk-Gonczaryk, B. (2019). Does participation in social networks foster trust and respect for other people—Evidence from Poland. *Sustainability, 11*(6), 1733. https://doi.org/10.3390/su11061733

McCowan, T. (2016). Three dimensions of equity of access to higher education. *Compare: A Journal of Comparative and International Education, 46*(4), 645–665. http://dx.doi.org/10.1080/030579 25.2015.1043237

Morris, T. H. (2019). Experiential learning – A systematic review and revision of Kolb's model. *Interactive Learning Environments*, May, 1–14. doi:10.1080/10494820.2019.1570279

Moseley, C., Summerford, H., Paschke, M., Parks, C., & Utley, J. (2019). Road to collaboration: Experiential learning theory as a framework for environmental education program development, *Applied Environmental Education & Communication*, March, 1–22. doi:10.1080/15330 15X.2019.1582375

Navarretea, J., Vásqueza, A., Montero, E., & Cantero, D. (2019). Significant learning in catholic religious education: The case of Temuco (Chile). *British Journal of Religious Education*, June, 90–102. doi:10.1080/01416200.2019.1628005

Neal, P. Justice, B., & Baron, K. (2019). How ethical leadership impacts student success. *New Directions for Community Colleges, 2019*(185), 97–105. doi:10.1002/cc

Osorio, S.L. (2018). Toward a humanizing education: Using Latinx children's literature with early childhood students. *Bilingual Research Journal, 41*(1), 5–22.

Rasooli, A., Zandi, H., & DeLuca, C. (2019). Conceptualising fairness in classroom assessment: Exploring the value of organisational justice theory. *Assessment in Education: Principles, Policy & Practice, 26*(5), 1–28. doi:10.1080/0969594X.2019.1593105

Renger, D., Mommert, A., Renger, S., Miché, M., & Simon, B. (2019). Voicing one's ideas: Intragroup respect as an antecedent of assertive behavior. *Basic and Applied Social Psychology, 41*(1), 34–47. doi:10.1080/01973533.2018.1542306

Renner, A., Brown, M., Stiens, G., & Burton, S. (2010). A reciprocal global education? Working towards a more humanizing education through critical literacy. *Intercultural Education, 21*(1), 41–54.

Robson, J., & Martin, E. (2019). How do early childhood education leaders navigate ethical dilemmas within the context of marketised provision in England? *Contemporary Issues in Early Childhood, 20*(1), 93–103.

Roux, C., & Becker, A. (2016). Humanising higher education in South Africa through dialogue as praxis. *Educational Research for Social Change (ERSC), 5*(1), 131–143.

Salazar, M. D. C. (2013). A humanizing education: Reinventing the principles and practice of education as a journey toward liberation. *Review of Research in Education, 37*, 121–148.

Samara, G., & Paul, K. (2019). Justice versus fairness in the family business workplace: A socioemotional wealth approach. *Business Ethics: A European Review, 28*, 175–184.

Shih, Y-H. (2018). Towards a education of humanizing child education in terms of teacher–student interaction. *Journal of Education and Learning, 7*(3), 197–202.

Usman, M., Iqbal, M. M., Iqbal, Z., Chaudhry, M. U., Farhan, M., & Ashraf, M. (2017). E-assessment and computer-aided prediction methodology for student admission test score. *EURASIA Journal of Mathematics Science and Technology Education, 3*(8), 5499–5517.

Zembylas, M. (2018). Decolonial possibilities in South African higher education: Reconfiguring humanising pedagogies as/with decolonising pedagogies. *South African Journal of Education, 38*(4), 1–11.

ABOUT THE AUTHORS

Patrick Blessinger, Ed.D., is an Adjunct Associate Professor of Education at St. John's University, a Math and Science Teacher with the New York State Education Department, and Chief Research Scientist of the International Higher Education Teaching and Learning Association (in consultative status with the United Nations). He is the editor and author of many books and articles and is an Educational Policy Analyst and contributing writer with UNESCO's *Inclusive Policy Lab, University World News, The Hechinger Report, The Guardian,* and *Higher Education Tomorrow,* among others. He teaches courses in education, leadership, and research methods, and serves on doctoral dissertation committees. He founded and leads a global network of educators focused on teaching and learning and is an expert in inclusion, equity, leadership, policy, democracy, human rights, and sustainable development. He provides professional development workshops to teachers and professors and regularly gives presentations and keynote addresses at academic conferences around the world. He has received several educational awards, including Fulbright Senior Scholar to Denmark (Department of State, USA), Governor's Teaching Fellow (Institute of Higher Education, University of Georgia, USA), and Certified Educator (National Geographic Society, USA).

Luisa Bunescu has been working as Policy and Project Officer at the European University Association (EUA) in Brussels, Belgium, being mostly in charge of initiatives in higher education learning and teaching across Europe, with a focus on teaching enhancement and student diversity, since 2016. Prior to joining EUA, Luisa was Research Assistant in Macroeconomics at the Berlin School of Economics and Law, Germany, and Assistant to the Director at Centre International de Formation Européenne in France. She is an Aspen Institute fellow, with M.A.s in Political Economy and International Relations.

Alison Robinson Canham is a highly experienced educator, strategist, and change agent with extensive experience in the higher education and professional body sectors. She has undertaken academic and professional development work in the UK, Europe, Australasia, and South Africa, and has led the design and implementation of numerous academic and professional development initiatives in higher education and professional learning contexts. Her Principal Fellowship of the Higher Education Academy was awarded for, among other things, her strategic leadership of learning and teaching and her commitment to fair access and equal opportunity in higher education. She is a freelance educator and higher education enhancement consultant, most recently Head of Learning and Teaching Enhancement and Support at the Royal Veterinary College, University of London. She has held senior positions in the Higher Education Academy (now Advance HE) and the Association of University Administrators, and previously worked at the Open University and the University of Hull.

Timothy J. Fogarty is a Professor in the Accountancy Department at the Weatherhead School of Management, Case Western Reserve University. He is also the Thomas Dickerson Faculty Fellow at that school. He has published over 270 articles on a wide variety of topics, in both academic and practitioner journals. His research interests include accounting education, the sociology of business organizations, and the regulation of professionals. He has served on the editorial boards of over 20 journals, including several outside the United States. He has served in several capacities at the national level for the American Accounting Association, including as Vice President – Education and as President of three sections. He has worked on research projects for the Financial Executives Research Foundations and on educational matters for the American Institute of Certified Public Accountants (CPA), including extensive work with the design and content of the CPA exam. He also has been involved with the accreditation of business schools. At Case Western, he previously served as department chair and associate dean, teaches across the curriculum, and has served in several university-level capacities. He has been an attorney for 45 years and a CPA for 40 years.

Hope J. Hartman is a Professor Emerita of The City College of New York (CCNY) and The Graduate Center of the City University of New York in the Educational Psychology Doctoral Program. At CCNY, she was the Director of the Center for Excellence in Teaching and Learning and the City College Tutoring and Cooperative Learning Program. She obtained her doctorate in Cognitive Psychology from the Institute for Cognitive Studies at Rutgers University. Her Ph.D. has been used primarily in educational psychology for developing and researching methods of improving thinking and learning by children, adolescents, and adults, and helping teachers at all school levels and in all subject areas apply a repertoire of instructional methods which enhance thinking and learning. Her primary specializations are faculty development, metacognition, and instructional technology. She spent several years as a Research Specialist in the Research, Evaluation and Testing Offices of the Board of Education in Newark, New Jersey. She has four books currently in print and has authored many peer-reviewed chapters and journal articles. Her most recent book is *A Guide to Reflective Practice for New and Experienced Teachers*.

Leanne R. Havis is a Professor of Criminal Justice in the School of Arts and Sciences at Neumann University. She earned her B.A. in Political Science from the University of Kansas, her M.A. and Ph.D. in Comparative Criminology and Criminal Justice from Bangor University in Wales, and most recently, her M.B.A. from Holy Family University. She has been teaching in higher education for over 20 years and her interactions with students routinely provide the inspiration for her scholarly activities. Her professional and research interests include metacognitive pedagogy, assessment methods, and intercultural competence development. She is the creator of the "exam autopsy" method, an integrative post-exam assessment tool designed to promote self-regulated learning in undergraduate students.

Moeketsi Letseka holds a Doctorate in Philosophy of Education from UNISA, where he teaches and conducts research in philosophy of education and African philosophy. During 2002–2008, he served as a Senior Research Specialist at the Human Sciences Research Council (HSRC) where he conducted large-scale multi-year, multi-stakeholder research projects that were supported by external donor funders. During 2003–2005 He served as a Senior Researcher in the HSRC's Carnegie Foundation-funded study on "Higher Education-Industry partnerships in South Africa." In 2005, he served as joint Guest Editor with Dr Glenda Kruss (HSRC) of the Special Issue of the London-based scholarly journal, *Industry & Higher Education*, volume 19, number 2, which disseminated the findings to the global audience. During 2005–2008, he served as Principal Investigator and Project Leader of the "Student Pathways Study," which was co-funded by Ford Foundation and Council on Higher Education (CHE). The study investigated the question "Why University students drop out?" at seven universities. It yielded a book, which he co-edited: Letseka, M., Cosser, M., Breier, M., & Visser, M. (Eds.) (2010). *Student retention and graduate destinations: Higher education and labour market access and success*. Cape Town: HSRC Press; During 2014–2016, he received a research grant from South Africa's National Research Foundation in support of the "Archaeology of Ubuntu" study, in which he served as a Principal Investigator. The study was conducted in Botswana, Lesotho, Namibia, Swaziland, Zambia, Zimbabwe, and in five provinces in South Africa, namely, Eastern Cape, Kwazulu-Natal, Limpopo, Mpumalanga, and North West. He is Editor-in-Chief of *Africa Education Review*, an international scholarly journal that is jointly published by UNISA Press and Taylor & Francis in the United Kingdom. He has over 100 publications in the form of peer-reviewed articles in national and international scholarly journals and peer-reviewed book chapters. He has published the following additional scholarly books:

- Aluko, R., Letseka, M., & Pitsoe, V. (Eds.). (2016). *Assuring institutional quality in open distance learning (ODL) in the developing contexts*. New York, NY: Nova Publishers.
- Letseka, M. (Ed.). (2015). *Open distance learning (ODL) in South Africa*. New York, NY: Nova Science Publishers.
- Letseka, M. (Ed.). (2016). *Open distance learning (ODL) through the philosophy of Ubuntu*. New York, NY: Nova Science Publishers.

Vimbi Petrus Mahlangu holds a B.A.Ed. (Vista University), B.Ed., M.Ed., & Ph.D. degrees from the University of Pretoria. He is an Associate Professor at the University of South Africa, Department of Educational Leadership & Management. He is responsible for teaching and research. He presented papers at national and international conferences. He is a recipient of Dean's Award for Excellence in Teaching in the Faculty of Education (2011) at the University of Pretoria. He has published extensively in accredited journals and contributed a book, book chapters, and editor of a book titled *Reimagining Professional Development in Teacher Education.*

Mandla S. Makhanya was appointed Principal and Vice Chancellor of the University of South Africa on January 1, 2011, and is a prominent proponent of higher education leadership and advocacy, nationally, continentally, and globally, more especially as it pertains to Open, Distance and eLearning. He is a past President of the International Council for Distance Education and is also Treasurer of the African Council for Distance Education. He is also the President of the HETL – International body for higher education professionals. Despite his busy schedule, he maintains active scholarship through regular publications in accredited journals. he has been awarded honorary doctorates from the University of Athabasca, Canada, and Thomas Edison State University, USA.

Veronica Margaret Makwinja (Ed.D.) is the Director of Postgraduate Studies at Botswana Accountancy College (BAC). She worked as the Head of Department in Education at Botho University in the Faculty of Health and Education. She holds an M.S. in Educational Administration from Syracuse University, NY; and an ED.D. in Educational Administration from Ohio University (OU), Athens, USA. She was voted the most outstanding student in the College of Education in 2006 at OU, USA. She is an Educator with more than 30 years teaching experience in both secondary (high schools) and tertiary institutions in Botswana. She has co-authored books in social studies with Pearson publishers and Guidance and Counselling with MacMillan Botswana. She has been involved in several projects including a partnership between the University of Botswana and the University of Pennsylvania on HIV and AIDS Partnership for capacity building for HIV/AIDS/STIs prevention for Batswana adolescents. She taught online education courses at Botho University and sill does so at BAC, supervises masters' students' dissertations, and provides community service to the Botswana Open University on part-time basis. Her research interest is on improving basic education in Botswana and catering for the children of the marginalized communities in the country.

Victor Pitsoe is a Professor in the Department of Educational Leadership and Management at the University of South Africa and a Deputy Editor of *Africa Education Review.* A member of The World Institute for Nuclear Security, he has published more than 40 articles and 10 book chapters and co-edited 2 books. He has published in an array of areas including management, citizenship and human rights education, philosophy of education, open distance learning, teacher education, and teacher professional development.

Carolyn L. Sandoval is the Associate Director of the Teaching + Learning Commons. She has worked in higher education for over 25 years and has extensive experience in teaching and in developing and leading programs aimed at faculty and student success. Prior to her appointment at UC San Diego in 2018, she worked in the Dean of Faculties unit at a large research institution where she provided individual and departmental consulting on a variety of topics, including curriculum redesign, inclusive and equitable teaching practices, and peer review of teaching. She worked several years in the areas of outreach and retention for Chicanx/Latinx students at the University of New Mexico and the University California, Riverside. She has taught graduate- and undergraduate-level courses in learning theories, qualitative research methods, and social justice education, both online and face-to-face. She has provided educational consulting at various colleges and universities across the country and internationally. Her research interests include transformative learning, adult learning and development, women and mass incarceration, and social justice.

Jennifer Schneider earned her B.S. in Economics and Finance at New York University's Stern School of Business and her J.D. from the New York University School of Law. She holds an M.Ed. (Learning and Technology) and an M.S.CIN (Curriculum and Instruction) from Western Governors University. She is currently working on her Ed.D. (Curriculum and Instruction) at the University of South Carolina. She currently serves as a Faculty Team Lead and an Adjunct Faculty member at Southern New Hampshire University. She also serves as a Subject Matter Expert and Faculty Member at the University of the People. She has over 15 years of curriculum development, instructional design, and teaching experience in online learning and blended environments. She has taught and developed a wide variety of justice studies, critical thinking, legal research, business, and law courses. She has published widely in a variety of scholarly and literary journals. Her research interests are broad and include online support and student retention, student efficacy, online pedagogies, online learning communities of practice, and issues associated with grading (including characteristics, bias, and efficacy).

Enakshi Sengupta, Ph.D., serves as the Associate Director of Higher Education Teaching and Learning Association (HETL) and is responsible for the advancement of HETL in Asia, Middle East, and Africa. She works closely with the executive director to fulfill the mission of HETL. She is also the Director of the Center for Advanced Research in Education, Associate Series Editor of the book series, Innovations in Higher Education Teaching and Learning, Emerald Group Publishing. She is the Managing Editor of the *Journal of Applied Research in Higher Education*, Emerald Publishing, and serves as the Vice Chair of the Editorial Advisory Board of the Innovations in Higher Education Teaching and Learning book series, Emerald Publishing. She is the Senior Manager of the Research, Methodology, and Statistics in the Social Sciences forums on LinkedIn and Facebook responsible for managing all aspects of those forums. She is a Ph.D. holder from the University of Nottingham in research in higher education, prior to which she completed her M.B.A. with merit from the University of Nottingham and Master's degree in English Literature from the Calcutta University, India. She has previously held leadership positions in higher education institutions.

Cameo Lyn West is a Diversity Education Specialist and a Postdoctoral Scholar with the UC San Diego Engaged Teaching Hub. Her work investigates how student learning outcomes are developed and deployed for Diversity, Equity, and

Inclusion (DEI) courses, and develops promising practices to support DEI instructors in achieving their outcomes. She is also an Adjunct Professor of History and Black Studies for the San Diego Community College District, and her research interests include historical memory, audience reception theory, and cultural studies.

NAME INDEX

SUBJECT INDEX